Diggin' Up Bones

Obituaries of
Kendall, Lydia German Lutheran,
Lydia Lutheran, Lydia Methodist,
And Shockey Cemeteries
Book IV

Betty Barnes

HERITAGE BOOKS
2008

HERITAGE BOOKS
AN IMPRINT OF HERITAGE BOOKS, INC.

Books, CDs, and more—Worldwide

For our listing of thousands of titles see our website at
www.HeritageBooks.com

Published 2008 by
HERITAGE BOOKS, INC.
Publishing Division
100 Railroad Ave. #104
Westminster, Maryland 21157

Copyright ©2001 Betty Barnes

Other books by the author:

Diggin' Up Bones: Obituaries of Deerfield, Fairview, and Miscellaneous Kearny County Cemeteries, Kearny County, Kansas

Diggin' Up Bones, Part I and II: Obituaries of Lakin and Hartland Cemeteries, Kearny County, Kansas

All rights reserved. No part of this book may be reproduced or transmitted in any form or by any means, electronic or mechanical, including photocopying, recording or by any information storage and retrieval system without written permission from the author, except for the inclusion of brief quotations in a review.

International Standard Book Numbers
Paperbound: 978-0-7884-1878-5
Clothbound: 978-0-7884-7041-7

DIGGIN' UP BONES
BOOK IV

TABLE OF CONTENTS

	PAGE
KENDALL CEMETERY	2
KENDALL CEMETERY MAP	3
LYDIA GERMAN LUTHERAN CEMETERY	93
LYDIA LUTHERAN CEMETERY	98
LYDIA LUTHERAN CEMETERY MAP	99
LYDIA METHODIST CEMETERY	129
LYDIA METHODIST CEMETERY MAP	130
SHOCKEY CEMETERY	145
BIBLIOGRAPHY	190

KENDALL CEMETERY

Kendall Cemetery is located in Hamilton County, Kansas, on a 5 acre tract in the NE/c of NE/4 of Section 25, Township 24, Range 39.

It is located on a hill just north of the small town of Kendall. On Highway 50 it is located at mile marker 28 1/2.

The first burials were in 1886 but the ground was not deeded until May 10, 1901, to the City of Kendall from Arkansas Valley Town and Land Company for $25.00.

(The Kendall Gazette, August 4, 1887) It is time the people of Kendall were doing something about our cemetery. The site is a beautiful and fitting one, and could easily be made a most suitable resting place for our dead. As it is now the land is owned by the railroad and has never been laid out into lots. About thirty persons have been buried there with little regard to order or even direction. None of these are marked, and in a few years it will be impossible to distinguish them. The longer this is neglected the worse it will become. Let us in some way procure a title to the land, have it platted in lots and fenced. This is a matter in which every one should be interested. Let some one start it and we think he will find many who are more than willing to aid in the work. Don't put it off.

KENDALL CEMETERY

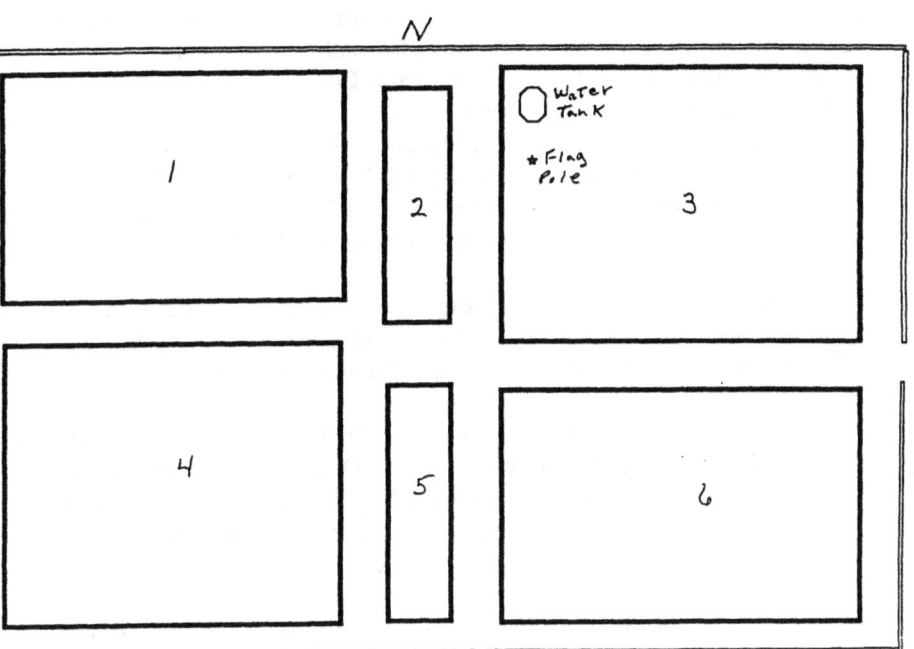

KENDALL CEMETERY

ADAMS, ETHEL GERTRUDE - (Sec. 4) (The Lakin Independent, March 18, 1993) Gertrude Adams, 99, died March 7, 1993, at Cheyenne, Wyoming.
She was born September 11, 1893, at Burlington, the daughter of Charles B. and Artie West Sinclair. She was a 1925 graduate of Union College, Lincoln, Nebraska, with a degree in elementary education. A Cheyenne resident since 1985, formerly of Kendall, she was a pioneer school teacher for many years. She was a Seventh-day Adventist.
On September 4, 1927, she married Milo Conrad Adams at Boulder, Colorado. He died October 24, 1964.
Survivors include: a son, David James Roby, Stoneham, Massachusetts; three daughters, Margaret Bernice Olson and Shirley Darlene Thompson, both of Cheyenne, and Theresa Marie Affolter, Knoxville, Tennessee; seven grand-children; and eight great grandchildren.
Graveside service was at 11 a.m. MST Monday in the Kendall Cemetery, Kendall, with Pastor David Ritter presiding. Kehr-Greene Funeral Home, Syracuse, was in charge of arrangements.

ADAMS, MILO CONRAD - (Sec. 4) (The Garden City Telegram, Oct. 27, 1964) Milo Conrad Adams, 67, died October 24, 1964, at the Donohue Memorial Hospital, Syracuse, after four weeks illness. Born March 24, 1894, in Phillips County, he was married September 4, 1927, at Boulder, Colorado. He was a retired clerk.
Member: Seventh-day Adventist Church. Survivors: daughters, Mrs. Terressa Marie Assolter, Boulder, Colorado, Mrs. Margaret Bernice Olson, Cheyenne, Miss Shirley Darline Adams, Kendall; sons, David James, Syracuse, Roby, Stoneham, Massachusetts; sister, Mrs. Ina Armstrong, Lincoln, Nebraska; six grand-children.
Funeral was held at the Methodist Church, Syracuse; Rev. Carl Johnson and Harry Walz. Burial: Kendall Cemetery. Call: Tuesday evening, McFadden Funeral Home, Syracuse.

ADKISSON, CECIL LEROY - (Sec. 4) (The Lakin Independent, May 16, 1985) Funeral for Cecil Leroy Adkisson, 65, was at 2 p.m. (MDT) Monday at the Kendall Methodist Church, the Rev. Alvin Smith officiating. Burial was in Kendall Cemetery.
He died Friday, May 20, 1985, at Hamilton County Hospital, Syracuse.

KENDALL CEMETERY

Born December 1, 1919, at Anthony, he married Bonnie Delores Stevens, May 23, 1959, at Syracuse. For four years prior to October 1984, Cecil and Bonnie were the owners and operators of the Capri restaurant in Syracuse. Cecil retired last October and planned to travel and do some fishing. Things he loved and had never had time to do.

Mr. Adkisson was a member of the Baptist Church, Argonia, and was a U.S. Army Air Force Veteran of World War II. He spent 36 months in Europe in an Air Force Reconnaissance division.

Survivors include his wife, of the home; a son, Randy Pieratt, Calhan, Colorado; a daughter, Joyce Mason, Ellicott, Colorado; four brothers, Harold, Anthony, Don, Gary, Indiana, and Dale, Teneyville, Missouri; a sister, Maxine Ruckle, Winfield, and four grandchildren.

Greene Funeral Home, Syracuse, was in charge of arrangements.

ALEXANDER, ROY "Elmer" - (Sec. 5) (The Lakin Independent, Feb. 19, 1998) Roy "Elmer" Alexander, 83, died at his home in Kendall on Sunday, February 15, 1998.

He was born February 21, 1914, on a homestead north of Kendall, the son of James W. and Carrie Schwab Alexander. He had been a lifetime resident of Kendall.

Elmer was a mechanic and had owned his own garage in Kendall for 70 years. He was a member of the Kendall Methodist Church.

On March 11, 1933, he married Jewell Wilma Rogers in Chickasha, Oklahoma. She survives.

Other survivors include a son and daughter-in-law, Jerry and Donna Alexander of Wheatland, Wyoming; a daughter, Mona Trussell of Kendall; brother, Wilber Alexander of Santa Rosa, California; half brother, Wallace Alexander of Ogden, Utah; five grandchildren and six great grandchildren.

He was preceded in death by one brother, Carl Alexander; a sister, Agnes; a son-in-law, Ronald Trussell and a daughter-in-law, Emiko Alexander.

Graveside services were held at 10:00 a.m. (MDT), Wednesday, at the Kendall Cemetery with the Rev. William Salmon officiating. Greene Funeral home of Syracuse in charge of arrangements. Memorials to the Kendall Methodist Church.

ALEXANDER, UTO - (Sec. 5) (The Garden City Telegram, Sept. 25, 1966) Uto Alexander, 39, died Friday night, September 23, 1966, in

KENDALL CEMETERY

Hamilton County Hospital following surgery Friday morning. Born Oshima, Japan, March 11, 1927, she lived in Japan and Okinawa most of her life. She has lived in Kendall eight months. She was married to Jerry Alexander January 14, 1953, in Naha, Okinawa. Survivors: the widower, Fleet Post Office, New York, New York; parents, Mr. and Mrs. Kibonhima Miijima, Oshima; sister, Mariko, Okinawa; brother, Tomihiro, Oshima.

Funeral Monday 2 p.m. First Methodist Church, Syracuse, Rev. Harry Walz. Burial in Kendall Cemetery.

ALLEN, ALLON - 1915-1916 (Sec. 3)

ALLEN, HENRY - (Sec. 3) (The Lakin Independent, March 23, 1961) Henry Allen, only child of Charles M. Allen and Catherine Harris, was born on February 25, 1898, at Stafford and passed away at the Donahue Memorial Hospital in Syracuse on March 20, 1961, at the age of 63. He had been stricken nine days before with a heart ailment from which he did not recover.

Henry came with his parents in 1906 to western Kansas where they homesteaded west of Kendall. On November 1, 1915, he married Miss Martha M. Roth at Kinsley. For the past 45 years Mr. and Mrs. Allen have farmed north of Kendall in Kearny County.

Mr. Allen enjoyed his farming and his home. He was a good neighbor and friend to all. His chief hobby, which he thoroughly enjoyed, was hunting.

Mr. Allen is survived by his wife, Martha, a number of cousins, and many friends.

Funeral services were held from the Kendall Methodist Church, Wednesday afternoon at 2:00 o'clock, with Dr. E. F. Markley officiating. Interment was in the Kendall Cemetery.

ALLEN, KATHERINE - (Sec. 3) (Syracuse Journal, April 28, 1911, Kendall News) After a lingering illness of almost all winter, Mrs. C. M. Allen who resided two miles west of town, died at eleven o'clock a.m. and was buried at Kendall at 5 o'clock, Wednesday. A large concourse of friends attended the funeral. Rev. T. H. Lent preached a very interesting sermon.

Mr. and Mrs. Amon Allen of Stafford, Kansas, came up on the stub Wednesday afternoon to attend the funeral of his brother Charles' wife.

KENDALL CEMETERY

(Kearny County History Book II) Kathrene Harris Allen, wife of Henry Allen came to Kearny County, Kendall, in 1906.

ALLEN, LEROY - (The Syracuse Journal, Feb. 23, 1917) Mrs. C. M. Allen of Kendall awoke Monday morning (February 19, 1917) to find her baby boy dead in bed with her. Mr. Allen was at Hartland doing some carpenter work and had left Mrs. Harry McCommon of Hartland with is wife. When the ladies retired at bed time the baby was apparently well but awoke once during the night and cried a little then dropped off to sleep again, but was found to be dead when they awoke in the morning.

Mr. and Mrs. C. M. Allen's baby's funeral was held at the church Tuesday at 2 p.m. conducted by Rev. White, pastor of the Lakin Christian Church of which Mrs. Allen is a member. Quite a large crowd of friends and neighbors were in attendance.

ALLEN, MARTHA M. - (Sec. 3) (The Lakin Independent, Thursday, March 6, 1980) Funeral service for Martha M. Allen, 84, was held Saturday afternoon, March 1, 1980, at the Kendall Methodist Church with the Reverend Loren Chapman officiating. Burial was in the Kendall Cemetery.

Born Martha M. Roth, February 14, 1896, she was married to Henry Allen, November 1, 1915, at Kinsley. He died in 1961. She died at her home in near Kendall, February 26, 1980. She had lived there since 1917.

Martha and Henry lived on her father's place until January 1917, when they moved to their own ranch. They continued to farm her father's place and care for him until his death, May 1937. The old home place was purchased by Mr. and Mrs. John Gingerich, who still reside there.

Martha liked cattle and was a rancher all her life but had to sell them because of failing health.

Her husband passed away on March 20, 1961, and in 1964 Martha rented the rest of her land to the Gingeriches but continued to live on the ranch.

Martha was a member of the Kendall Methodist Church but had not attended for some time because of her health.

Martha, Henry, her father, Charles Allen, and her brothers, Paul and Tom, helped to build the Methodist Church in Kendall. Martha had

KENDALL CEMETERY

lived all her life in Kearny County.

AMOS, FRANKLIN - 1887-1960 (Sec. 2)

AMOS, THELMA K. - 1907-1961 (Sec. 2)

AUSTIN, AURORA E. - (Sec. 3) (Lakin Investigator, Kendall News, Aug. 19, 1910) Mrs. G. H. Austin died at Syracuse, August 14, 1910. She was born March 17, 1887, and was married to G. H. Austin, three years ago, whom she leaves with one child, two years old; also, father, two brothers and one sister. She was a niece of D. E. Gard. The cause of her death was lock jaw, caused by stepping on a nail, about ten days before. She was taken to Syracuse for treatment, and everything possible done, but with out avail. The husband and little one, brothers, sister and other relatives, have the sympathy of the entire community, in this, their hour of sorrow.

AUSTIN, GILBERT HENRY - (Sec. 3) (The Lakin Independent, Sept. 14, 1961) The life of Gilbert Henry Austin began March 22, 1873, in White County, Illinois. His parents were Alex and Emily Vaught Austin. He moved to Western Kansas about 1906, and settled near Menno, Kansas, in the vicinity of Kendall.

By profession he became a water well driller and lived in Pierceville, Coolidge, Syracuse, Lakin and Garden City, drilling many of the wells on the then very dry Kansas plains.

In 1908, on February 10, he was united in marriage with Miss Aurora E. Bachman in Lakin. Into this happy home was born one daughter, Agnes. Sorrow soon visited this new home and eighteen months later, on August 14, 1910, Mrs. Austin was taken from her family by death.

Mr. Austin continued his occupation of well drilling, but always kept his daughter with or near him. Neighborly women and close friends were a great help in caring for and rearing this young lady. Mr. Austin never remarried, but chose to be both father and mother to his only child.

In 1935, he left the western area for Carbondale, Kansas, to be near his daughter. When she moved to Pratt, he joined her there to spend the remainder of his life.

Mr. Austin's health was good until a few weeks prior to his passing. Mrs. Morgan cared for him at their home for sometime, but when his condition became such as to demand more medical care, he was taken to

KENDALL CEMETERY

the Pratt County hospital. On Sunday afternoon, September 3, Mr. Austin died at the age of 88 years, five months and 12 days.

He is survived by his daughter, Mrs. Clem Morgan, four grandchildren and four great grandchildren.

KENDALL CEMETERY

BIRD, SAMUEL - (The Hamilton County Republican, Sept. 9, 1886) Samuel Bird, colored, died September 2d. Mr. Bird had a very severe attack of typhoid fever and was on the high road to recovery, but gave way to his appetite and brought on a new complication, which soon proved fatal.

(The Kendall Weekly Signal, Friday, Sept. 3, 1886) Samuel Bird was interred in the Kendall Cemetery.

BLODGETT, MRS. SAMUEL - (The Kendall Boomer, November 10, 1886) Last Thursday Mrs. Blodgett, wife of Samuel Blodgett, died at her home in the Veteran addition. She leaves a family of seven children motherless, and the youngest is an infant. Mrs. Blodgett was known as an amiable lady and a kind and affectionate mother and wife.

Died November 4, 1886.

BRIERY, GIRL - (The Lakin Independent, Oct. 1, 1926) The people of this community extend sympathy to Mr. and Mrs. Briery and family in the death of their daughter. Funeral services were held Friday by Rev. Mawdsley and interment was made in the Kendall Cemetery.

BROWN, CHILD - (Kendall Weekly Signal, Sept. 10, 1886) A little child of Mrs. Brown (colored), wife of John Brown, late deceased, died Tuesday morning (September 7, 1886) and was interred Wednesday.

BROWN, GRACE - (Sec. 3) Died December 22, 1897, 30 years old.

BROWN, JOHN H. - (Pioneer Democrat, Lakin, Finney County, Kansas, July 17, 1886) A colored man named John H. Brown was killed at his home three miles east of Kendall, on the 6th of this month, by his twenty two year old son, Henry T. Brown. It seems that the old man was whipping his wife when the boy took a .32 caliber revolver and shot his father in the head, and after he was dead, Henry took a horse and dragged the body by the feet, about seventy-five yards from the house, where it was buried. He then went to Kendall and drew $75 from the bank and took a train at Hartland for Kansas City. A few days after the old woman and the sixteen year old boy said Mr. Brown had left them but their movements were rather suspicious, and upon being accused of the crime, the boy, Charles, acknowledged the whole affair. He was bound over to the charge of accessory to the murder.

KENDALL CEMETERY

John H. Brown killed by his son, July 6, 1886. Buried in the Kendall Cemetery. Served in the Civil War.

(Grant County Register, Ulysses, Hamilton County, Kansas, July 17, 1886) A colored man named Brown was killed by his son at Kendall last week and all the family took a hand in burying the body. It is claimed that the father was beating his wife, and in order that his mother may have time to get breath, one of the sons made his pater's muscles relax. All the family but the old man are in jail. This may boom poor old Kendall.

(Hartland Herald, July 24, 1886) John T. Brown, colored, who murdered his father some 10 days ago near Kendall and then fled to Goldsboro, North Carolina, his father's old home, has been arrested. His whereabouts were learned from a half brother who is confined in the jail at Garden City as an accessory to the crime, and the sheriff of this county, who went after him will arrive with him in a few days.

BUCKNER, GEORGE - (The Kendall Bloomer, Saturday, September 15, 1888) George Buckner died in this city of pneumonia last Friday (September 7, 1888). He was in very destitute circumstances.

BURGESS, MRS. E. A. - (Kearny County Advocate, Kendall News, March 3, 1911) Died at her home, ten miles south of Kendall, Thursday, February 23rd, Mrs. E. A. Burgess, after a long illness. She was laid to rest last Saturday in the Kendall Cemetery. Deceased leaves a husband and three small children to mourn her loss.

(Syracuse Journal, March 3, 1911) Mrs. Burgis, who lived near Charles Spencer, 10 miles southeast of Kendall, died last Friday (February 24, 1911) of diabetes and was buried at Kendall. She was about 33 years old.

BURROWS, EMMA C. - (Sec, 3) (Lakin Investigator, Feb. 11, 1910) Emma C. Burrows, born in Astubury Lane End, Congleton, Chessire, England, August 7, 1811, departed this life February 6, 1910, aged 98 years, five months and 29 days. She was married at the age of 30 years to W. H. Clayton. To this union four children were born, three of whom are still living: Peter Clayton of New Harmony, Indiana, Mrs. A. C. Helmick and W. H. Clayton, of Lakin. They came to America in 1845, and first settled at Lewisville, Kentucky, and lived there one year and from there they moved to New Harmon, Indiana, here her husband died

KENDALL CEMETERY

in 1850, leaving her with four children. In 1851 she was married to Hugh Burrows, and to this union six children were born, and three of them are still living. Mrs. Sarah Spillman and Hugh Burrows, both of Padueah, Kentucky, and Mrs. Emma Peters, of St. Louis, Missouri. She was parted from her second husband in 1865. From New Harmony she moved to Paducah, Kentucky, from there to Skiatook, I.T. and from there to Kearny County, where she made her home with her son, W. H. Clayton, where she was living at the time of her death. Very early in life she united with the Wesleyan Methodist Church of England, to which she was a faithful, burning light till she came to America. At New Harmony, Indiana, she united with the Baptist Church of which she was a member at the time of her death. She seemed to view life on the bright side and always had a good word for everybody. Her illness only lasted a few days and the end was due to extreme old age. Before her death she told those at her bedside many times that she had "a building of God, not made with hands, eternal in the heavens." The funeral was conducted by Rev. John Hiner, at the Dodge school house. The text was taken from First Corinthians 15. 55, 56, and 57. She was dressed for the grave in a fine silk dress she had had for 79 years. After the services her body was laid to rest in the cemetery at Kendall, Kansas.

KENDALL CEMETERY

CHERRY, FLOYD VICTOR - (Sec. 3) (Garden City Telegram, Tues. Nov. 9, 1971) Floyd Victor Cherry, 71, Tribune, died Sunday, November 7, 1971, at the Greeley County Hospital, Tribune, after a long illness.
    Born July 13, 1900, in Marietta, Ohio, he married Lorinda Hazen, October 2, 1925, at Tribune.
    Survivors include the widow; two sons, Donald and Harry, both of Leoti.
    Funeral was held Wednesday at the Weinmann-Price Funeral Home, Leoti, the Rev. Glen Epp officiating. Burial in the Kendall Cemetery.

CHERRY, LORINDA - (Sec. 3) (Garden City Telegram, Wed. July 19, 1972) Funeral services for Mrs. Lorinda Cherry, 64, was held Thursday at the Weinmann-Price Funeral Home, the Rev. Glen Epp officiating. Burial in the Kendall Cemetery.
    Mrs. Cherry died July 17, 1972, at St. Catherine Hospital.
    Born October 2, 1907, in Greeley County, she was married to Floyd V. Cherry October 2, 1925, at Tribune. He died in 1971. She lived here (Leoti) two years.
    Survivors include two sons, Donald and Harry, Leoti; a brother, Will Hazen, Lamar, Colorado; and one sister, Mrs. John Courtney, Onalaska, Washington.

CHERRY, VIRGIL LEE - (Sec. 3) September 23, 1932 to June 3, 1935.

CLAAR, CHARLOTTE IDA - (Syracuse Journal, Oct. 1, 1926) Charlotte Ida Briery was born at Brewster, Thomas County, Kansas, July 30, 1903. In 1911 she moved with her parents to Hoxie, Sheridan County, Kansas, where they lived until 1922, when she was married to Alva Claar on November 10th. Two children came to bless and brighten the home, Marie Irene, aged 2 years and Anna Maxine, aged 1 year.
    Mrs. Claar was converted at the age of 18 years and united with the Christian Church at Paola, Colorado.
    She was sick about eight months, during which time everything was done that loved ones knew to do, but it seemed to avail nought. She gradually slipped away. Some seven weeks ago she came to the home of her parents, Mr. and Mrs. Briery who live about 16 miles southeast of Syracuse, but after about three weeks she was taken to Colorado, but growing steadily worse, she was brot back Saturday, September 18. She passed away Wednesday, September 22, age 23 years, 1 month and 22

KENDALL CEMETERY

days.

Besides her husband and two children she leaves her father and mother, five brothers and three sisters and several other relatives and many friends, to mourn her going. All the immediate family, several other relatives and many friends from the old home near Hoxie attended the funeral services which were held in the Kendall Church, Friday at 10 o'clock, conducted by the pastor, P. L. Mawdsley, and the body was laid to rest in the Kendall Cemetery to await the resurrection.

CLORE, MR. - (The Kendall Bloomer, Saturday, September 1, 1888) As we go to press we learn that Mr. Clore who was sick in town here for a long time during the early part of the summer was found dead at 5 o'clock Friday evening. He leaves a wife and seven children.

COFFING, CLYDE - (The Kendall Boomer, June 23, 1886) Mr. and Mrs. J. C. Coffing's baby, Clyde, died last Saturday noon (June 19, 1886). Its age was eleven months. Grieved parents and kind friends laid the tired little body in the Kendall Cemetery last Sunday afternoon; Rev. C. W. Garten said the benediction.

COFFING, GEORGIE - (The Kendall Boomer, June 29, 1887) Last Thursday morning at an early hour (June 23, 1887), death enter the home of Mr. and Mrs. J. C. Coffing and took from them their infant son, Georgie, aged four months. The funeral took place in the afternoon and the tired little body was laid to rest among the flowers in the Kendall cemetery. The stricken parents have the sympathy of the entire community in this, their second bereavement since their residence here and we fervently hope that in this their hour of sorrow and suffering, the world will not seem all shrouded in gloom but that they will see even in these dark clouds a silvery lining.

COGHILL, MARY PAULINE GROPP - (Sec. 3) Born in March 1913, and died in October 1999, at Montrose, Colorado.

CORBETT, CLESTIAN CLARENCE - (Sec. 3) (The Advocate, Feb. 17, 1922) The father of Mr. Dan Corbett passed away Saturday afternoon. The remains were laid to rest in the Kendall Cemetery. Mr. Corbett and family have the sympathy of their many friends, in their sorrow.

(Funeral Record) Retired farmer, married, no doctor in attendance,

KENDALL CEMETERY

died February 11, 1922, at the age of 78 years, 26 days.

CORBETT, INFANT - (The Lakin Independent, Nov. 17, 1922) The infant of Mr. and Mrs. Corbett was buried in the Kendall Cemetery, Thursday. The Kendall people extend their sympathy to the bereaved parents.

COZAD, CLAUD - (Hartland Herald, October 13, 1888) On Wednesday last, Rev. Marsh was called to Kendall to preach the funeral sermon of the infant son of Mr. and Mrs. L. J. Cozad. The remains were buried from the house at 10 a.m.

(Kendall Boomer, Oct. 13, 1888) Died in Kendall, Ks., Tuesday, October 9, 1888, at 3 o'clock p.m., Claud Leonard, infant son of Mr. and Mrs. T. J. Cozad, aged 5 months, 14 days.

The funeral service was held at their residence Wednesday morning at 10 o'clock, Rev. W. B. Marsh of Hartland, preached a sermon appropriate to the occasion to a large audience.

Beautiful in life-too pure for earth-lovely, in death-Claude has gone to the land of bright spirits, after a long season of intense suffering, to join the angelic choir in realms of eternal bliss.

OUR LITTLE DARLING
In memory of little Claud Cozad
Sorrow and sadness shall reign through the house,
As we move with a soft, gentle tread,
There's a void in our hearts that can never be filled
Oh! whisper it, Claudie is dead,
No more shall we hear his sweet, gentle voice,
For the soul that so loved us has fled;
No more shall we see his dear loving face,
For the darling we loved is dead.
Bitter the tears we shed on his grave,
While kind words of comfort were said,
But naught can fill the deep grief in our hearts;
We are lonely now, Claudie is dead.

CRITES, SON - (The Kendall Boomer, Sat. Feb. 11, 1888) Mr. Crites of Bear Creek, son of Mr. A. J. Crites, lost his little 3 year old boy last week, his death being caused by a kick from a horse. We have not learned the particulars as Mr. A. J. Crites has been with the bereaved family since the sad occurrence.

KENDALL CEMETERY

CURRY, JAMES - (Kendall Boomer, Aug. 18, 1888) James Curry, an employee of John Brady, died from a bullet wound received July 4, 1888, at Coolidge. This is indeed a sad culmination of a day's fun. On the morning of the Fourth, James Curry, John Toohey and a few more friends got together to celebrate the day over a keg of beer. The best of feeling prevailed and the boys were having a big time. Curry and Toohey engaged in a friendly scuffle and in some manner Toohey's revolver was discharged, the ball entering Curry's body in the region of the stomach. He seemed to be rapidly improving for a time, then a relaps came and inflammation set in. In this condition he lingered several weeks when death came to his relief. He was in the prime of manhood, and a man of more than ordinary intelligence. He had a natural talent for carving and his efforts in that direction were the wonder and admiration of all who saw them. Being of a roaming disposition he never reaped any substantial benefit from his artistic skill, but contented himself with his trade, that of stonemason. He was particularly attached to his employer, Mr. John Brady, who cared for him during his fatal illness.

KENDALL CEMETERY

DAVIS, CHARLES H. - (The Kendall Boomer, July 6, 1887) Charles H. Davis, formerly of Michigan, died at the home of his father-in-law, Mr. Ira Parish, three miles north of town. He was about thirty-four years old. Mr. Davis became quite well known during the short time he resided here. He was a victim of consumption long before he came west and was very feeble. He had followed dentistry in Michigan and intended to open an establishment here but his health would not permit. The funeral took place on Friday and the Kendall cemetery now contains all that is mortal of Mr. Charles H. Davis, whose lamp went out in the prime of his manhood.

DODGE, GLADYS - (Sec. 3) (The Syracuse Journal, Jan. 13, 1911) Gladys, the 13 year old daughter of Mr. and Mrs. Thomas Dodge, died at their home six miles east of town, Saturday evening and was buried in the Kendall Cemetery, Sunday afternoon.

Kearny County Advocate, Jan. 13, 1911) Died Saturday, January 7th, at the home of her parents, Gladys, the eldest daughter, age 13 years, of Mr. and Mrs. Thomas Dodge living 5 miles east of Kendall, after a short illness.

Funeral services were conducted at the Dodge school house Sunday, by the Rev. Hiner. The funeral was attended by a large number of friends and neighbors. The bereaved parents have the sympathy of the entire community.

DODGE, WARREN K. - (The Lakin Independent, Nov. 29, 1990) Graveside service for Warren Keith Dodge, 33, Garden City, was held at 1 p.m. MST, Tuesday at Kendall Cemetery, the Rev. Laurie Armstrong officiating.

He died November 24, 1990, in a traffic accident three miles west of Garden City.

Born May 22, 1957, at Syracuse, he was a millwright for Triple S. Steel. He had been a Garden City resident for three years, moving from Kendall.

Survivors include his father, Keith Dodge, Syracuse, His mother, Neva Maerz, Lakin; a brother, Larry Dodge, Garden City; two sisters, Lisa Bell and Connie Dodge, both of Lakin; his grandmothers, Ruth Dodge, Lakin, and Florence Boese, Syracuse; and his great grandmother, Carrie Graber, Syracuse.

KENDALL CEMETERY

DUNN, EDGAR - (Sec. 3) (Kearny County Advocate, Kendall News, Dec. 22, 1911) Died on Saturday, December 16, at Kansas City, Edgar Dunn, age 13 years. Funeral services at the school house conducted by Rev. E. E. Carter of Syracuse, interment in Kendall Cemetery. Deceased was born and raised here and has been sick for about seven months. The bereaved family have the sympathy of the whole community.

DUNN, F. E. - (Sec. 3) (The Syracuse Journal, Sept. 9, 1898) Died at Kendall, Monday, September 5th of typhoid fever, F. E. Dunn, aged 31 years. He leaves a wife and seven children, the oldest 12 and the youngest three months. Those who knew him best, say he was a good neighbor, a true friend, honorable and upright, an exceptional father and husband. The whole community and especially the wives and mothers sympathize with Mrs. Dunn and her children in their great sorrow.

DUNN, IDA LOIS - (The Kearny County Advocate, April 30, 1915) Ida Lois, three month old baby of Mr. and Mrs. Phil Dunn, died at Syracuse, Kansas, where she was taken for medical treatment, April 19th. The remains were brot to Kendall and the funeral services held at the church, conducted by Rev. Blair, and interment made in the Kendall Cemetery.

DUPREE, JACQUELINE DENISE - (Sec. 4) Died April 15, 1983. Daughter of Robert and Anita (Bezona) Dupree.

DURHAM, MRS. D. H. - (The Lakin Independent, Sept. 7, 1923) Mrs. C. H. Durham died at her home in Kendall Tuesday morning. She has been failing in health since early spring. Her daughter from Ohio arrived on Wednesday morning.

DYCK, EDGAR - (Sec. 2)

DYCK, ELLA - (Sec. 2) (The Syracuse Journal, May 6, 1959) Mrs. Pete (Ella) Dyck died Thursday, April 30, at the Donohue Memorial Hospital after a two days illness.
  Mrs. Dyck was born March 17, 1888, in Broken Bow, Nebraska. She had been a resident of Syracuse for the past 20 years. She was a member of the Church of the Latter Day Saints, Coolidge, and while her health permitted, took an active part in the church organization.
  She is survived by her husband, Pete; a son, George R. Burns; two

KENDALL CEMETERY

daughters, Mrs. Alice Smithers of Costa Mesa, California, Mrs. Dorothy Henderson, Galesburg, Illinois; 6 grandchildren; 12 great grandchildren; 2 step children; and 10 step grandchildren; and 10 step great grandchildren.

Funeral services were held at the Church of the Latter Day Saints in Coolidge at 2 p.m. Sunday, Elder Glen Ryan officiating.

Burial was in the Kendall Cemetery.

DYCK, ERVIN - (Sec. 2) (The Syracuse Journal, May 30, 1941) Funeral services were conducted for Ervin Dyck, son of Mr. and Mrs. Henry Dyck, at the Kendall church Monday afternoon, and burial was in the Kendall Cemetery. Rev. Wells of Syracuse was in charge of services. Mr. Dyck, 29 years old, died from complications arising from an accident in a sawmill at Eugene, Oregon. His leg was broken on May 16, and five days later he died from a blood clot.

Ervin Dyck was born on the family farm south of Kendall, and attended the Hamilton County rural school. In October 1937, he went to Oregon, and had been there since that time working in the lumber industry. He is survived by his parents, Mr. and Mrs. Henry Dyck, two sisters, Mrs. Thelma Warner of Kendall and Miss Verna Dyck of Syracuse, and many other relatives and friends.

DYCK, HENRY - (Sec. 2) (The Lakin Independent, March 21, 1963) Retired Syracuse farmer Henry Dyck, 76, died March 12, 1963, at Donohue Memorial Hospital in Syracuse after an illness of a year. He was born April 29, 1886, at Burrton and moved to the Menno community from Inman in 1906. He married on September 1, 1904, and his wife, Mary, died in 1955.

Mr. Dyck was a member of the Mennonite Brethren Church.

Survivors are daughters, Mrs. Thelma Warner of Ulysses and Mrs. Verna Gregg of Syracuse; a sister; five half sisters; a brother, Pete Dyck of Lakin; two half brothers; five grandchildren and six great grandchildren. Funeral was held at 1:30 p.m. Saturday from the Pilgrim Holiness Church in Syracuse with the Rev. Heckart officiating. Burial was in Kendall Cemetery.

DYCK, MARY - (Sec 2) (The Syracuse Journal, Aug. 11, 1955) Mrs. Henry Dyck, a resident of the Menno community for 49 years, died last evening, August 10, at the age of 71. She had not been ill, and was

KENDALL CEMETERY

working about the house. Mrs. Dyck was alone in the house at the time of the attack and was found dead last evening by members of the family.

She is survived by Mr. Dyck, who lives on the family farm one mile south and one mile west of the Menno Community building; two daughters, Mrs. Wayne Gragg of Syracuse and Mrs. Clifford Warner of Ulysses; a brother, Edward Knackstedt, of Redwood City, California; five grandchildren and five great grandchildren. Preceding Mrs. Dyck in death were two sons, Irvin and Clarence.

Mrs. Dyck was born in Inman in 1884, the daughter of Mr. and Mrs. William Knackstedt. She was a member of the Evangelical Church.

Funeral services will be held at 1:30 p.m. Saturday in the Syracuse Methodist Church. Burial will be in the Kendall Cemetery. The Cory-McFadden Funeral Home is in charge of the funeral arrangements.

DYCK, RAYMOND LEROY - (Sec. 2) Born April 19, 1929, and died May 19, 1935.

KENDALL CEMETERY

EARNEST, CLEO LOUISE - (Sec. 2) (The Lakin Independent, Nov. 2, 2000) Cleo Louise Earnest, 84, of Kendall, Kansas, died October 25, 2000, at Western Prairie Care Home in Ulysses, Kansas.

She was born December 24, 1915, at Penalosa, Kansas, the daughter of Eli Herman and Gracie Mae (Hiatt) Tope.

A lifelong resident of Kendall, she was a homemaker and a cook at the Kendall school for many years. She had been a resident of High Plains Retirement Village at Lakin for seven years and at Western Prairie Care Home in Ulysses for the past year. She belonged to the Kendall United Methodist Church.

Survivors include two sons, Floyd Pointer of Holcomb and Dean Pointer of Ulysses; a daughter, Shirley Williams of Rolla; 13 grandchildren; 17 great grandchildren; and a great-great grandchild.

She was preceded in death by two brothers, a sister, one grandchild and two great grandchildren.

Funeral services were Saturday, October 28, 2000, at Roselane Church of God in Ulysses with Pastor Mike Wirt and John Duran presiding. Burial was at Kendall Cemetery.

The family suggests memorials be given to Western Prairie Care Home Chaplains Fund in care of Garnand Funeral Home, Ulysses.

EATON, CYNTHIA C. - (Sec. 3) DOD 6/8/1934 age 72 years, 6 months, 9 days. Second wife of John Eaton, Cynthia Hanna.

EATON, JOHN GAVEN - (Sec. 3) (Syracuse Journal, Friday, Nov. 25, 1921) John Gaven Eaton died at the home of William Jones in this city early Friday morning at the age of 81 years. His death was due to a complication of diseases.

Mr. Eaton came to Hamilton County in the spring of 1886, and filed on a homestead nine miles northwest of Kendall. He proved up his claim, sold it, and moved to Kendall where he was engaged in the mercantile business. He was postmaster at Kendall from 1896 to 1906, and was one of the best known citizens in that part of the county. At the expiration of his term as postmaster he went to New Mexico, where he remained about two years. He returned to Kendall where he resided until 1920, when he was admitted to the Old Soldiers home at Ft. Dodge on account of failing health.

John Eaton was married to Miss Marion Kendrick shortly after the close of the Civil War and to them were born three children, all of who

KENDALL CEMETERY

are living. December 19, 1894, he was united in marriage with Miss Cynthia Hanna of Kendall.

Mr. Eaton was a soldier in the Civil War, enlisting in Co. A 8th Missouri Infantry, and served four years in the defense of his country. Born in 1840.

ENZ, HANS - (Sec. 3) (The Kendall Boomer, Feb. 16, 1887) Mr. John Enz's child, Hans, aged about four years, died the first part of this week (February 14, 1887) and was buried in the cemetery here Tuesday afternoon.

EVANS, CHARLES - (Sec. 3) (Kendall Weekly Signal Friday, Aug. 6, 1886) Mr. Charles Evans, aged about 52 years, died at his place four and one half miles north of town yesterday (August 5, 1886) and was buried in the cemetery north of town today. He leaves a wife and six little children almost destitute, any aid rendered the family will be thankfully received and greatly appreciated. Our citizens are a wholesouled people and Mrs. E. can rest assured that they will not be neglected in the time of their affliction.

KENDALL CEMETERY

FERRELL, BESSIE - Died in October 1940, cremated, age 78 years, 2 months and 10 days, buried at Kendall.
(The Lakin Independent, Nov. 29, 1940) Friends of Bessie Ferrell will be interested to know of her death. The remains were cremated in San Bruno, California, and the ashes were sent to Kendall and burial will take place Sunday, December 1 at 2:00 p.m.

FOREMAN, DANIEL - (Sec. 2) (The Lakin Independent, Dec. 25, 1969) Daniel Foreman, 72, died Sunday, December 20, 1969, at Hamilton County hospital following a long illness.
Born March 19, 1897, in Ogalla, Oklahoma, he married Mary Frances Hendreckson, July 5, 1924, in Kansas City, Mo. She died in 1957. A retired rancher, he had been a Kendall resident for 20 years.
He was a member of the Methodist Church and Masonic Lodge, Kendall, and was a veteran of World War I.
Survivors include a daughter, Mrs. Jerry Valentine, Kendall; three sisters, Mrs. Olie Bullard, Arnett, Oklahoma, Mrs. Elsie Adams, Parsons, and Mrs. Delia James, Ogden, Utah; five brothers, Jessie and Johnnie, Altamont, Leonard, Oswego, Delbert, Plymouth, Michigan, and Clifford, Altamont; and three grand-children.
Funeral was Tuesday at the United Methodist Church, Syracuse, the Rev. Charles Chipman officiating. Burial was in Kendall Cemetery.

FOREMAN, MARY FRANCES - (Sec. 2) (The Lakin Independent, March 29, 1957) Funeral services for Mrs. Jack Foreman of Kendall was held Sunday afternoon at 2 o'clock at the Kendall Methodist Church with the Rev. Mary Ellen Markley officiating. Rev. Markley was assisted by Dr. E. F. Markley.
Mrs. Foreman died at her home near Kendall Sunday. Her death was not connected in any way with the storm. She had been ill for some time.
The body was brought to Garden City by the CIG helicopter Monday afternoon.

FUNSTON, DAVID RALPH - (Sec. 2) (The Lakin Independent, April 17, 1953) Graveside funeral service were held at the Kendall Cemetery, Saturday morning at 11 o'clock for David Ralph Funston, 61, who was killed April 10 by a hit and run motorist, 20 miles east of Winfield.
Funston's body was found along the highway the morning of April

KENDALL CEMETERY

10. He was the son of Charles and Elizabeth Funston and was a former resident of the Kendall vicinity.

Survivors include his mother, one brother, two daughters and five grandchildren.

FUNSTON, MAY - (Sec. 2) (The Syracuse Journal, May 17, 1940) Plans of two Hamilton County families for Mother's day holidays ended in tragedy Sunday morning when their motor car sideswiped the steel guard rail on the Arkansas River bridge four miles west of Hutchinson, killing two and injuring five others, one seriously.

The dead: Mrs. May Funston of Kendall, 47 years old; V. I. Williams, Syracuse, 44 years old. Five members of the Frank Stevens family of Kendall were injured. Of the injured, only Letha Stevens, 9, was seriously hurt. She regained consciousness Sunday afternoon at the Grace Hospital, Hutchinson, and her chances for recovery are good.

Mr. and Mrs. Stevens, their small daughter, Bonnie, and a son, Ronald Stevens, 22, were treated for minor injuries and dismissed from the hospital.

The accident happened about 7 o'clock Sunday morning. Stevens was driving. The car crashed into the iron guardrail at the west end of the bridge approach where there is a marked curve. The entire right side of the car was ripped away by the force of the sideswiping.

Williams, who accompanied the party to help with the driving, was on the right side front seat with Mrs. Stevens in the center and Stevens behind the wheel. In the rear seat Mrs. Funston was also on the extreme right and was crushed by the tremendous impact of the railing against the side of the machine.

Mrs. Funston apparently died almost instantly. Williams was still alive when he was brought to the hospital but died within a few minutes.

A dairy truck came upon the scene a few seconds after the crash, as did Ernest Towse, farmer living 19 miles west of Hutchinson. The truck driver hastily removed his load of bottles, placed six of the victims in the truck and started for the hospital. The seventh was taken to the hospital in Towse's car.

Both Mr. Williams and Mrs. Funston were badly crushed. The man apparently had his head crushed between the side of the car and railing and he was also thrown clear of the wreckage. Others not so close to the steel rail were less seriously hurt and those seated on the extreme left escaped with minor hurts.

KENDALL CEMETERY

The Stevens family went to the O. B. Graham home in Hutchinson, Mrs. Graham being a daughter of Mrs. Funston. Late Sunday Sheriff R. D. Warner of Syracuse and Ralph Funston of Kendall arrived.

Mrs. Funston had planned to spend Mother's day at the home of her daughter in Hutchinson. The Stevens family intended to go to Wichita to visit Mrs. Stevens' mother.

Stevens told officers he was traveling about 50 miles an hour as he approached the bridge and claimed another car was coming off the bridge from the east and was near the center of the pavement crowding him to one side and causing him to strike the railing.

The iron guardrail is placed along the south shoulder of the highway in such a manner as to prevent motorists from heading straight into the bed of the Arkansas River at the point where the highway starts its S-curve route over the bridge.

Mr. Williams has been a resident of Hamilton and Kearny Counties since 1909. He lived on a farm near Kendall part of this time, and four years ago moved to Syracuse to enter the employee of Gould Implement Company. He is survived by his wife. Funeral services were conducted at the Lakin Methodist Church Wednesday afternoon and burial was in the Lakin Cemetery.

Mrs. Funston has been a resident of Kendall for many years. Funeral services were held at the Kendall church Friday afternoon. She is survived by her husband and two daughters.

Mrs. Funston was born in 1893.

KENDALL CEMETERY

GALLAGHER, HENRIETTE - (Sec. 3) (The Syracuse Journal, April 5, 1956) Mrs. John Gallagher was buried by the side of her husband in the Kendall Cemetery, Wednesday afternoon. She died at Salt Lake City, and graveside services were held at the cemetery. Her husband was buried at Kendall in 1904.
She was born November 12, 1869, and died March 31, 1956.

GALLEGHER, J. - (Sec. 3) (The Syracuse Journal, June 9, 1905) J. Gulegher, son-in-law of Mrs. M. H. Ward, died at the hospital in Kansas City, after an operation for stomach trouble. They are expecting his body here to be buried in the Kendall Cemetery. He leaves a wife and son to mourn his loss.
(Syracuse Journal, June 16, 1905, Kendall Items) Mrs. Gallegher and Hugh Gallegher, a brother of Mr. Gallegher, arrived Friday morning with the body of her husband, which was buried here at ten o'clock that day. Mr. Gallegher who is a Santa Fe Engineer, returned at once, to his home in Chicago. Mrs. Gallegher is still here with her mother, Mrs. Ward.

GALLEGHER, TWINS -

GARNER, LESLIE S. - (Sec. 4) (The Lakin Independent, Dec. 13, 1973) Leslie S. Garner, 75, Kendall, died Friday at Hamilton County hospital, Syracuse.
Born February 4, 1898, in Sugar Creek Township, Ohio, he married Edith Donnell, April 15, 1932, at Eads, Colorado. He was a retired Santa Fe station agent and had lived here since 1937.
Mr. Garner was a member of the Kendall Methodist Church, Masonic Lodge, American Legion, and was a World War I veteran.
Survivors include the widow; two daughters, Mrs. Glenda Pointer, Holcomb, and Mrs. Linda Vance, Phoenix, Arizona; three sisters, Mrs. Lucille Werner, Wapakoneta, Ohio, Mrs. Grace Harrod, Elida, Ohio, and Mrs. Lois Hover, Maumee, Ohio; four brothers, R. V. Garner, Myrtle Beach, South Carolina, Dr. R. W. Garner, Port Alberni, British Columbia, Canada, George Rupel and Clarence Rupel, both Gomer, Ohio; and five grandchildren.
Funeral services were held at 10:30 a.m., Dec. 10, at the Kendall Methodist Church, the Rev. Duane Harms officiating. Burial was in Kendall Cemetery.

KENDALL CEMETERY

GARR, LAWRENCE P. - (Sec. 3) (Kearny County Advocate, Jan. 17, 1913) Lawrence P. Garr born June 20, 1840; was married 25th of October 1863, to Leucinda J. Parkhurst, eleven children was born to them, one dying in infancy, the other ten lived to be grown and eight are still living. He died January 7, 1913. He was 73 years, 6 months, and 17 days old. Funeral services were held at the Dodge Schoolhouse by Rev. I. R. Williams and the remains were laid away in the Kendall Cemetery to await the resurrection morn.

He was a Corp. with the 7th Ind. Inf. Co. F. in the Civil War.

GARRISON, ALONZO LEE - (Sec. 3) (Syracuse Journal, Dec. 19, 1919) Alonzo Lee Garrison was born October 9th, 1868, in Logan County, Kentucky, and died at his home near Kendall, Kansas, Wednesday morning, December 10, 1919.

In 1870, with his parents, he was moved to Cedar County, Missouri, where they lived until the death of the parents. (Illegible)

He was converted at the age of 24 and united with the Presbyterian Church, later uniting with the Methodist Church in which he has remained a faithful member until his death.

He was united in marriage to Edith May Swinney in Grant County, Kansas, January 15th, 1900. To this union one child, Carrol, was born whom, with the mother, two sisters and five brothers of the deceased, remain to mourn his going.

About four years ago Mr. Garrison's eyes began to fail and he consulted the best specialists but nothing seemed to give him relief and with in less than a year he became totally blind and has remained so since. About ten months ago partial paralysis seemed to develop and since than he has been bedridden and helpless. Funeral services were held at Kendall, Thursday the 11th by the pastor, A. A. Hankins of Syracuse and the body was laid away in the Kendall Cemetery.

Card of thanks signed: Edith M. Garrison, Carrol W. Garrison, Martha A. Goostree.

GARRISON, EDITH - (Sec. 3) (The Lakin Independent, Oct. 19, 1923) Mrs. Edith Garrison died at the home of her father, Capt. T. W. Sweeney, of Eureka Springs, Arkansas. The remains were brought home and buried Tuesday at Kendall. We have not been able to obtain an obituary for publication.

Born January 20, 1870 and died October 13, 1923.

KENDALL CEMETERY

GOINS, LORAINE - (Syracuse Journal, Jan. 12, 1917) Miss Loraine Hayden was born in Bartlesville, Oklahoma, November 16, 1891. She was, at the time of her death, 25 years, 1 month and 18 days of age. She was married to Mr. Austin Goins at the age of 16. To this union were born four children, three sons and one daughter. Two sons preceded her to the great beyond, where all is bright.

She was converted in the Pentecostal Church four years ago, and lived a devoted Christian from that time until the day of her death on January 3, 1917.

She leaves a husband and two children, a son and a daughter, a mother, two sisters and four brothers to mourn their loss. Her mother took the little girl to live with her and be a mother to her. This is doubly hard on her, but the Lord is able to comfort our bruised hearts, and bind up the wounds that have been made in our hearts.

Loraine, being the name the departed was best known by among her friends as well as relatives, was loved by all who knew her, as she, owing to her cheerful disposition and smiling face, created an atmosphere of sunshine wherever she went. She will be greatly missed by us all but we do not mourn as those having no hope, for we know we shall meet her again, where there will be no more sorrowing.

Funeral services were held January 7th at 1 p.m. conducted by Rev. Frank Trotter. Interment was made in the Kendall Cemetery.

GOINS, NOT NAMED - Stillborn December 7, 1914. Mother Loraine Goins.

GOINS, NOT NAMED - Died in December 1916. Mother Loraine Goins.

GOOSTREE, GEORGE - (Sec. 3) (The Lakin Independent, Dec. 18, 1925) Another immortal spirit has winged its way from the low grounds of earth to the evergreen hills of God beyond the dark river. At about 4 o'clock Sunday, December 6, the emancipated soul of Mr. George Goostree passed on to Jesus. The funeral was held in the Kendall Church Wednesday, conducted by the pastors, Rev. Mawdsley and Rev. Calkins. The remains were laid to rest in the Kendall Cemetery. The many friends extend sympathy to the family and relatives.

He was born in 1847.

KENDALL CEMETERY

GOOSTREE, MARTHA ADELINE - (Sec. 3) (Syracuse Journal, May 25, 1928) Martha Adeline Garrison was born in Allen County, Kentucky, July 7, 1848, where she grew to young womanhood. She was united in marriage to George W. Goostree, October 18, 1866, and to this union was born six children, four girls and two boys. The father, two girls and two boys preceding her in death.

In 1878 the family moved to Butler County, Kansas, where they resided for a brief period. They moved to Hamilton County, Kansas, in 1879, where she lived until the day of her death, May 22, 1928, at the age of 80 yrs., 10 months and 15 days.

She leaves to mourn her death, two daughters, Mrs. Mary Hennebergh of Syracuse, Kansas, and Mrs. Pearl White of Kendall, Kansas; 10 grandchildren and 25 great grandchildren.

When but a child, Mrs. Goostree united with the Methodist Episcopal Church and ever remained a faithful member until she was called home. She was a good, kind and affectionate mother and neighbor and was loved by all who knew her. Her presence will be greatly missed in our community.

Funeral services were held in the Methodist Church at Kendall at 12:30 o'clock, May 24. Rev. Wiley of Syracuse officiating. Burial was made in the Kendall Cemetery.

GROPP, AMELIA - (Sec. 3) (Hamilton County Bulletin, Syracuse, Hamilton County, Ks., Friday, Feb. 19, 1892, Kendall News) Died at her home north of Kendall, Mrs. Amelia Gropp, last Sunday morning at 5 o'clock, aged 43 years. She leaves a large family of children and a sorrowing husband to mourn her loss. She was always known as a loving mother and an affectionate wife. The bereaved family have the sympathy of the community.

Born September 14, 1849.

GROPP, CHARLES OTTO - (Sec. 3) (Syracuse Journal, July 8, 1954) Otto Gropp, 74, resident of Coolidge, died at Donohue Memorial Hospital, Wednesday, July 7, 1954, at about 1:30 p.m. In failing health for some time. Mr. Gropp was admitted to the hospital Sunday.

He had been a resident of Hamilton County for 23 years, most of which were spent in ranching and farming in the Coolidge community.

Funeral services were held Saturday afternoon at 2:00 p.m. in the Baptist Church in Syracuse, with Rev. Al Wells in charge. Burial in the

KENDALL CEMETERY

Kendall Cemetery.
Survivors include his widow, Mrs. Nina Gropp of Coolidge; five sons, Clyde of Scott City, Enos of Kendall, Fred of Syracuse, Samuel of Lakin and Donald of Holly; and four daughters, Mrs. F. M. Patton of Scott City, Mrs. Pauline Coghill of Montrose, Colorado, Mrs. Myrtle Miller, Watsonville, California. and Mrs. Roberta Reynolds of Syracuse.

GROPP, DONALD - (Sec. 3) (The Lakin Independent, Jan. 16, 1975) Sam Gropp received word of the death of his brother, Don Gropp, 47, who died of pneumonia Tuesday in Arkansas City, Kansas. Funeral service will be Friday at 10 o'clock at the United Methodist Church in Syracuse. Burial will be in Kendall Cemetery.
Donald was a Cpl. in the U.S. Army. Born September 16, 1928 and died January 13, 1975.

GROPP, FRED O. - (Sec. 3) (The Lakin Independent, Oct. 6, 1988) Fred O. Gropp, 69, longtime state highway department employee, died on September 30, 1988, at St. Catherine Hospital, Garden City.
A lifetime resident of the Syracuse and Kendall area, Mr. Gropp retired after working 35 years for the highway department. He was born September 8, 1919, at Lakin and married Venus Herren on February 4, 1939, at Syracuse.
He was a member of Veterans of Foreign Wars, Holly, Colorado, and the Barbed Wire Association.
Survivors are his wife of the home; a son, Terry, Scott City; a daughter, Mary McCrary, Topeka; a brother, Enos Gropp, Bloomington, Illinois; two sisters, Pauline Coghill, Montrose, Colorado, and Roberta Kirby, Tucson, Arizona; three grandchildren and seven great grandchildren.
Funeral was held Monday at the Wesleyan Church, Syracuse, with the Revs. Rodney Collins and Stephen Darr officiating. Burial in the Kendall Cemetery. Greene Funeral Home, Syracuse, was in charge.

GROPP, HENRIETTA ANNA - (Sec. 3) (The Lakin Independent, Jan 11, 1955) Henrietta Anna Gropp, also known and Emma Gropp, was born on June 5, 1862, at Insterburg, Germany, the daughter of Martin and Dorothy Pritzkat, and departed this life on Thursday evening, January 6, 1955, at the age of 92 years, seven months and one day.
She was brought to her Savior in infancy and was made a member of

KENDALL CEMETERY

His Kingdom of Grace through baptism. At the age of 13 years she renewed her baptismal covenant in confirmation.

From her home in Europe she made the journey alone, to Western Kansas in 1893 when she was 30 years of age and was joined in marriage on April 6 of that year to John Samuel Gropp. Her children by this marriage are: Myrtle, of Nyssa, Oregon; Richard, of Lakin; George and Emma, of Deerfield; Arthur of Washington, D.C.; and Martha (who died in infancy). However, her duties as mother began immediately at marriage in that she gave a mothers care to the children of her husband's first marriage: Amelia, Otto, Albert, Rudolph, Elizabeth, and Adolph. At the time all but Amelia were yet in the home. Of these, Rudolph of Lakin and Elizabeth of Dalton, Kansas, are the only survivors.

They made their home on the farm 10 miles north of Kendall. While living there she had to lay to rest her husband who died March 26, 1923. Since 1938 and until the time of her death she had made her home in Lakin.

Mrs. Gropp was signally blessed with a long and peaceful life during which she gained countless friends, but during which also she faithfully and devotedly served her Savior in her home and her church. As a family in the rural area they were instrumental in bringing church services to that community. The services were generally held in the little school house, but many times she opened her home to serve this purpose also. These services were held during five pastorates of Immanuel Lutheran Church in Deerfield, and always remained a cherished memory to her.

She leaves to mourn her passing: her children, six grandchildren, one great grandchild, the children and grandchildren of her husband's former marriage, and many, many friends. Besides her husband and daughter who preceded her in death, there was also one brother, Fritz Fredrick Pritzkat, who died soon after she came to the United States.

To honor her memory many friends and relatives presented gifts in the form of Memorial wreaths to the Lutheran Hour, and the Lutheran Children Home in Winfield, Kansas, so that the good works that she did in this life may still follow after her.

GROPP, JOHN SAMUEL - (Sec. 3) (The Advocate, March 30, 1923) Samuel Gropp, an old and highly respected citizen of this county, passed away Tuesday morning at 4:30 o'clock, at his home 20 miles Northwest of Lakin. The deceased has resided in this county for over 35 years and

KENDALL CEMETERY

was in his seventy-sixth year when death called him. He leaves a large number of relatives and a host of friends to mourn his loss, and The Advocate extends heart felt sympathy to the bereaved ones, in this, their hour of sorrow. Funeral services were held in the Kendall Church Wednesday afternoon, conducted by Rev. Karl Karstensen, Lutheran Minister, and interment in the Kendall Cemetery.

Samuel Gropp was born June 19, 1848, at Insterburg, Germany. He served in the reserve army in the Franco-Prussian war in 1871, after which he lived in Dortmund three years with his family before coming to America.

In 1885 he came with his family to America, making his home in Iowa for two years, and in the spring of 1887 coming to Kearny County, where he took up government land and resided until his death on Tuesday morning, March 27, age 74 years, 9 months, and 8 days.

Mr. Gropp was married at the age of twenty-five to Mille Szagun, and nine children were born to this union, five of whom are still living: Otto, Albert and Rudolph Gropp, all of Lakin: Mrs. Millie Bridgeman of Cotter, Arkansas; and Mrs. Elizabeth O'Brien of Conway Springs, Kansas.

His wife died in 1892, and the following year he was married to Emma Pritzkat. Eight children were born to this union, of whom five are living: Richard, George, Emma and Arthur Gropp, all living at home, and Mrs. O. J. Kurz of Kendall. He also leaves a sister in Berlin, twenty five grandchildren, and one great grandchild to survive him.

The deceased was a member of the Evangelical Lutheran Church. The funeral services were conducted by Rev. K. J. Karstensen of Deerfield, assisted by Rev. Manka of Garden City, and the remains laid to rest in the Kendall Cemetery.

GROPP, MARTHA - (Sec 3) (Lakin Investigator, Dec. 21, 1906) The little two year and nine months old daughter of Mr. and Mrs. Samuel Gropp, living seventeen miles northwest of here, was found dead on the prairie Sunday afternoon last, three miles from home, where she had perished from hunger and exposure. The parents went away from home last Friday, leaving two children to the care of a farm hand. A short time after dinner the little one was missed by the man left in charge, and a search at once begun, and which was kept up until the body was found Sunday by members of the Kendall searching party. Funeral services were held Tuesday, and the remains laid to rest in the Kendall Cemetery.

KENDALL CEMETERY

The parents and immediate family have the sympathy of all our people in their affliction.

GROPP, NANCY ELIZABETH - (Sec. 3) (The Garden City Telegram, April 10, 1967) Funeral for Mrs. Nancy Elizabeth Gropp 79, of Lakin, who died Friday (April 7, 1967) at the Kearny County Hospital following a three week illness, will be at 10 a.m. (MST), tomorrow at the First Christian Church, Lakin.

The Rev. W. G. Ferguson will officiate, with burial at the Kendall Cemetery.

Mrs. Gropp was born August 16, 1887, at Winchester, Indiana. She had lived in Lakin most of her life. She was married there to Charles Otto Gropp May 29, 1910. He died in 1954.

She was a member of the First Christian Church, Lakin and the VFW Auxiliary, Lakin.

Surviving are five sons, Clyde, Scott City, Enos, Kendall, Fred, Syracuse, Samuel, Lakin, and Donald, Holly, Colorado; three daughters, Mrs. Helen Miller, Salinas, California, Mrs. Roberta Kirby, Colorado Springs, Colorado, and Mrs. Pauline Coghill, Montrose, Colorado; a brother, Fred Chessman, Lynn, Indiana; two sisters, Mrs. Jennie Marquis, Lynn and Mrs. Edith Miller, Dunkirk, Indiana; 26 grandchildren; and 11 great grandchildren.

The Davis Funeral Home, Lakin, is in charge of arrangements.

GROPP, TWINS - (Kearny County History Book, Volume I) Daughters of John Samuel and Henrietta Pritzkat Gropp, died at birth, January 27, 1902.

GUERNEE, CHILD- (Kendall Weekly Signal, Aug. 1886) A little child of Mr. Guernee's, living south of the Thompson house, died Wednesday night (August 18, 1886).

GUERNEE, MAGGIE - (The Kendall Boomer, April 28, 1886) Maggie, aged 5 years, died yesterday evening (April 27, 1886) of tubercular meningitis. The funeral will take place today from the family home on Kelley Street and the remains will be interred in the Kendall Cemetery.

(The Kendall Weekly Signal, Fri, April 30, 1886) Little Maggie Guernee, aged five years, died last Tuesday afternoon, the remains were interred on Wednesday, in the City Cemetery. The bereaved family have

KENDALL CEMETERY

the sympathy of the entire populace.

KENDALL CEMETERY

HANNA, MRS. JAMES - (Sec. 3) (Kendall Boomer, Oct. 13, 1886) Mrs. James Hanna, who had been sick for about two weeks, died last Friday (October 8, 1886) and the funeral took place Saturday afternoon. Three children are left motherless by this sad and untimely demise and a whole community extends the warmest sympathy to the stricken ones.

HANNA, WILLIAM - (Sec, 3) Died April 29, 1891, age 56 years, 17 days. A Sgt. in Co. F. 82nd Regt. Ind. Inf., Civil War.

HANSON, PETER J. - (The Kendall Boomer, Aug. 10, 1887) Died Peter J. Hanson on Friday morning, August 5, 1887, aged 32 years.

Hanson, as he was familiarly called, was a good and true man and it is no task for us to write these few words in his memory. In such a life as Hanson's the recital of his good qualities in the plainest and simplest words is the finest eulogy that mortal hand can indite. If he were living he would want nothing else. He was a plain, matter of fact man; scrupulously honest, candid, more than ordinarily intelligent, and earnest in every purpose. He had few failings and if a friend were asked to name them it would be difficult for him to do so.

Mr. Hanson was a native of Sweden. After coming to this country he spent some time at a school in Indiana. He came to this place a couple of years ago without means but as he was a good blacksmith he was provided with a shop and very soon paid for it. He followed his trade at intervals, proving up a pre-emption south of town last summer. At the time of his death he was in flourishing circumstances. His death was caused by catarrh which settled in his brain and was sudden and unexpected.

HARDING, LENORA AILEEN - (Syracuse Journal, Dec.12, 1930) Lenora Aileen Harding, daughter of Mr. and Mrs. James H. Harding, died Tuesday morning at the age of 8 years, 4 months, and 22 days. Her death was caused by leakage of the heart.

Lenora Aileen's heart was left weak after having the scarlet fever a year ago last February. She had been bedfast for the past 16 months. All during her illness she was very patient. She leaves to mourn her death her father, her mother, four sisters, all of Syracuse, also a number of relatives and friends. Funeral services were conducted Thursday afternoon by Rev. Danner at the Methodist Church.

KENDALL CEMETERY

HAZEN, DAVID - (Sec. 3) Born November 13, 1870 and died May 31, 1939.

(The Garden City Daily Telegram, Friday, June 2, 1939) Syracuse, June 2 - Friends here have been informed of the suicide of David Hazen, former Hamilton County resident who until recently made his home with a son, L. G. Hazen of near Coolidge.

Hazen hung himself from the rafter of a barn at the home of another son, William Hazen, of near Holly, Colorado. Friends said he had been in poor health more than a year and frequently had threatened to take his life.

He was 70 years old. Burial at Kendall.

HAZEN, EVA A. - (Sec. 3) Born September 8, 1875 and died April 2, 1968.

HAZEN, GARETT - (Sec. 3) Born April 3, 1897, 61 years old.

HEISINGER, ELSIE - (Sec. 4) (The Lakin Independent, July 26, 1979) Elsie Heisinger, 79, died Saturday at Syracuse. Born Elsie Mayhill, March 2, 1900, at Ingerham, Illinois, she married Henry Heisinger, October 7, 1920, at Lakin. He died September 6, 1972. She lived in Hamilton County since 1914.

She was a member of V.I.P. Club and Kendall United Methodist Church.

Survivors include a sister, Mrs. Vesta Allen of Syracuse, and nieces and nephews.

Funeral was held at 10 a.m. Wednesday, July 25, 1979, at the United Methodist Church, Syracuse; Rev. Tom Sheldon. Burial in Kendall Cemetery.

HEISINGER, HENRY - (Sec. 4) (The Lakin Independent, Sept. 14, 1972) Henry Heisinger, a long time resident of Kendall, died Wednesday morning, September 6, 1972, at Hamilton County hospital after a long illness.

Funeral services were held Saturday at 2 p.m. in the Kendall United Methodist Church with Rev. Duane Harms officiating. Interment was in the Kendall Cemetery, with military graveside rites by Lakin veterans.

Mr. Heisinger, who was 83, was born August 19, 1889, at Hartford and was married to Elsie Mayhill at Lakin, October 7, 1920.

KENDALL CEMETERY

He was a retired Santa Fe railroad employee and had lived in Kendall for 50 years. He was a veteran of World War I and was a 50 year member of the Lakin American Legion post.

His wife is his only survivor.

HELMICK, ALLEN - (The Kearny County Advocate, Jan. 30, 1920) Allen Helmick, aged seventy-four years and a veteran of the Civil War, passed away Saturday last, at his home in northwest Kearny. He has not been in the best of health for some time, and about two weeks ago, grew worse. Funeral services were held at the home Sunday last conducted by Rev. I. R. Williams, and interment in the Kendall Cemetery in charge of the Masonic order.

(Funeral Record) Died January 24, 1920. He was married, a mechanic and died Northeast of Kendall of paralysis of long duration, at the age of 74 years, 7 months, and 25 days.

HELMICK, ANNA - (The Lakin Independent, Nov. 17, 1922) Anna Clayton was born October 12, 1845, at Manchester, England, and died November 5, 1922, at the home of her niece, Mrs. F. L. Gold, near Springfield, Colorado. On December 25, 1865, she was united in marriage with Allen C. Helmick at New Harmony, Posey County, Indiana. Six children were born to the union. Three preceded her in death. Mr. Helmick died near Lakin, January 24, 1920. Of the immediate family she leaves to mourn her passing; one daughter, Mrs. E. F. Cornthwaite of Jenks, Oklahoma; two sons, Amos Helmick of Emmett, Idaho, and Audley Helmick of Wichita; one brother. W. H. Clayton of Lakin, Kansas; two half sisters; one half brother; two grandsons and three granddaughters.

Mrs. Helmick came to their homestead in Kearny County with her husband in 1908 where she lived until 1920. Her last residence was in Wichita, Kansas.

Mrs. Helmick united with the Reorganized Church of the Latter Day Saints, July 6, 1890, at Caney, Kansas. She was always a faithful advocate of her belief and interested in all kinds of religious work.

She was always ready and willing to help the needy and sick. She spent a great part of her life relieving the suffering of others. She was anxious to see all entertainments given by children and if necessary give what aid she could to encourage them. She took great delight in remembering the children on special days by giving them gifts.

KENDALL CEMETERY

Mrs. Helmick and son, Audley, were on their way to Phoenix, Arizona, to spend the winter when she became ill. She had been very delicate the last three years.

Funeral services were conducted by Rev. B. E. Willoughby at Kendall, Wednesday, November 8th, and the body was laid to rest in the Kendall Cemetery.

HENNEBERGH, ADOLPHUS P. - (Sec. 3) Syracuse Journal, Aug. 31, 1917) Wednesday forenoon at the little house on Ave. B, where the family had taken up their temporary residence a little more than one week before, one of the best citizens of Hamilton County was called from life to eternity. Dolph Hennebergh, as he was affectionately known by all his friends, many of whom had known him for more than a quarter of a century, was injured on July 5, when a horse he was riding stumbled and fell with him, causing internal injuries, the seriousness of which were not at first appreciated. Three weeks after he was hurt, he began to go about a little but he was obliged to give up and return to his bed. Last Saturday a surgical operation disclosed the fact that the bladder had been torn in his fall of July 5, and all this time a condition bordering on blood poison had existed and while all that was possible to be done was done, little hope was entertained that in his weakened condition he would be able to survive. Only his clean, abstemious life and perfect physical condition, his nurse said, enabled him to hold on to life as he did.

Adolphus Pinckard Hennebergh was born in Camden Point, Platte County, Missouri, April 21, 1855, and died in Syracuse, August 29, 1917, aged 62 years, 4 months. and 8 days. He came to this part of Kansas in 1883 and has lived in the neighborhood of Kendall ever since, a period of 34 years. He was one of the most successful stockmen in this county and had accumulated a nice compesency. On January 15, 1901, he was married to Mrs. Mary J. Dunn, who with two little daughters, Faye 14, and Hazel 12, survive him. He was kind and devoted husband and father and his home life was ideal and he took the place of father for the seven children of his wife by her former marriage, ever manifesting a keen interest in their welfare.

He was kind and benevolent and never missed an opportunity to contribute to any good cause, and his word was as good as a bond. He lived his life as we knew him with one hand, the other having been amputated in early life, because of blood poison necessitated the operation, but he always performed a man's work.

KENDALL CEMETERY

Of his own relatives one brother and two sisters survive him, namely, William H. Henneberg, Leon Springs, Texas; Mrs. C. S. Grubb, Barnes City, Iowa, and Mrs. L. J. Carter, Centralia, Missouri, the latter being with him when he passed away.

The funeral was held Thursday afternoon from the little church at Kendall, which he helped to build and support, and it was much too small to hold the friends who came to pay tribute of respect to their life long neighbor and friend. The services were conducted by Rev. A. A. Hankins of Syracuse. He was laid to rest in the Kendall Cemetery.

HOGBIN, INFANT - (The Kendall Boomer, May 19, 1886) The infant child of Mr. and Mrs. D. E. Hogbin died last week, aged 8 months, 11 days, and was buried Sunday, Rev. Gramley preaching the services.

(The Kendall Weekly Signal, Friday, May 21, 1886) Died on Friday, May 14th, 1886, Charles Freeport, son of Daniel E. and Mrs. Emma Hogbin, aged 8 months and 11 days. The funeral services were conducted at the City Hall, last Sabbath by Rev. C. H. Gramley, after which, a large procession of sympathizing friends followed the little body to the City Cemetery north of town, where he was softly laid away in the bosom of mother earth, and left to the care of the angels. The bereaved family have the sympathy of the entire people.

> The little life has passed away,
> From this life and its care;
> But 'twill live again in heaven above,
> More bright, and pure, and fair;
> So kindred, do not weep,
> In anguish nor in pain,
> The little one so gently sleeps;
> 'Twill be sweet to meet again.

HOPPE, FRED F. - (Sec. 3) (The Kearny County Advocate, Nov. 22, 1918) Fred Hoppe, our Santa Fe Agent, died Friday morning at Topeka after having two operations. He was buried in the Kendall Cemetery, Monday morning, by the Masons.

Miss Gladys Hoppe returned from Howell, Kansas, Friday night to attend her fathers' funeral. She has been working as operator at Howell.

HOPPE, LELAND F. - (Sec. 3) (Lakin Index, March 11, 1898) Mr. and Mrs. Fred Hoppe, of Kendall, have the heartfelt sympathy of their large circle of friends in the loss of their infant son, Monday last. He only

KENDALL CEMETERY

lived to beam in their home a couple of days, but the blow was none less severe or hard to bear. Dr. Johnson informs us that the grief-stricken mother is doing as well as could be expected.

HOUCK, CHARLOTTA F. - (Sec. 6) (The Lakin Independent, October 27, 1944) Mrs. Lottie Houck, 74, passed away Monday, October 23, 1944, at the Donahue Memorial Hospital in Syracuse. Funeral service was Thursday afternoon in the Lakin Methodist Church.

Mr. and Mrs. Houck came to Kearny County in 1915 and settled on a farm North of Kendall. Her husband, John M. Houck, and two children, Mrs. Marguerette Ferrin and Dale Houck, survive her passing.

(The Syracuse Journal, Aug. 11, 1944) Charlotta Frances, daughter of Jacob J. and Sarah E. Sanders was born December 7, 1869, at Danville, Illinois. She came with her parents to Kansas in 1877, when the parents emigrated to Burlington. Here she grew to womanhood and on January 7, 1891, she became the bride of John Houck. To this union was born a son, Jesse Dale and a daughter, Marguerite.

The family left Coffey County, Kansas, in 1911, and lived for four years at Cotter, Arkansas. The call of the newer west reached them and in 1915 they moved to a farm in Kearny County, Kansas, north of Kendall, where they have resided for nearly 30 years.

Nearly 75 years of labor and care bore heavily on this wonderful mother. Recent months of ill health used up her vitality and in spite of loving care by relatives on October 23, 1944, she entered the rest that God has prepared for all who labor and are heavy laden. Death came while she was having the care of skillful physicians and nurses at Donohue Memorial Hospital in Syracuse.

Those who will cherish her memory are: the aged companion, who had walked by her side for nearly 54 years, the daughter, Mrs. Marguerite Ferrin and family, the son, Jesse Dale Houck and family, a sister, Caroline, of Mitchell, California, six grandchildren along with other relatives and friends.

A tender memorial service was held at Lakin Methodist Church on October 26, by Rev. R. L. Wells and Rev. L. S. Cowan. Interment was at Kendall Cemetery. The body was borne to its final rest by the following neighbors: Herb Kurz, Roy Kurz, Carl Palmer, Harry Palmer, Henry Bennett and Henry All.

HOUCK, JOHN M. - (Sec. 6) (The Lakin Independent, May 18, 1945) J.

KENDALL CEMETERY

M. Houck passed away Monday, May 14, 1945, in the hospital in Lakin. He had been ill a long time but two weeks ago he fell and fractured a hip.

Mr. Houck came to this county from Arkansas about 30 years ago and settled on a farm north of Kendall with his family. Mrs. Houck preceded him in death last October.

Funeral service was Thursday afternoon in the Lakin Methodist Church.

John Mansfield, youngest son of John and Caroline Houck, was born in Ohio, July 23, 1860, and departed from this life May 14, 1945, at Lakin, Kansas, at the age of 84 years, 9 months and 21 days.

When he was three years of age, the family moved to Illinois where he grew to manhood. In the year of 1877 they moved to eastern Kansas, near the town of Burlington, where he lived until 1911, moving to Cotter, Arkansas, in that year. In 1915 they came to Kearny County, Kansas, settling on a farm in the northwest part of the county, where he has since lived.

On January 7, 1891, he was united in marriage to Charlotta Frances Sanders. To this union were born two children, Dale Houck and Marguerette Ferrin, both of Kendall, Kansas. His wife preceded him in death last October 23. He had five brothers and two sisters.

He leaves to mourn his passing, his two children, five grandchildren and many nieces and nephews. Also many neighbors and friends.

HUBER, MIKE - (Sec. 3) 1878-1898.

HUBER, THOMAS VICTOR - (Sec. 3) (The Lakin Independent, Sept. 26, 1963) Thomas Victor Huber was born to Mike and Wilhelmina Huber on August 12, 1885, in Chicago, Illinois. He died after only a few days of illness, on September 19, 1963, at the Donahue Memorial Hospital in Syracuse, Kansas. Tom came to Kendall, Kansas, with his parents as one of the early settlers in 1886 and lived his entire life in and around Kendall. His life was devoted to farming and cattle.

Those who survive him are: a sister, Martha M. Allen; a brother, William P. Roth; two nephews, William and Tom Roth; one niece, Ellen May Kauffman, all of Kendall community. There are also cousins, Geo. Fehrenbacher of Seward, Kansas, and Howard Fehrenbacher of Syracuse, Kansas, as well as many friends.

Funeral services were held at the Kendall Methodist Church at 2:00,

KENDALL CEMETERY

September 21, 1963, with burial in the Kendall Cemetery. Rev. Paul G. Brooks presided.

HUGHBANKS, OLIVER - (Lakin Investigator, July 3, 1908) Oliver Hughbanks, living eight miles south of Kendall, died at his home, Thursday June 25th, of dropsy. Interment in Kendall Cemetery, J. E. Johnson, presiding.

(The Kearny County Advocate, July 2, 1908) Hughbanks died on his homestead south of Kendall, June 24, aged about 50 years.

HULBERT, MRS. - (The Kearny County Advocate, July 28, 1933) Mrs. Hulbert, mother of Ed Mitchell, passed away at her home in Syracuse, last Thursday evening, and was laid to rest in the Kendall Cemetery. The community extends heart felt sympathy to the bereaved ones.

KENDALL CEMETERY

JOHNSON, ABIGAIL - (Sec. 3) (The Syracuse Journal, Feb. 1, 1901, Kendall News) Died, Grandma Johnson, mother of J. E. and H. M. Johnson of Kendall. She had been sick a long time and passed quietly away Saturday evening to a land where there is no sickness or sorrow. She patiently bore her cross to the very last, aged 82 years, 1 month and 8 days. She leaves many friends and relatives to mourn her death.
She was born December 18, 1818, and died January 26, 1901.

JOHNSON, ALICE - (Sec. 3) 1873-1908

JOHNSON, CHARLIE - (Sec. 3) 1872-1936

JOHNSON, FRANKLIN P. - (Sec. 2) (The Lakin Independent, Kendall News, Sept. 20, 1940) The community extends their sympathy to the family of Frank Johnson whose funeral services were held September 7, at the Kendall Methodist Church.
He was born in 1853.

JOHNSON, MRS. HENRY - (The Kendall Weekly Signal, Aug. 13, 1886) Died on Monday, 9th day of August 1886, in the Veteran addition, Mrs. Henry Johnson. She leaves a husband and six children to mourn her departure. Although in poor circumstances financially, Mrs. Johnson was a kind and indulgent mother, and as most of the children are small she will be doubly mourned. And we feel sure that our good people will kindly look to their wants and comforts. But it is indeed a sad and painful task to us to be called upon to chronicle the departure of life, leaving to the cold unfeeling world, motherless, little children who have had the care and protection of a kind and indulgent parent, depriving them of a something that can never be replaced nor recalled. The place of a real mother can never be filled by proxy, no matter how kind and true and indulgent the world may be, it can never give back the real happiness and simplified confidence of a mother. Oh, I tell you if there is an angel saint taking shape and form of the human being, and dwelling upon a material earth breathing a material air it is a true mother, if there is truth in life a reality in death and an affection for like it is the affinity of mother and child whose very existence are essential one to the other-- one the plant, one the flower.

> Tears fell when thou wert dying,
> From eyes unused to weep.

KENDALL CEMETERY

And long, where thou are lying,
Will tears the cold turf steer.
When hearts, whose truth was proven,
Like thine, are laid in earth.
There should a wreath be woven,
To tell the world their worth.

JOHNSON, MARGARET J. - (Sec. 2) (The Kearny County Advocate, Jan. 17, 1930) The friends and neighbors were sorry to hear of the death of Mrs. Maggie Johnson, who passed away Saturday, January 4, 1930, at her home in Kendall. She had been a resident of this county for many years and an active church worker. Funeral services were conducted by Rev. Wiley, January 6th, and she was laid to rest in the Kendall Cemetery. She leaves to mourn her loss, her husband, two sons, two daughters, Mrs. Minnie Slate, of Kendall, and Mrs. Florence Pugh, of Coolidge.

(The Lakin Independent, Jan. 17, 1930) Margaret Jane Hall was born March 31, 1861, in Columbiana County, Ohio, and departed from her friends to be with Jesus on January 4, 1930, at the age of 68 years, nine months, and 4 days. In June 1884, she was united in marriage to Franklin Pierce Johnson, who is left to go when the Master calls. Eight children were born to this union, four of whom still survive, and four of whom have crossed the border land of eternity to live in the spirit realm. She and her husband have lived in Hamilton County for the past 45 years.

Those to mourn her going are her husband; and children, Charles Christopher Johnson and Mrs. Minnie Pearl Slate of Kendall, Kansas, Elmer H. Johnson of Bellflower, California, and Mrs. Florence Pugh of Coolidge, Kansas; and 13 grandchildren.

(Highland News) Neighbors and friends of Mrs. Maggie Johnson were sorry to learn of her death Saturday night, January 4th, at her home in Kendall. She had lived there a good many years and was an active worker in the church. Funeral services were held the following Monday in the church by Rev. Wiley, and the body was laid to rest in the Kendall Cemetery. She leaves to mourn her departure: her husband, Frank Johnson; two sons, Charley of Kendall and Elmer of California; two daughters, Mrs. Minnie Slate of Kendall and Mrs. Florence Pugh of Coolidge.

JOHNSON, STEPHEN - (Sec. 3) (The Syracuse Journal, Feb. 9, 1894)

KENDALL CEMETERY

Died on Tuesday morning, February 6, 1894, Mr. Stephen Johnson, in the 78th year of his age.

The death of Grandpa Johnson closes a long and useful life. His native state was Ohio, which he left when quite a young man, to seek his fortune in the then boundless and unsettled west. In the years of his life he has witnessed great changes, which are more astonishing when considered that they are all embraced within the span of one human life. The civilization of the beginning of the nineteenth century, in which he was born, and that of its close, which witnessed his demise, are quite different to human liberty and human progress. Mr. Johnson is the father of George Y. Johnson of Brown County, J. E. and H. M. Johnson of Kendall and Charles Johnson, at present in Wyoming. He leaves the aged partner of his joys and sorrows through all these years of their married life, to mourn his loss, and to form another link of affection between here and the spirit land, where youth is eternal and partings are unknown. The funeral was held on Thursday and the worn out body was laid to rest in the Kendall Cemetery.

JOHNSON, THOMAS - (Sec. 3) Died December 20, 1892, 43 years, two months and 16 days old.

JOHNSON, WILLIE H. - (Sec. 3) Son of T. & L. B. Johnson, died May 27, 1891, age 10 months and 8 days.

KENDALL CEMETERY

KAUFFMAN, CHARLES ORREN - (Sec. 2) (The Lakin Independent, Oct. 1, 1961) Charles Orren Kauffman, son of Mr. and Mrs. George Kauffman, was born at Larned, Kansas, January 9, 1915, and passed away at Garden City, Kansas, September 30, 1961, at 46 years of age.

Charles spent four years, nine months and 28 days in the service of his country in World War II. One year of that time was spent in the hospital in Germany near Berlin, after which he was flown back to the states,

On January 8, 1947, he was united in marriage to Ellen Roth at Syracuse, Kansas. To this union four children were born but only two survive. They are Charles, 13, and Margarette, 8, of the home. Other survivors besides his wife, Ellen, include three brothers and three sisters. One aunt, Mrs. Lizzie Phillips of Kendall, also survive

He had worked at the carpenter trade for the last five years. He worked a full day the last day of his life.

His parents, three brothers and two of his own children have preceded him in death.

KAUFFMAN, ELLEN M. - (Sec. 2) (The Lakin Independent, Sept. 9, 1965) Funeral services for Mrs. Ellen M. Kauffman, 35, her daughter, Margarette Ellen Kauffman, 12 and Linda Kay Nichols, 2, were held at 2 p.m., Wednesday, at the Syracuse Methodist Church, the Rev. Harry Walz officiating. Burial was in the Kendall Cemetery.

They were killed Saturday morning in a car train collision one mile east of Syracuse.

Mrs. Kauffman was born October 5, 1929, at Kendall. Her husband, Chas., died four years ago. She and her daughter had lived in Kendall since moving here from Garden City.

Margarrette Ellen Kauffman was born January 26, 1954, at Syracuse.

Survivors of Mrs. Kauffman and her daughter include a son and brother, Charles, of the home; her parents, Mr. and Mrs. Willie Roth, her brothers, Thomas and William, all of Kendall.

They were members of the Methodist Church in Kendall.

Linda Kay Nichols was born June 28, 1963, at Abilene. Her mother died in 1963. Her family moved to Kendall after Mrs. Nichol's death.

Her survivors include the father, James, two sisters, Margaret and Mary Alice; a brother, Lawrence, all of the home; and her grandmother, Mrs. Hazel Nichols, Satanta.

KENDALL CEMETERY

KAUFFMAN, MARGARETTE ELLEN - (Sec. 2) (See obit of Ellen M. Kauffman.

KAUFFMAN, MARTHA ANN - (Sec. 2) (The Lakin Independent, Feb. 2, 1951, Kendall News) Martha Ann Kaufman, daughter of Mr. and Mrs. Charley Kaufman, passed away, Sunday, January 28, 1951, at the Donahue Hospital at Syracuse. Funeral services were held at Kendall, Tuesday afternoon. They have the sympathy of the entire community.
She was born May 31, 1947.

KAUFFMAN, PAUL EDWARD - (Sec. 2) (Lakin Independent, Friday, Dec. 16, 1955) Paul Edward Kauffman, son of Charlie and Ellen Kauffman, was born January 22, 1952, and departed this life December 8, 1955, after an extended illness. (Headstone has birth date of 1951)
He will be sadly missed by his parents who live in Kendall, Kansas, his brother, Charles, and sister, Margaret, his grandparents, Mr. and Mrs. Bill Roth of Kendall, his great grandmother, Mrs. Lizzie Phillips of Kendall, and a number of aunts and uncles.
One sister, Martha, preceded him in death.

> "O not in cruelty, not in wrath,
> The reaper came that day;
> 'Twas an angel visited this green earth
> And took the flowers away." Longfellow

Funeral services were conducted at 2 p.m., December 9, 1955, by the Rev. Mary Ellen Markley at Kendall Methodist Church. Interment was in the Kendall Cemetery.

(Syracuse Journal, Thurs, Dec. 8, 1955) Paul Eddy Kauffman, small son of Mr. and Mrs. Charles Kauffman of Kendall, died early this morning in Donohue Memorial Hospital. Born January 22, 1952, the little boy had been an invalid since birth and suffered from spastic convulsions.
He was brought to the hospital about 10:30 last night and passed away at 4 o'clock this morning. Funeral services held at the Kendall Methodist Church, Friday, at 2:00 p.m., and burial in the Kendall Cemetery.

KLASSEN, HERB - (Sec. 5) (The Lakin Independent, July, 1964) Herb Klassen, a farmer in the Menno community in Hamilton County most of his life, died Thursday on his 60th birthday anniversary in Donahue Hospital in Syracuse, where he had been a patient eight days. He had

KENDALL CEMETERY

been in ill health six years. He had lived in Kendall one year.
He was born July 16, 1904, in Medford, Oklahoma. He was a member of the Menno Methodist Church.

Survivors include the widow, Ruth; a son, John of the home; two sisters, Mrs. Hilda Wiens, Reedley, California, and Mrs. Lena Laisure, Wichita; three brothers, Adolph, Hamilton County; Elmer, Sacramento, California; Henry of Redding, California.

Funeral services were held at 2:30 p.m. (MST) Saturday in the Syracuse Methodist Church, Rev. Harry Walz officiating. Burial was in the Kendall Cemetery.

KLASSEN, RUTH C. - (Sec. 5) (The Garden City Telegram, Sept. 5, 1980) Ruth C. Klassen, 82, died Wednesday, September 3, at the Hamilton County Hospital, Syracuse.

Born Ruth C. Hyle, December 17, 1897, in Lyons County, she married Herb Klassen May 9, 1931, at Saffordville. He died in 1964. She was a resident of the area for 38 years.

Mrs. Klassen was a member of the Eastern Star, Syracuse.

Survivors include a son, John, Grover City, California; a brother, George Hyle, Eureka; two sisters, Mrs. Leona Wells, Elmdale, and Mrs. Dorothe Myers, Spokane, Washington; and three grandchildren.

Funeral was held at 10 a.m. (MST) September 8, at the First United Methodist Church, Syracuse, Mr. Albert Lambeth officiated. Burial at the Kendall Cemetery.

Greene Funeral Home, Syracuse, took care of arrangements and memorials were made to the Hamilton County Long Term Care Home, Syracuse.

KURZ, CARL - (Sec. 6) Carl W. Kurz died from influenza in Camp Fort Crook, at Omaha, Nebraska, on October 18, 1918. He was the son of Joseph B. Kurz and Rosa Kurz (pioneer family who farmed north of Kendall)

Carl William was born March 2, 1897, at Savannah, Missouri.

KURZ, CONRAD W. - (Sec. 6) (The Kearny County Advocate, May 28, 1937) Con Kurz, a well known northwest Kearny County farmer, who has been ill for several months, passed away at a hospital in Colorado Springs, Tuesday, May 25th, 1937. His remains were brought to his old home, and interment was made in the Kendall Cemetery. The Advocate

KENDALL CEMETERY

extends heartfelt sympathy to the bereaved ones, in this, their hour of sorrow.

(The Lakin Independent, June 4, 1937) Conrad Walter Kurz was born at Nodaway, Andrew County, Missouri, on July 10, 1895, and departed this life May 24, 1937, at Colorado Springs, Colorado.

While he was a small boy he migrated to Kearny County, Kansas, with the family and here he grew to manhood.

He was an active farmer and rancher for several years in the community of Kendall and in 1918 he was drafted into the service of the United States as a soldier of the World War, being stationed at Camp Funston, Kansas.

In 1919 he was united in marriage with Margueriette Houck and to this union two children were born Donald Dean and Walter Dale. The latter preceded him in death.

He had been ill for several years and for the last six months he had been bedfast, yet he was patient in all his suffering, never complaining, always appreciating everything that was done for him.

He is survived by his mother, Mrs. Rosa Kurz of Kendall; six brothers and two sisters, one brother, Carl, having preceded him in death: Oscar of Nyssa, Oregon, Albert of Chicago, Illinois, Edward of Omaha, Nebraska, Lydia Lindquist of Kansas City, Missouri, Sylvia Roth of Lakin, Kansas, and Herbert and Roy of Kendall, Kansas; also a host of other relatives and loyal friends.

The local American Legion post attended the funeral services at Syracuse and conducted the burial rites at the grave in Kendall Cemetery where interment was made.

KURZ, DONALD DEAN - (Sec. 6) Donald Dean Kurz was born December 8, 1926, near Kendall, Kearny County, Kansas. He departed this life October 6, 1953, at Bassano, Alberta, Canada, at the age of 26 years, nine months and 28 days.

He attended the public schools of Syracuse, Kendall and for a time at McClave, Colorado.

He answered the call of his country and entered the Navy, December 15, 1943. He was discharged from that branch of our armed forces on April 25, 1946.

He was joined in holy wedlock on June 28, 1946, to Louise Leslie, also of Syracuse. To this happy union were given two beautiful daughters, Deanna Lou, born June 24, 1948, and Debra Marlene, born

KENDALL CEMETERY

January 15, 1953. With these to mourn this great loss remain his wife, Louise, his devoted mother, Marqueritte Ferrin and a kindly stepfather, Burt Ferrin. Dean's father, Conrad Walter Kurz, and a younger brother preceded him in death.

Dean, a quiet, lovable boy, was liked and respected by all. The sad news of his early passing from this world came as a shock to the community where he had spent almost his entire life. One who knew him well remarked that Dean never harmed any human being by either word or deed. Could a greater tribute be given?

O! not in cruelty, not in wrath, the reaper came that day; 'twas an angel visited the green earth and took our Dean away. -- A friend

KURZ, JOSEPH BENEDICT - (Sec. 5) (The Lakin Independent, Nov. 20, 1936) Joseph Benedict Kurz was born in Worb, Canton Bern, Switzerland, on July 15, 1865, and passed away from this life at his home on November 14, 1936, at 8:30 p.m., at the age of 71 years, 3 months and 29 days.

He emigrated to the United States of American in 1881 accompanied by his brothers, Fred and John. They settled near Amazonia, Missouri, and prepared a home for the rest of the family who followed later.

He was baptized in infancy, at the age of 15 was confirmed to the Reform Church and later was united with the St. John's Reform Church in which faith he remained until his death.

He was united in marriage to Rose Oppliger of Nodaway, Missouri, on April 5, 1893, and to this union nine children were born, all of whom are living except Carl who preceded him in death at Fort Crook, Omaha, Nebraska, during the World War.

On May 1, 1906, he came with his family to Kearny County, Kansas, to make his home. He resided here until his death.

He leaves to mourn: his faithful wife, Rosa; six sons and two daughters, Oscar of Nampa, Idaho, Conrad of Kendall, Mrs. Leslie Lindquist of Kansas City, Missouri, Albert of Chicago, Illinois, Edward, Herbert, Mrs. Carl Roth, and Roy, all of Kendall; three grandsons; two granddaughters; and two brothers, Alex of Thun, Switzerland, and Godfred of Savannah, Missouri; and a host of other relatives and friends.

He was devoted to his family and a true friend to all who knew him. His life has been lived as an open book and could join with other valiant spirit who sang:

KENDALL CEMETERY

> Under the wide and starry sky
> Dig the grave and let me lie.
> Glad did I live and gladly die
> And I laid me down with a will.
> This be the verse you grave for me,
> "Here he lies where he longed to be,
> Home is the sailor, home from the sea,
> And the hunter, home from the hill."

Relatives who came to attend the funeral were: Mrs. Oscar Kurz, Nampa, Idaho; Mrs. and Mrs. Leslie Lindquist, Kansas City, Missouri; Messrs, Fred, Eric, Heinz, Elmer, and Ernest Kurz of Savannah, Missouri; Mr. and Mrs. Oscar Oppliger and son, John, Mrs. Lillie Yost and sons, Fred and Ulrich, daughter, Mrs. Ernest Jahde, and Mrs. Clarence Whistler, all of Ransom, Kansas.

KURZ, ROSA ANNA - (Sec. 5) (Garden City Telegram, Feb. 8, 1964) Mrs. Rosa Anna Kurz, 90, of Syracuse, died February 6, 1964, at Sabo Manor, Lakin, after three years' illness. Born April 22, 1873, at Nodaway, Missouri, she had lived on a farm in Kearny County from 1906 to 1946 and had been a resident of Syracuse for 15 years before moving to the nursing home. Her husband, Joseph, died in 1936.

Member: Syracuse Methodist Church.

Survivors: daughters, Mrs. Lydia White, Ocala, Florida and Mrs. Sylvia Roth, Nyssa, Oregon; sons, Oscar, Nyssa, Albert, Oak Forest, Illinois, Edward, LeMars, Iowa, Herbert, Weiser, Idaho, Roy, Kendall; and a sister, Mrs. Lillie Yost, Ransom.

Funeral: 2 p.m. (MST) Monday, at the church, Rev. Harry Walz. Burial: Kendall Cemetery.

KURZ, WALTER DALE - (Sec. 6) (The Lakin Independent, February 5, 1932) Walter Dale, the little son of Con and Marguerite Kurz, died on January 25th, 1932, at the early age of 1 year, 8 months and 3 days. The child took seriously ill with intestinal flu on January 15th. He was later taken to the Donohue Memorial Hospital at Syracuse and there passed from this life. He was a very lovable child and a bundle of joy in the home, where he will be greatly missed by his parents and his five year old brother, Dean.

Funeral services were held Wednesday afternoon, January 27, from the Kendall church, with Rev. Warren Conn in charge, and the little body was laid to rest in the Kendall Cemetery.

KENDALL CEMETERY

LAUTZENHEISER, ADAM - (Sec. 6) (1910 Census of Hamilton County, Ks., Kendall Twp.) Adam was 69 yrs old. born in Ohio, wife Florence E., 60, son William E., 22.
Born April 15, 1839 and died August 4, 1916.

LAUTZENHEISER, FLORENCE - (Sec. 6) Born April 4, 1849 and died May 7, 1936.

LAUTZENHEISER, PEARL - (The Syracuse Journal, April 9, 1969) Graveside services was held at Kendall Cemetery at 2:30 p.m., Friday, for Mrs. Pearl Lautzenheiser, a former resident of Kendall and Syracuse who died Monday at the La Junta hospital. Mrs. Lautzenheiser, who was 81, had been hospitalized for several weeks.
 She was born at Stuart, Iowa, on July 22, 1887, and moved to Kendall in 1910. She was married in 1913 to William Edgar Lautzenheiser. He preceded her in death on May 29, 1935.
 The Lautzenheisers lived in Kendall and Syracuse until 1922, when they moved to La Junta. He was employed by the Santa Fe Railroad.
 Mrs. Lautzenheiser is survived by eight nieces and nephews and a good friend, Mrs. Agnes Morgan of Pratt.
 Funeral services were held at 9:30 a.m., Friday, at the Peacock-Green Memorial Chapel in La Junta, with interment in the Kendall Cemetery.

LAUTZENHEISER, WILL - (The Lakin Independent, April 5, 1935) Will Lautzenheiser died last Friday, May 29, 1935, at La Junta from blood poisoning that developed as a result of an automobile accident. Mr. Lautzenheiser formerly was a resident of this county, living three miles north of Kendall, and for six years was a partner of Henry Austin in the well drilling business. In 1920 he moved to La Junta and became a railroader. He leaves his wife, his aged mother, three sisters, and a brother. Funeral services were held Monday afternoon at Kendall by the Methodist minister from Syracuse and burial was made in the Kendall Cemetery by the Masonic Lodge of Syracuse of which he was a member.
 He was 47 years, 9 months and 20 days old.

LAWRENCE, SAMUEL - (Sec. 3) (The Lakin Investigator, Kendall News, Feb. 25, 1910) Died, at his home in Kendall, Tuesday, February 22d, after a long illness, Samuel Lawrence, aged 52 years. Deceased was born in North Girard, Pennsylvania, November 8, 1857, where he

KENDALL CEMETERY

resided until he came to Kearny County in 1908. He leaves a wife and one daughter to mourn his loss. Funeral services were held at Kendall school house, Wednesday at 2:00 p.m., Rev. E. E. Carter of Syracuse, officiating.

LAWRENCE, VALLEDIA D. - (Sec. 3) Date of birth 1860.

LEMONS, FRANCES R. - (Sec. 2) (The Lakin Independent, February 16, 1995) Frances R. Lemons, 63, Kendall, died February 11, 1995, at St. Catherine Hospital, Garden City.

She was born September 21, 1931, at Olney, Illinois, the daughter of Elva and Alta Ann Trenary Mayhill. She lived in Kendall before moving to Brea, California, for 30 years. She moved back to Kendall in 1989. She was a homemaker.

She attended Church of the Nazarene, Brea, California.

On August 31, 1950, she married Charles D. Lemons at Raton, New Mexico. He survives.

Other survivors include: three sons, Chuck, Moreno Valley, California, Joe, Syracuse, and Bill, Kendall; two daughters, Anne L. Mack, Kansas City, Missouri, and Betty F. Kaufman, Argenta, Illinois; two brothers, John Mayhill, Syracuse, and Joe Mayhill, Oakland, California; six sisters, Joan Siddons, Cisco, Illinois, Mary Hinterscher, Ingerham, Illinois, Donna K. Alexander, Wheatland, Wyoming, Marie Ewalt, Crane, Missouri, Linda Swisher, Fairgrove, Missouri, and Donna Fisher, Argenta, Illinois; 12 grandchildren; and two great grandchildren.

Funeral was at 1 p.m., MST, Wednesday, at Kendall United Methodist Church, Kendall, with the Rev. Leroy Smoot presiding. Burial was in the Kendall Cemetery.

LEMONS, WILLIAM RILEY - (Sec. 1) (Garden City Telegram, April 11, 1997) Icy road conditions contributed to two injury accidents in southwest Kansas Thursday.

A 41 year old Kendall man, William R. Lemons, was killed Thursday in a two vehicle crash on icy roads near Lakin,

Three Lakin residents were injured. Barbara Stipe, 46, Lakin, was in good condition and Rosa Graham, 70, was in fair and stable condition at Kearny County Hospital, Lakin. Kelly Stipe, 18, was treated and released with minor injuries.

Kansas Highway Patrol said Lemons was eastbound on U.S. 50

KENDALL CEMETERY

highway at 8:10 p.m. about four miles east of Lakin when his 1979 Chevrolet pickup truck slid out of control and into the path of Barbara Stipe, westbound in a 1992 Buick station wagon.

Kelly Stipe and Graham were passengers in the Buick. The pickup was demolished and the Buick sustained more than $500 damage.

Lemons and Kelly Stipe were not wearing their seat belts, Barbara Stipe and Graham were.

(The Garden City Telegram, April 14, 1997) Graveside service for William Riley Lemons, 41, was to be at 2 p.m. CT today at Kendall Cemetery, with the Rev. Leroy Smoot officiating.

Mr. Lemons died Thursday, April 10, 1997, from injuries suffered in a traffic accident near Lakin.

Born May 23, 1955, at Lakin, he was the son of Charles Dean and Frances Rachel Mayhill Lemons. He had been a resident of Hamilton and Kearny counties for five years, moving from Estacada, Oregon, where he had lived since 1979.

Mr. Lemons was a journeyman welder and pipe fitter for Diversified Construction Inc., Garden City. He was a veteran of the U.S. Army.

He is survived by a son, William Riley Lemons, Jr. and a daughter Stephanie Lemons, both of Estacada; his father, Kendall; two brothers, Charles Dean Lemons, Jr., Moreno Valley, California, and Joe Monte Lemons, Syracuse; two sisters, Anne Mack, Kansas City, Missouri, and Betty Kaufman, Argenta, Illinois; and his companion, Katherine Kisel, Lakin. He was preceded in death by his mother.

Greene Funeral Home, Syracuse was in charge of arrangements.

LIGGETT, EFFIE SIDERS - (Sec. 3) (Kendall Gazette, July 28, 1887) Mrs. C. F. Liggett died last Sunday and was buried Monday afternoon in Kendall Cemetery. Mrs. Liggett had many friends in this town, all of whom were shocked to hear of her death. The remains were followed by a large crowd to their last resting place.

(Kendall Boomer, July 27, 1887) Died Mrs. Effie Liggett, wife of C. F. Liggett on Sunday afternoon, three miles northeast of town of inflammation of the bowels, after an illness of about two weeks.

Mrs. Liggett was for nearly a year a resident of this town and ably assisted her husband in the publication of the Signal. She was highly regarded by all who knew her and the sad news of her death was received with regret on every hand. The family consisting of husband and wife, moved on their claim last spring and were making an honest

KENDALL CEMETERY

endeavor to acquire a title to the land.

Deceased was first attacked with fever a couple of weeks ago and when a physician was summoned she was unconscious and at times violent and no hope was entertained for her recovery. She was interred in the Kendall Cemetery on Monday afternoon. The funeral was largely attended.

LITTLE - (The Kendall Boomer, Dec. 8, 1886) Mr. Frank Little's son, aged 21 years, died last Sunday, (December 5, 1886) of malarial fever at his home south of here and was buried in the Kendall Cemetery, Tuesday.

LOWERY, LOIS MOLLY - (Sec. 2) (The Garden City Telegram, Feb. 2, 1982) Lois Molly Lowry, 55, died Monday at Hamilton County Hospital, Syracuse, after a short illness. She was a cafe owner/operator and had been a resident of Syracuse since 1967.

Born Lois McMillian, April 4, 1927, at Jerusalem, Arkansas, she was married to Irvan Meyers. He died in 1971. She was married to Richard Lowery, April 3, 1975, at Garden City.

Mrs. Lowery was a member of Southern Baptist Church, Syracuse.

Survivors are her husband, of the home; a son, Frank Meyers, Syracuse; two daughters, Lois Louise Harris, Chouteau, Oklahoma, and Nora Lewis, Pratt; her mother, Effie McMillian, Syracuse; two half brothers, Kenny McMillian, Hugo, Oklahoma, and W. L. McMillian, Pawhuska, Oklahoma; two half sisters, Barbara Coppage, Broken Arrow, Oklahoma, Wanda White, Tulsa, Oklahoma; two step sisters, Nora Perry, Little Rock, Arkansas, and Ruby McMillian, Coweta, Oklahoma; thirteen grandchildren and three great grandchildren.

Funeral at 10 a.m., MST, Wednesday at the Southern Baptist Church, the Rev. Louis Davis officiating. Burial at Kendall Cemetery, Kendall.

LOWERY, RICHARD - Second husband of Lois Molly Meyers, married in 1975.

KENDALL CEMETERY

MARRS, ETHEL LOUISE - (Sec. 4) (The Lakin Independent, Oct. 19, 1978) A Kendall woman was killed and her two daughters injured in a traffic accident northwest of Lakin on a Kearny County road Monday night, October 16, 1978.

Ethel Marrs, 33, Kendall, died Tuesday evening at Denver General Hospital where she had been transferred from St. Catherine Hospital at Garden City.

Kansas Highway Patrol officials said one of the daughters, Joanna, 5, was also transferred to Denver General from St. Catherine. Information about her condition was not available.

A second daughter, Sharon, 7, was treated and released from Hamilton County Hospital.

Officials said the accident occurred about 8:20 p.m. Monday on a county road approximately 14 miles northwest of Lakin. The Marrs car was northbound when it swerved to avoid a vehicle parked in the road and another vehicle parked on the side of the road.

Ethel Louise Marrs was born October 2, 1945, at Syracuse and died October 17, 1978, in a Denver, Colorado, hospital as a result of injuries received in a car-truck collision northwest of Lakin on October 16.

She married George Marrs on June 15, 1969, and to this union two daughters were born.

Ethel was only with those she loved, and who loved her for a short while. Her gentle hands and loving heart will never be forgotten by those who lives she touched.

Ethel loved animals and working with children.

She leaves to mourn: her husband, George; daughters, Sharon and Joanna of the home; parents, Buck and Althea Lane of Syracuse; three sisters, Mrs. John (Margaret) Carter of Lakin, Mrs. Catherine Stimatze of Syracuse, Gayle Lane of Syracuse; a brother, Jim Lane of Kendall; grandmother, Mrs. George Fuller of Syracuse; many aunts, uncles, cousins and friends.

Funeral services were held Saturday at the Syracuse Methodist Church with Rev. Loren Chapman of Lakin officiating. Burial was in Kendall Cemetery.

MARTINSON, BELLE - (Kendall Boomer, Saturday, Nov. 24, 1888) On Wednesday, November 21, 1888, Mrs. Belle Martinson, wife of Severin Martinson, died, aged 26 years, 9 months and 10 days. The family are recent arrivals in Kendall and the sudden and untimely taking

KENDALL CEMETERY

off of the young wife and mother is a very distressing loss, especially to the two children, one of whom is but a week old. The funeral took place on Friday, and the good, kind-hearted ladies of Kendall performed another of the many little acts of kindness of which the recording angel alone keeps account, and which, after all, make up the sum of true Christianity.

MASIS, VICTORIA - Died 4/5/1917, age 25, buried at Kendall.

MAYHILL, BILLY - (Sec. 2) (The Lakin Independent, Feb. 9, 1951) Billy Mayhill, the twelve year old son of Mrs. Alta Mayhill was fatally injured when the tractor on which he was riding overturned. He was taken to the Donohue Hospital in Syracuse where everything possible was done for him. He only lived about two hours after the accident. The entire community extends their sympathy.

MCCAIN, JAMES - (Sec. 1) (The Lakin Independent, May 27, 1932) James McCain was born September 15, 1879, in Kankakee, Illinois, and died May 18, 1932, at his daughter's home in Syracuse, Kansas. He had reached the age of 53 years, 8 months, and 3 days.

He spent his boyhood days in Illinois, later moving to Paris, Missouri. On September 18, 1906, he was united in marriage to Annabelle Tiegs. To this union three children were born, two of which survive him: Mildred, age 24, who lives in Syracuse, and Leslie, age 16, who is at home. Everett, who preceded his father in death, died at eight years of age at Starbuck, Canada.

He was a loving husband and father. He gave his best in loving and sacrificial service to all. He always tried to do what was right and was said to be fair and honest by his friends and neighbors.

In August 1926, he moved to the Fegan ranch, south of Kendall, and since that time has been the foreman.

He leaves to mourn his departure, his wife; his daughter and son-in-law, Mr. and Mrs. Stockwell; his son, Leslie; and other relatives; besides a large host of friends.

Funeral services were held on Saturday afternoon at the Kendall M.E. Church, with the pastor, Warren A. Conn, in charge. Burial was in the Kendall Cemetery.

MCCORT, FLORENCE ELVA - (Sec. 1) Born in 1885 and died January

KENDALL CEMETERY

16, 1931.

MERRIMAN, WILLIS - (The Syracuse Journal, March 15, 1918) Willis Merriman died at his home near Kendall, Tuesday. He was sick but a few days. He had been a resident of this county eight or ten years and was around 65 years of age. He leaves a wife and two sons and two daughters.

MEYERS, IRVAN T. - (Sec. 2) (The Garden City Telegram, Jan. 11, 1972) Funeral for Irvan T. Meyers, 54, was held at 2 p.m. Saturday at the Southern Baptist Church, Syracuse, the Rev. John W. Lurtz officiating. Burial in Kendall Cemetery.

Mr. Meyers died Wednesday at Stella's Care Home here after a long illness. He had been a former resident of Kendall.

Born January 1, 1917, in Boyd, he was a retired Santa Fe Railroad laborer and had lived in Kendall 11 years before moving to Garden City about a year ago.

Survivors include two daughters, Mrs. Lois Harris, Tulsa, Oklahoma, and Mrs. Nona Lewis, Hutchinson, two sons, Labin, Holcomb, and Frank, Syracuse; a sister, Mrs. Savilla Lee, Garden City; two brothers, Grant, Deerfield, and LaVern, Dighton; and 11 grandchildren.

MEYERS, LABIN H. - (Sec. 2) (The Garden City Telegram, June 26, 1976) Funeral for Labin Hilvan Meyers, 31, was held June 28, at Garnand Funeral Chapel, the Rev. Alvin L. Daetwiler officiated. Burial in Kendall Cemetery.

Mr. Meyers died Friday evening, June 25, 1976, at St. Catherine Hospital from a self-inflicted gunshot wound to the head, Finney County Sheriff Grover Craig said. The shooting occurred at the Meyer's home at Whatley's Trailer Park.

Born October 28, 1944, at Garden City, he married Jackie Brewer, July 14, 1968, at Scott City. He was an employee of the Garden City park department and a member of the Southern Baptist Church of Syracuse.

Survivors include the widow, of the home; two sons, Timmy and Bill, both of the home; four daughters, Denise, Pam, Becky, and Tammy, all of the home; his mother, Mrs. Lois Lowery, Eminence Rt.; a brother, Frank Meyers, Eminence Rt.; two sisters, Mrs. Lois Harris, Chouteau, Oklahoma, and Mrs. Nora Lewis, Pratt; grandmother, Mrs. Effie

KENDALL CEMETERY

McMillian, Coweta, Oklahoma; and great grandfather, Hilvan L. Victory, Coweta, Oklahoma.

MEYERS, THOMAS ROY - (Sec. 2) (The Garden City Telegram, Sept. 28, 1963) Wilse Alvin and Thomas Roy Meyers, sons of Mr. and Mrs. Irvan Meyers of rural Kendall, were killed instantly Thursday, September 26, 1963, in a car-motorcycle collision near Kendall. Both were students at Kendall High School.

Wilse Alvin, 17, was born February 23, 1946, at Coweta, Oklahoma.

Thomas Roy, 16, was born March 16, 1947, at Coweta. Both were members of the Bible Baptist Church, Coweta.

Survivors: the parents; sisters, Mrs. Lois Harris, Tulsa, and Nora, of the home; brothers, Hilvan, Deerfield, and Frank of the home; grandparents, Mr. and Mrs. Walter McMillian, Coweta.

Funeral: 2:30 p.m. (MST) Monday, First Baptist Church, Syracuse; Rev. Clifford Monroe. Burial: Kendall Cemetery.

MEYERS, WILSE ALVIN - (Sec. 2) (The Garden City Telegram, Sept. 28, 1963) Wilse Alvin and Thomas Roy Meyers, sons of Mr. and Mrs. Irvan Meyers of rural Kendall, were killed instantly Thursday, September 26, 1963, in a car-motorcycle collision near Kendall. Both were students at Kendall High School.

Wilse Alvin, 17, was born February 23, 1946, at Coweta, Oklahoma.

Thomas Roy, 16, was born March 16, 1947, at Coweta. Both were members of the Bible Baptist Church, Coweta.

Survivors: the parents; sisters, Mrs. Lois Harris, Tulsa, and Nora, of the home; brothers, Hilvan, Deerfield, and Frank of the home; grandparents, Mr. and Mrs. Walter McMillian, Coweta.

Funeral: 2:30 p.m. (MST) Monday, First Baptist Church, Syracuse; Rev. Clifford Monroe. Burial: Kendall Cemetery.

MILLER, WILLIAM U. - (The Syracuse Journal, September 25, 1914) William U. Miller died September 19, 1914, at 3 o'clock from the burns received in his house fire the Tuesday before. His funeral was held at the church Sunday afternoon at 2 o'clock, conducted by Rev. M. S. Blair, the first funeral to take place in the new church, which was dedicated on the 21st of last September. The church was crowded with the friends of Mr. Miller.

He was born in 1863 in Coshocton, Ohio, and came to Kansas in

KENDALL CEMETERY

1886, proving up a homestead 13 miles north of Kendall. Three years ago he opened a blacksmith shop in Kendall. He was a bachelor and half-brother of George Phillips.

(The Syracuse Journal, September 18, 1914) On Tuesday about 5 o'clock p.m. W. N. Miller, the blacksmith had some vegetables boiling on the oil stove in his living room adjoining his shop. He was over at the Mitchell auto garage when some one discovered smoke coming out of his room and gave the alarm of fire. Miller went to his room and went in to save his trunk, which contained $160 in money and valuable papers. In doing so he became badly burned about the head, face and hands, the sleeves of both of his shirts being burned off to the shoulders. Hair, eyelashes, whiskers and mustache all burned off. Dr. Harrison was called and dressed the burns. Had it not been for the timely arrival of Roscoe Mitchell and George Hixson he would have been past saving, as he had jerked the trunk through among tables and boxes to the door but could not get the door open. A bucket brigade soon had the fire extinguished without any great damage to the building, although the contents were badly damaged by fire and water.

MITCHELL, FILLMORE - (Sec. 3) (The Lakin Independent, June 29, 1916) Fillmore Mitchell, father of Roscoe Mitchell, the Kendall merchant, who died latter part of last week, was laid to rest at that place Sunday afternoon at 2:30 o'clock. The funeral was largely attended by friends, relatives and neighbors. J. J. Nash had charge of the funeral arrangements.

Fillmore Mitchell was born May 12, 1851, near Louisville, Kentucky, being at the time of his death, 65 years, 1 month and 12 days old. He was married in Mayview, Missouri, October 1873, to Miss Weltha Ann Read. To this union six children were born, of which four are now living: Edward P., Roscoe, Charles, William and six grandchildren.

(Funeral Record: June 23, 1916) He was a farmer and hardware merchant.

MITCHELL, WELTHA - (Sec. 3) Wife of Fillmore Mitchell. Born April 16, 1854 and died July 19, 1933.

MOBERLY, MRS. F. M. - (The Advocate, Sat., July 23, 1887) Mrs. Moberly, wife of F. M. Moberly who a couple of weeks ago took charge of the depot at this place, died Sunday night or early Monday morning

KENDALL CEMETERY

(July 17 or 18, 1887) under particularly sad circumstances. She had been confined to bed by an attack of fever but was much better on Sunday evening when the family retired. During the night the baby woke Mr. Moberly who got up to quiet it and not succeeding in this he tried to wake his wife and made the distressing discovery that she was dead. The remains were interred in the Kendall Cemetery Tuesday morning.

MULLINIAX, INFANT BOY - (The Kendall Boomer, May 26, 1888) The infant son of Mrs. Mulliniax died last Tuesday evening and was buried on Wednesday. His illness was of only a few hours duration.

(The Kendall Boomer, April 21, 1888) Born on Sunday night to Mr. and Mrs. T. C. Mulliniax, a boy and a girl.

MULLINIAX, FRANK - (The Kendall Boomer, Oct. 27, 1888) Died on Tuesday morning at 3 o'clock, Frank, infant son of Mrs. and Mrs. Mulliniax, aged 1 yr. 10 mos.

> Sweet bud of promise early gone,
> Torn from the parent stem
> The casket moulders in the earth
> But heaven claims a gem.

Less than two years ago the little form now lying cold and still in death came to bring joy and gladness to the hearts of the parents. Each day as the little one grew in strength and beauty it entwined itself around the heartstring of the parents and was the light and joy of the household. But the grim messenger of Death was hovering near on silent wing to snatch the little treasurer from its earthly parents and transplant him in his infant beauty into the bright home where there is no sorrow or trouble, and where, in the light of God's presence, he will await for those left behind and welcome them when they cross the dark river of death.

The sorrowing parents have the sympathy of the entire community in their bereavement. The little one had been sick five weeks and at one time it was thought he was out of danger but a relapse came and the young spirit left its earthly tenement and winged its flight to the God who gave it. Jana Patton

KENDALL CEMETERY

NICHOLS, LINDA KAY - (Sec. 2) (The Lakin Independent, Sept. 9, 1965) Linda Kay Nichols was born June 28, 1963, at Abilene. Her mother died in 1963. Her family moved to Kendall after Mrs. Nichols death. Her survivors include the father, James, two sisters, Margaret and Mary Alice; a brother, Lawrence, all of the home; and her grandmother, Mrs. Hazel Nichols, Satanta.

(see obit of Ellen M. Kauffman)

NUCKLES, MARY ETHEL - (Sec. 3) (Kendall Free Press, April 19, 1890) Mr. and Mrs. M. E. Nuckles desire to extend their thanks to the people of Kendall for their kindness and sympathy extended to them in their great sorrow in the loss of their daughter, Ethel.

She died April 13, 1890, at the age of 4 months and 2 days.

KENDALL CEMETERY

PACKER, SARAH ANN - (The Lakin Independent, Jan. 28, 1921) Sarah Ann Rosenberry was born in Philadelphia, Pennsylvania, Sunday morning, March 23, 1829, and died in Kendall, Kansas, at the home of her daughter, Mrs. Laura Deever, Sunday evening, January 16, 1921, aged 91 years, 10 months and 18 days. She with her parents moved to Ohio in 1838. When eleven years old she was converted and joined the church of which her father was the pastor, and has ever since lived a consistent Christian life.

July 1st, 1852, she married Isaac C. Packer. To them seven children came to bless their home, four still live to mourn their loss, the husband preceding her 38 years.

Those remaining are B. F. Packer, of New Albany, Kansas; J. H. Packer, of Liberty Missouri; Mrs. Rosa Thomas of Turney, Missouri; and Mrs. Laura Deever, of Kendall, Kansas; and 12 grandchildren.

She with her husband came to pioneer Kansas the fall of 1856, settled in Allen County, where Humboldt now is, lived there till 1862, went to Lawrence, Kansas, a few months, then to Leavenworth, where she lived many years. In 1893 she moved to Topeka and 1909 came to Stanton County. She truly was imbued with the spirit of Kansas thrift and Kansas sacrifice, and loved her adopted state more truly than she did her native state.

She lived a long life of usefulness and service for her Lord and Master, passed away happy in the knowledge that she was going home to her Savior and her loved ones gone before.

(The Lakin Independent, Jan. 21, 1921) Mrs. Sarah Ann Packer, of Kendall, was buried there Tuesday. Death was due to old age. She was the mother of Mrs. Deever, who is conducting a general store at that place, at which place the deceased was making her home. She was aged 91 years, 10 months and 18 days. The Syracuse Undertaking Company had charge of the funeral arrangements.

PAPENDYCK, JOHN - (Sec. 4) (The Syracuse Journal, Oct. 4, 1940) John Papendyck, 90 years old, a resident of Kendall for more than twenty years, passed away at the Donohue Memorial Hospital, Friday. Mr. Papendyck had been a patient at the hospital for more than six months. Funeral services in charge of Rev. Lyman S. Johnson were conducted at the Kendall Cemetery, Monday. Mr. Papendyck had lived alone in Kendall and leaves no near relative in this county. Friends say he is survived by an estranged wife and son, neither of whom were

KENDALL CEMETERY

present for the funeral.
He was 90 years and 54 days old.

PEREZ, ENRIQUE - Died July 19, 1920, buried at Kendall.

PHILLIPS, MARGRET ANNE - (Sec. 3) (The Syracuse Journal, May 24, 1907) Margaret Anne Phillips was born in Harrison County, Ohio, May 3rd, 1844. She died in Kendall, Kansas, May 15, 1907, at the age of 63 years and 12 days. She was twice married and the mother of six children, four of whom survive her. She and her children and also a grandson came to Hamilton County about twenty years ago. She has been a member of the Methodist Church for twenty-five years and has often said she was ready at any hour to welcome her Father's call home.

PHILLIPS, VIOLA - (The Lakin Independent, Mar 30, 1916) Viola, the five year old daughter of Calvin Phillips and wife of the Kendall district, was the victim of scarlet fever, Sunday. Burial took place at Kendall, Monday.

PITT, JOHN - (The Kendall Boomer, Oct. 15, 1887) Died, John Pitt, at the home of Mr. and Mrs. J. P. Francis, on last Saturday (October 8, 1887) at the age of 77 years, of Bright's disease.

Mr. Pitt's life work is ended and as his sun sank peacefully to rest it was the golden sunset of the prairie, emblematical of a long and well spent life. Father Pitt had the Christian's faith in a life beyond the grave and when his eyes closed in mortality they opened in immortality beyond the grave. All is peace with the weary soul after a long and troublous journey on the sea of life.

The old gentleman was a familiar site in town and until his complaint turned its last stage two or three weeks ago he seemed quite hearty. His two daughters, Mrs. Francis and Miss Goff cared for him and soothed his declining days.

Mr. Pitt was born in London, England, October 15, 1810, and if he had lived seven days longer he would have been 77 years of age. The funeral took place on Monday and the remains were interred in the Kendall Cemetery. Rev. W. B. Marsh preached the sermon.

(Card of Thanks) We extend grateful thanks to our neighbors and friends for the many kindnesses shown us during the illness and burial of our father. Mr. and Mrs. J. P. Francis and Miss Estella A. Goff.

KENDALL CEMETERY

PORTER, DELLA - (Sec. 3) (Syracuse Journal, Jan. 3, 1902, Kendall Items) The five months old daughter of Mr. and Mrs. T. E. Porter died last Tuesday from some cause unknown.

PORTER, HAZEL - (Sec. 3) (Syracuse Journal, June 29, 1900, Kendall News) Hazel, daughter of Mr. and Mrs. Ed Porter of Kendall, died last Saturday, aged one year and seven months. The little body was laid to rest on Sunday, Rev. E. E. Robbins conducting the services. The bereaved family have the sympathy of the entire community.

PORTER, LENORA M. - (Sec. 3) Died August 3, 1905, age 2 months and 23 days.

(The Syracuse Journal, August 4, 1905) T. E. Porter's three months old baby died at Kendall Thursday evening at 8 o'clock.

PORTER, LORAINE - (Sec. 3) (The Syracuse Journal, March 20, 1903) The infant son of Mr. and Mrs. Ed Porter was found dead in bed Friday morning, of last week, March 13, 1903. He was well on retiring and the cause of death is assigned to heart failure. The funeral was held Saturday.

PORTER, MERVIN - (Sec. 3) (Lakin Investigator, Aug. 18, 1905) Little Mervin, the 15 months old son of Mr. and Mrs. T. E. Porter, died at 4 o'clock Thursday morning, August 10, 1905. This being the second child they have lost in the past week, and the fifth one in the last six years. They have the heartfelt sympathy of this entire community in their bereavement. Kendall News in Syracuse Journal.

PORTER, THOMAS EDWARD - (Sec. 3) (The Lakin Independent, Apr. 6, 1916) Edward Porter, a brother of Will Porter of this neighborhood, died at his home near Kendall, March 30. Funeral services were held at Kendall, April 1, after which interment was made in the Kendall Cemetery.

Ed Porter, of Kendall District, who was in the East for his health, died Friday shortly after he returned home. He is survived by a brother and family. He was very well known here and was liked by all who knew him. J. J. Nash furnished the coffin. He was buried at Kendall, Saturday morning, the funeral was largely attended.

(Funeral Record) He was 40 years of age, married and died of cancer

KENDALL CEMETERY

of jaw.

PUGH, EMMA L. - (Sec. 1) (Syracuse Journal, Sept. 4, 1948) Funeral for Mrs. G. A. Pugh, who died Tuesday, were conducted at the Kendall church this morning. Rev. O. Ray Pomeroy delivered the funeral sermon, and burial was in the Kendall Cemetery.

Emma Loretta Johnson was born October 15, 1870, in Neosho County, Kansas, to William and Diantha Johnson and departed from this life August 31, 1948, age 77 years, 10 months and sixteen days. She was married May 26, 1897, to George Almond Pugh. One son was born to this union, Murrell Emett Pugh, now living in La Junta, Colorado.

Mr. and Mrs. Pugh made their home in Neosho County, Kansas, until the fall of 1916, when they moved to Hamilton County, Kansas, and lived there until their death. Mr. Pugh passed away October 5, 1947.

She leaves to mourn her death, her son and his wife, three granddaughters, two great grandchildren and one sister, Mrs. Lillie Oliphant, of Erie, Kansas. Mrs. Pugh was baptized and joined the church when just a child.

> Hundreds of dew drops to greet the dawn
> Hundreds of lambs in the purple clover
> Hundreds of butterflies on the lawn
> But only one Mother the wide world over.

PUGH, GEORGE A. - (Sec. 1) (The Lakin Independent, Oct. 10, 1947, Kendall News) Our community was saddened by the death of George Pugh, who died Sunday morning, October 5, 1947. Out of town people attending the funeral included Mr. and Mrs. Bill Reynolds of Yates Center and Mr. and Mrs. Fred Jones of La Junta, Colorado.

KENDALL CEMETERY

ROTH, HENRY PAUL - (Sec. 3) (The Kearny County Advocate, Jan. 20, 1918) Henry Paul Roth was born April 28, 1893, at his home six miles north east of Kendall, Kansas, and died January 14, 1918, at Barnes Hospital, St. Louis, Missouri, where he was taken for treatment for his eyes, caused by an explosion of a welding machine on last thanksgiving night, pneumonia setting in at the last, causing his death. He was 24 years, 8 months, 13 days old, having lived here during his life. He leaves a father and mother, Mr. and Mrs. W. J. Roth; two brothers, William and Tommie; one sister, Mrs. Martha Allen to mourn his loss. He became a member of the Methodist Church of Kendall, Kansas, some six years ago. His remains were laid to rest in the Kendall Cemetery, Friday afternoon, January 18th.

(Lakin Independent, Jan. 18, 1918) Paul Roth, who went to St. Louis sometime ago to undergo an operation on one of his eyes, died Monday on the operating table, it is said. The remains were shipped to his home near Kendall and the funeral was held Wednesday. The deceased was formerly employed at the Ford garage at this place. Last summer while approaching the river bridge south of Lakin one Sunday night in his automobile he missed the bridge and fell into the river. He was very well known here and was a very industrious young man.

ROTH, JOHN HENRY - (Sec. 2) (The Lakin Independent, May 23, 1941) John Henry, little son of William and Lillian Roth, was born at Lakin, Kansas, on February 22, 1941.

The little one was welcomed by two sisters and a brother into a happy family circle. Days passed quickly and happily until a critical illness laid hold of the little one. Kindly and skilled care of loved ones and physicians were given, but on May 15 the spirit left its tenement of clay to return to the Father who gave it. The parental home was north of Kendall.

Those who will cherish the memory of this brief but sweet life are the parents; the brother, William George; and sister, Ella May and Wilma Elizabeth; grandparents, Mr. and Mrs. George Phillips; and a number of aunts and uncles, among whom are Mr. and Mrs. Henry Allen who have helped care for the little one with solicitous care.

Funeral services were held at Kendall Methodist Church on May 18 by Rev. R. L. Wells. Mrs. Earl Ross and others arranged for comforting songs. The little body was laid to rest in the Kendall Cemetery. Nash Mortuary in charge.

KENDALL CEMETERY

ROTH, LILLIE M. - (Sec. 2) (The Lakin Independent, October 23, 1986) Lillie Margaret Roth, 76, a lifelong resident of Kendall, died Thursday at St. Catherine Hospital, Garden City. Born Lillie Margaret Phillips on July 9, 1910, she married W. P. Roth in 1928, in Lakin. He died in 1981.

Survivors are two sons, William and Tom, both of Kendall; five grandchildren; and three great grandchildren.

Funeral was held at the United Methodist Church, Syracuse, the Rev. Dale Ellenberger officiating. Burial in Kendall Cemetery. Greene Funeral Home, Syracuse, in charge of arrangements.

ROTH, WILHELMENA - (Sec. 3) (The Kearny County Advocate, Jan. 14, 1909) Mrs. W. J. Roth committed suicide by hanging herself at the home of her husband north of Kendall in this county, on Friday afternoon.

Her husband left home at noon for Kendall and the children were at school, leaving her alone; and when the little girl returned in the afternoon she found her mother hanging to the joist in the broom corn shed.

After adjusting the rope about her neck, Mrs. Roth jumped from the stack of broom corn and the fall broke her neck.

We learn that Mrs. Roth was a woman of about 53 years of age, and was formerly a Mrs. Huber and had one son, Thomas Huber, by her first husband.

Since her marriage to Mr. Roth, who was a widower at the time, she had three children, Willie, Paul and Martha, who survive her untimely death.

Mrs. W. J. Roth, living nine miles north of Kendall, was found dead by her daughter, on coming home from school last Friday afternoon. She had hung herself in the barn. Coroner C. H. Waterman was summoned, and accompanied by Dr. Richards went to her late residence, and after making a careful examination and examining the husband, daughter, Mrs. Wells and Mrs. Mitchell, a verdict was returned that she came to her death by her own hand, probably caused by despondency, brought on by ill health.

Mrs. Roth was fifty-four years old and leaves three sons and one daughter. For some time her health had been very poor, considerable of the time not being able to move about. She was a member of the Catholic Church. A long concourse of friends gathered at the funeral

KENDALL CEMETERY

Sunday to pay their last respects and offer their sympathy to the husband and children. Mr. Roth is one of the old settlers and much respected in the community where he resides.

ROTH, WILLIAM JOHN - (Sec. 3) (Kearny County Advocate, Feb. 23, 1899) In 1888 William Roth, while at work on the dome of the state house missed his footing and fell 84 feet. A bill was introduced Tuesday in the house to give him $6,000 pension on account of his being "incapacitated" by reason of the fall. Mr. Roth is a resident of Kearny County.

(The Kearny County Advocate, May 28, 1937) William John Roth was born January 2, 1845, in Essen, Germany, and departed this life Monday, May 24, 1937. He came to this country when a young man and first settled in Chicago, Illinois, where he worked at the brick mason trade. In 1884 he came to Kearny County, Kansas, and homesteaded the land six miles northwest of Kendall where he has resided ever since.

On July 29, 1891, he was united in marriage to Wilhelmina Huber. To this union was born three children, William P. Roth, Henry Paul Roth and Martha M. Allen. His wife preceded him in death on January 10, 1909, also his son Henry Paul Roth, died January 14, 1918. Mr. Roth's health had been fairly good until about six weeks ago when he began failing and upon consulting a physician it was found he had heart trouble, from which he died suddenly.

He leaves to mourn his loss, his daughter, Martha M. Allen and husband; son, William P. Roth and family; one stepson, Tommy Huber; all residing near Kendall, Kansas; one niece, Mary Roth and family and a nephew, Bernard Helger, all of Lakin, Kansas.

Funeral services was held on Wednesday morning at the Methodist Church in Kendall, Kansas, conducted by Rev. Lyman Johnson, and interment in Kendall Cemetery beside his wife and son, Paul.

W. J. Roth who died Monday morning at his home in the Wonderland district was one of those rare individuals who could not be overcome by adversity. As an emigrant from Germany he homesteaded on the western frontier.

When the drouth and hot winds burned up his crops he went east to work at his trade and secured a job as a mason on the state house in Topeka, then under construction. While he was working there a wall gave way because of inferior materials used by the contractor and Mr. Roth fell to the basement, about 80 feet, receiving injuries from which

KENDALL CEMETERY

he never recovered, and for which the state never made adequate settlement.

Coming back to the farm, Mr. Roth managed so well he became known as the broom corn king of this county. Although crippled in the body, he had the spirit and determination to overcome the physical handicap and by adapting his farming methods to our climatic conditions and holding his crops for a favorable market he became a successful farmer.

Mr. Roth's latest philosophy was that the drouth is here to stay. The atmosphere, he said, had become unbalanced through extracting free nitrogen for the manufacture of explosives and munitions of war. The lower strata may hold in proper proportions but the upper strata, at this altitude, no longer have the thunderstorms of former years, said Mr. Roth.

ROTH, WILLIAM PETER - (Sec. 2) (The Lakin Independent, January 29, 1981) William Peter Roth, 90, died Sunday January 25, 1981, at Hamilton County Hospital, Syracuse. Born September 12, 1891, in Kearny County, he married Lilly Phillips in 1933, in Lakin. He was a retired farmer.

Survivors: widow, of the home; sons: William George Roth of the home; Tom Henry Roth, Sherlock, California; six grandchildren; two great grandchildren.

Funeral was held at 2 p.m. Friday at Syracuse Methodist Church, the Rev. Don O'Hara. Burial was in the Kendall Cemetery.

ROTH, WILMA ELIZABETH - (Sec. 2) (The Lakin Independent, Oct. 24, 1941) Wilma Elizabeth, nine year old daughter of Mr. and Mrs. Wm Roth, who live four miles north of Kendall in Kearny County, was fatally shot by the accidental discharge of a .22 caliber rifle in the hands of a six year old brother on October 19, at 12:30 p.m. The lad was carrying the rifle down a flight of stairs and it discharged, the bullet passing through a glass door and entering the forehead of the sister. An aunt and uncle, Mr. and Mrs. Henry Allen, rushed the child to the Kearny County Hospital, Lakin, but life was gone in a few minutes. The Roth family lost a baby by whooping cough in May of this year. A brother and sister remain in the home.

Funeral services were held at Kendall Methodist Church by Rev. R. L. Wells. A chorus from the high school, directed by Miss Courtright,

KENDALL CEMETERY

sang three selections. The following neighbors, Merl and Cliff Lindner, Dale Houck, and Roy Kurz, carried the body to its final resting place in Kendall Cemetery.

(The Lakin Independent, Nov. 7, 1941) Wilma Elizabeth, daughter of William and Lillian Roth, was born near Kendall, Kansas, December 8, 1932. Here she lived among a happy family knowing as an only sorrow the loss of a baby brother about five months ago. School days came on and the joys of life increased. Home tasks were accepted and her hands became a help in carrying on the numerous duties that come in a busy home with a growing family.

Sunday afternoon, October 19, 1941, joy turned suddenly into sorrow, when by accident the life of our little girl was taken and the friendly smile and contagious laugh faded away.

The memory of these nine years of sunshine will be cherished by the parents, the brother, Wm. R., Jr., and sister, Ella May, grandparents, Mr. and Mrs. Geo. Phillips, two aunts, Mrs. Henry Allen and Mrs. Florence Bone and five uncles.

RUNNELS, RICKEY RAN - (Sec. 5) (The Lakin Independent, Aug. 23, 1957) Rickey Ran Runnels, son of Mr. and Mrs. Bill Frank Runnels of Kendall, Kansas, was born Thursday, August 15, 1957 at 2:45 p.m. and died the same day at 8:15 p.m.

Besides his parents, Rickey Ran is survived by one brother, Morty, his maternal grandparents, Mr. and Mrs. Lovell Smith of Coche, Oklahoma, and his paternal grandparents, Mr. and Mrs. Odis Runnels of Coche, Oklahoma.

Graveside services were conducted at the Kendall Cemetery by Rev. Mary Ellen Markley at 4 p.m. Friday, August 16, 1957.

Mr. Runnels is Santa Fe depot agent at Kendall.

KENDALL CEMETERY

SAUNDERS, FRED - (Sec. 3) (The Syracuse Journal, August 28, 1896) Entered into rest at his home near Kendall, Friday, August 21, Fred Saunders, aged 21 years, 4 months and 5 days. He was taken with the inflammatory fever, which lasted about two weeks, but during the greatest of his afflictions, he bore them patiently unto the end when the angel of death came quietly and peacefully to bid him come home. Fred was a bright, industrious and worthy young man just entering upon the duties and responsibilities of manhood, but the One who doeth all things well saw fit to call him to his heavenly home. He left a host of friends who mourn his departure but it is a blessed consolation to all to think that their loss is his Eternal gain. Blessed are they that die in the Lord.

The funeral services were conducted by Rev. George E. Bicknell, after which the remains were interred in the Kendall Cemetery. Card of thanks signed: Dear friends of Fred Saunders, Mr. and Mrs. F. E. Dunn and family.

SCHWASINGER, TWIN - Stillborn 6/19/1927.

SHADLE, ALTA A. - (Sec. 2) (The Garden City Telegram, January 25, 1984) Funeral for Alta Ann Shadle, 76, was held at 2 p.m. (MST) Thursday at the Nazarene Church, Syracuse, the Rev. Ronald McElfresh officiated. Burial at the Kendall Cemetery.

Mrs. Shadle died Monday, January 23, 1984, at the Hamilton County Long-term Care Home, Syracuse after a short illness.

Born Alta Ann Ternary, December 9, 1907, at Olney, Illinois, she married Elva Mayhill in 1928. She married Wilbur Shadle. He died in 1962. Mrs. Shadle was a longtime Syracuse resident.

She was a member of the Bible Baptist Church, Syracuse.

Survivors are two sons, John Mayhill, Syracuse, and Joe Mayhill, Lafayette, California; seven daughters, Frances Lemons, Brea, California, Joan Williams, Cisco, Illinois, Mary Hentescher, Ingraham, Illinois, Marie Ewalt, Galena, Missouri, Donna Alexander, Wheatland, Wyoming, Linda Swisher, Springfield, Missouri, and Faith Fisher, Decatur, Illinois; a stepson, Jesse Shadle, Chicago, Illinois; a brother, Clark Ternary, Decatur; a sister, Violet Moats, Decatur; 27 grandchildren and 24 great grandchildren.

Visitation was at Greene Funeral Home, Syracuse.

SHINKLE, LEW WALLACE - (Sec. 3) (Kearny County Advocate,

KENDALL CEMETERY

Kendall News, Dec. 1, 1911) Died at the home of his parents, one mile east of here, Wallace Shinkle, age 16 years, 9 months and nine days, after an illness of three months. Deceased was loved and respected by all who knew him and his loss is greatly felt by our young people. The funeral services were conducted by Rev. Green, and he was laid to rest in the Kendall Cemetery. The bereaved parents have the sympathy of the whole community.

SLATE, BABY - (Sec. 3) (Hamilton County Cemetery Records) Son of Lewis Slate, born December 17, 1910, and died December 19, 1910.

(The Lakin Investigator, Kendall News, Dec. 23, 1910) Born to Mr. and Mrs. Lewis Slate, December 17th, a son. The baby lived but two days and was laid away in the cemetery here last Monday. The parents have the sympathy of the whole community.

SLATE, HARMOND F. - (Sec. 3) (The Lakin Independent, May 1, 1975) Harmond F. Slate, 56, died suddenly at his home Friday, April 25. Born May 3, 1918, at Kendall, he married Fay Lusk, March 2, 1944, at Hugoton. He was a retired railroad worker.

He was a member of the Kendall Methodist Church and was a World War II veteran.

Survivors are the widow; daughters: Mrs. Patricia Johnson, Sucib Bay, P.I., Mrs. Dixie Jury, Gulfport, Mississippi, Mrs. Shirley Jury, Quinter; son, Gene; sisters: Mrs. Hallie Reynolds, Yates Center, Mrs. Lillian James, Yates Center; brothers: Harold, Lakin, Leland, Lakin; seven grandchildren.

Funeral was Tuesday at the Kendall Methodist Church with Rev. Charles J. Chipman officiating. Burial was in the Kendall Cemetery.

SLATE, HAROLD L. - (Sec. 3) (The Lakin Independent, July 10, 1975) Services for Harold L. (Buck) Slate, 54, Kendall, who died Thursday at Lakin of an apparent heart attack were held at 2 p.m. Monday, July 7, at the Kendall Methodist Church by Rev. Duane Harms. Interment was in Kendall Cemetery.

Harold Leroy Slate, son of Lewis and Minnie Johnson Slate, was born on May 25, 1921, in Kendall, Kansas, and departed this life on July 3, 1975, at Lakin, Kansas.

He was a lifetime resident of western Kansas, residing with his mother until 1968 when she went to Yates Center, Kansas, to live with

KENDALL CEMETERY

her daughters. He then moved to Lakin where he lived with his brother, Leland, and family with frequent visits to eastern Kansas where Lillie and Hallie reside.

He is survived by two sisters: Lillian Jones and Hallie Reynolds, both of Yates Center, Kansas, and one brother, Leland, of Lakin; four nephews and four nieces, four great nephews and six great nieces. He was preceded in death by his parents and two brothers, one brother dying in infancy.

Being an avid outdoorsman he spent many hours hunting and fishing with his brother, cousins, nephews and friends.

He loved little children and all who knew him called him "Uncle Buck."

SLATE, KATHERINE FAY - (Sec. 3) (The Lakin Independent, March 5, 1981) Katherine Fay Slate, 67, died Tuesday at the Fall Memorial Hospital, International Falls, Minnesota. Born Katherine Fay Lusk, March 17, 1913, in Grant County, she married Harmond Slate, March 2, 1944, at Hugoton. He died April 25, 1975. She was a former employee of the Kendall elevator and was a resident of Kendall for 35 years.

Survivors: son; Harmond Slate, Lakin; daughters: Dixie Pullar, International Falls, Minnesota, Patricia Johnson, Oxnard, California, Shirley Jury, Hugo, Colorado; brothers: Dan Lusk, Vivian, Oklahoma, Ed Lusk, Pueblo, Colorado, John Lusk, Eads, Colorado; seven grandchildren.

Funeral was at 1 p.m. MST, Monday at the Kendall Methodist Church, the Rev. Clark Struebing. Burial at the Kendall Cemetery.

SLATE, HARMOND LEWIS - (Sec. 3) (The Lakin Independent, Sept. 27, 1946) Lewis Slate, son of Charles and Mary Slate, was born May 20, 1879, in Clinton County, Illinois. He departed this life at his home in Kendall, Kansas, September 15, 1946, at the age of 67 years and 26 days.

When he was 4 years old, his parents moved from Illinois to Hartland, Kansas. He grew to manhood in this vicinity, where he worked as a cowboy on various ranches.

He served 2 years in the Spanish American War, two months training in the States and 22 months with the 44th division in the Philippines under General Lawton. (Government marker has birth date of May 20, 1878.)

KENDALL CEMETERY

In 1909 he was united in marriage to Minnie Pearl Johnson at Syracuse, Kansas. To this union were born four sons and two daughters: Mrs. Hallie Reynolds of Yates Center, Kansas, Mrs. Lillian Jones of La Junta, Colorado; Lewis Lawton, deceased; Harold and Leland of the home and Harmond of Ulysses, Kansas. Three grandchildren, Lewis Jones, Gene and Patsy Slate, also survive him. He worked for the Santa Fe railroad for 34 years, retiring November 7, 1944.

Hunting and fishing were his hobbies and pastime at which he was active until the last week of his life.

Mr. Slate was known to be honest and dependable in all his dealing, which won for him many friends. He was a kind and loving father and will be sadly missed.

> Moonlight and evening star
> And one clear call for me.
> Yet may there be no moaning at the bar
> When I put out to sea.

SLATE, MINNIE PEARL - (Sec. 3) (The Lakin Independent, April 25, 1974) Minnie Pearl Johnson oldest daughter of Frank and Margaret Johnson, was born June 23, 1889, at Kendall, Kansas, and passed away April 18, 1974, in the Allen County hospital in Iola, Kansas, at the age of 84 years and ten months.

She accepted Christ as her Savior at an early age and attended church as long as her health permitted.

Minnie was united in marriage to Lewis Slate on June 10, 1909, at Syracuse, Kansas. She lived at Kendall until a few years ago when she went to Yates Center to make her home with her two daughters, Mrs. Hallie Reynolds and Mrs. Lillian Jones. She was a loving wife and mother and always ready and willing to help anyone in need.

Her husband, one son, parents, three brothers and one sister preceded her in death.

Those surviving are her two daughters, Hallie and Lillian; three sons, Leland of Lakin, Harmond and Harold of Kendall; seven grandchildren; ten great grandchildren; one brother, Elmer Johnson of Bellflower, California; one sister, Florence Pugh of La Junta, Colorado; several nieces and nephews and a host of friends. She will be sadly missed by all.

SLONIGER, GERTIE BELL - (The Kendall Gazette, May 5, 1887) Gertie Bell, the five year old daughter of Mr. and Mrs. J. H. Sloniger,

KENDALL CEMETERY

died Wednesday (May 4, 1887) on their claim twelve miles from town. The funeral took place today at noon from the school house. A large number of the friends of the family attended.

SMITH, EDNA - (Sec. 6) 1902-1918

SMITH, IDELLA ARTMAN - (Syracuse Journal, March 9, 1917, Kendall News) Mrs. Robert Smith, who lived six miles southwest of here died last Sunday with tuberculosis and was buried here Monday afternoon. She left a husband and three children, two girls, 8 and 14 years of age and a boy, between them, to mourn their loss of a wife and mother.

She was born June 20, 1883, in Putnam County, Missouri. She came with her parents to Grant County and was married to William Robert Smith on September 5, 1901. In 1916 they moved to a homestead in the Hixson school district.

SMITH, MARGARET - (Sec. 3) 1845-1916

SPENCER, AGNES - (Sec. 3) (Kearny County Advocate, Kendall News, Feb. 9, 1912) Mrs. Charles Spencer died at Natoma, Kansas, Tuesday, January 30, 1912, after a sickness of about a year. She leaves a husband and four children to mourn her loss, besides a father, mother and three sisters. Before her marriage she was Miss Agnes Weatherly, born at Gardener, Illinois, April 5, 1874, and was 37 years, 9 months and 25 days old at the time of her death. She was married to Charles H. Spencer in 1899 at Kendall. Their home life was of the happiest, and no sacrifice was to great for her to make, as can be attested by her neighbors and friends who happened to be sick or in distress. Funeral services was conducted by Rev. E. E. Carter, at Kendall, on Thursday, February 1, 1912, who preached a fine sermon on "The Mission of Tears," and eulogized the good life and character of the departed. The bereaved relatives have the sympathy of the entire community in their affliction.

SPENCER, CHARLES H. - (Sec. 3) (The Lakin Independent, November 15, 1957) Charles H. Spencer was born November 26, 1873, in Ohio, Illinois, and moved to Kearny County, Kansas, with his parents in 1888. He lived in the Southwest part of the county until 1948, when he retired from active farming and moved to Lakin, where he made his home near

KENDALL CEMETERY

his daughter, Grace.

Mrs. Spencer preceded him in death January 30, 1912, leaving him with the care and rearing of four small children. He was a member of the Presbyterian Church and the Modern Woodmen Lodge.

He is survived by two daughters, Dorothy (Mrs. P. C. Kiistner), Grace (Mrs. Howard Hutton) and two sons, Harry and Dick, a niece, Mrs. Leo Bass, Walnut, Illinois; ten grandchildren and fourteen great grandchildren, and many friends.

Mr. Spencer was a man of deep devotion to his family and also to his friends. He never failed to say some good word about some member of his family, and never lost interest in their welfare. He always had a hearty welcome for any of his many friends. May the good Lord of us all bless his memory and comfort his family.

Funeral services were held Tuesday, November 12, at the Presbyterian Church, with Dr. B. F. Henry in charge. Burial was in Kendall Cemetery.

SPENCER, HAROLD - (Sec. 3) (Kearny County Advocate, Jan. 14, 1892) Died at Lakin, Wednesday, morning, January 13, 1892, of bronchitis, Harry Spencer, aged 51 years. Mr. Spencer was born at Newport, Ile of Wight, England. He came to America in 1858 and married Miss Maria H. Moore, December 1, 1866, at Moorsheadville, Erie County, Pennsylvania. He settled in Ohio, Illinois; from there he came to Kendall and located in '87, where he worked at his trade of shoemaking; removed to Lakin, March 1, '85, where he has resided, working at his trade, giving good satisfaction to his patrons. Mr. S. was an honorable, upright man whom every person that knew him respected. He leaves a loving wife and two sons, Robert and Charles, and many friends to mourn his death. The Advocate extends condolence to the bereaved family.

SPENCER, MORNA H. - (Sec. 3) (Kearny County Advocate, Aug. 18, 1904) Mrs. Morna H. Spencer was born in Rock Island County, Illinois, November 20, 1835, where she resided until fourteen years of age, when she moved to Fulton, Illinois, where she made her home for sixteen years, when she was married, and died near Kendall, Kansas, August 6th, 1904, at the home of her son Charles, after an illness of two years. The deceased was among the oldest settlers of this county, and was highly esteemed by all who had the pleasure of her acquaintance.

KENDALL CEMETERY

During her long illness she never complained, knowing that He doeth all things well. She leaves one son to mourn her loss, which is great and the sympathy of the entire community goes out to him in this his hour of bereavement.

SPIRES, EMILY KATE - (The Syracuse Journal, July 1, 1932) Emily Dennison was born June 19, 1870, in Monroe County, Missouri, and departed this life June 26, 1932, at the age of 62 years and seven days.

In the year of 1888 she was married to Mick Spires, who preceded her in death July 17, 1920. To this union three children were born, Grace and Joseph, who preceded her in death and Clinton who now lives at Kendall, Kansas.

She moved to Oklahoma in 1896 and made her home there until December 25, 1930, when she came to Kansas to make her home with her sister. She has been in failing health for some time, and was taken to the Donohue Memorial Hospital at Syracuse, where she departed from this life.

She united with the Christian Church in early life. She leaves to mourn her departure one son, Clinton and family, of Kendall; two sisters, Mrs. W. T. Reynolds of Kendall, and Mrs. R. C. Schmeltzer of Hollywood, California; one brother, Robert Willis, of Paris, Missouri, and a host of friends.

Funeral services were held Monday afternoon at 2 p.m. at the Kendall M. E. Church, with the pastor, Rev. Warren A. Conn, in charge. Interment was in the Kendall Cemetery.

STEIGER, RALPH FELIX - (Sec. 6) Ralph Steiger, son of Felix Steiger died July 22, 1925, age 3 years, 6 months and 25 days of cholera infantum, north of Kendall. His mothers' maiden name was Hulda Ploeger.

STEVENS, DONALD JEAN - (Sec. 6) (Syracuse Journal, Feb. 24, 1928) Donald Jean Stevens, born October 8, 1927, at Kendall, Kansas, died at 3:45 Thursday evening, February 16, 1928, at the age of four months and eight days. He leaves to mourn his loss his father and mother; two brothers, Alva and Reynold, and other relatives.

Funeral services were conducted by Rev. Wiley in the Kendall church, Friday, February 17. Burial followed in the Kendall Cemetery.

KENDALL CEMETERY

"The little crib is empty now,
The little clothes laid by;
A mother's hope - a father's joy
In death's cold arm both lie,
Go little pilgrim to thy home,
On yonder blissful shore;
We miss thee here, but soon
Will come where thou has gone before."

STEVENS, FRANK - (Sec. 6) (The Lakin Independent, June 2, 1966) Frank M. Stevens, 77, Kendall, died last Thursday in the Hamilton County hospital, Syracuse, after a long illness.

He was born November 26, 1888, in Wallace County and had been a resident of Hamilton County for 35 years. He moved to Kendall after retiring 12 years ago.

Mr. Stevens married Hazel D. Ely, January 15, 1916, at Goodland.

Survivors include two daughters, Mrs. Latha Conklin, Flint, Michigan, and Mrs. Bonnie Adkinson, Kendall; two sons, Alva, Ottumwa, Iowa, and Renold, Kendall; three sisters, Mrs. Bessie Sneeringer, Mrs. Bertha Martin and Mrs. Mable Shumate, all of Wichita; a brother, Hurley, Morse, Texas; and seven grandchildren.

Funeral services were held Monday at the Pilgrim Holiness Church in Syracuse, with the Rev. Robert Heckart officiating. Burial was in the Kendall Cemetery.

STEVENS, HAZEL VERNA - (Sec. 6) (The Lakin Independent, March 24, 1983) Hazel Verna Stevens, 85, died March 19, 1983, at Stanton County Rest Home, Johnson, after a long illness. Born Hazel Ely, March 14, 1898, in Decator County, Nebraska, she married Frank Stevens, January 15, 1916, at Goodland. He preceded her in death. She had been a Kendall resident for over 60 years.

She was a member of the United Methodist Church, Kendall.

Survivors: sons, Alva, Syracuse, Ronald, Kendall; daughters, Letha Bozung, Flint, Michigan, Bonnie Adkisson, Kendall; brothers, Floyd Ely, William Ely, both of Fort Dodge, Iowa; six grandchildren; seven great grandchildren.

Funeral was at 2:30 p.m. MST Wednesday at Wesleyan Church, Syracuse; the Rev. Noel Bates. Burial at Kendall Cemetery.

STEWART, BOY - John Stewart, who lived ten miles north of town,

KENDALL CEMETERY

buried his little six year old son in the Kendall Cemetery today, November 17, 1886.

(The Kendall Boomer, Nov. 2, 1889) Word reached here yesterday that a small child of Mr. John Stewart had been fatally injured by falling from a chair. Dr. White was called but death occurred before he arrived. Mr. and Mrs. Stewart have the sympathies of this community.

SUTHERLAND, JOE VIRGIL - 1/1/1933-1/2/1933.

KENDALL CEMETERY

THOMPSON, JOHN F. (Sec. 3) (Kearny County Advocate, Feb. 27, 1908) Mr. Thompson, an old resident living near the headgate of the Amazon ditch, died Tuesday morning and was buried at Kendall, Wednesday.
(The Lakin Investigator, Feb. 28, 1908) J. F. Thompson, one of the old timers of Kearny County, and for many years a resident of Kendall, but for the last ten or twelve years living about four miles west of Hartland, died at three a.m., Tuesday morning at his home, aged 67 years. Mr. Thompson was born in Pennsylvania and has been a resident of this county about 25 years. He leaves a widow and two sons, Fred, now living in California and William, who lives near his father's home. They will have the heart felt sympathy of their neighbors and friends in their bereavement. The funeral was held at the home Wednesday and remains taken to Kendall for burial.

THOMPSON, ODEE - (Sec. 3) (The Lakin Independent, Hartland News, Sept. 5, 1924) The remains of Odee Thompson, who was killed in a motorcycle accident near Kansas City, will be sent here for burial at Kendall.

THOMPSON, SARAH ELIZABETH - (Sec. 3) Born 9/8/1865, wife of John F.

THOMPSON, VIOLET - (Sec. 3) (The Kearny County Advocate, June 11, 1920) Wednesday morning after having prepared and eaten breakfast, Mrs. Wm. Thompson of Hartland, got up from the table and procured a shotgun, loaded it and bumped the trigger against a portion of the foundation of the house and shot herself just above the heart, dying instantly. Mrs. Thompson had been ailing for several months and was subject to attacks of melancholia and the family and her father had watched her closely and taken precautions to hide the guns and shells but she had found the gun and some shells the family knew nothing of and eluded their vigilance. She was an industrious woman, a good neighbor and an excellent mother all of which makes the shock to her family the more severe and regretted by her neighbors.
(Funeral Record) Died June 9, 1920, 46 years, 3 months and 22 days old. Father: Chas Bates. Married, housewife, died in Kendall Township by suicide by shooting.

KENDALL CEMETERY

TOPE, ELI H. (Sec. 2) (The Lakin Independent, Jan. 4, 1962) Eli H. Tope, 78, died Saturday at Bent County General Hospital at Las Animas, Colorado, where he had been a patient three weeks.

He had been a resident of Hamilton County 38 years. He was a retired farmer and had lived at Kendall for 13 years.

Mr. Tope was born May 18, 1883, in Jackson County, Ohio.

Survivors are two daughters, Mrs. Gladys Elston, Hasty, Colorado, and Mrs. Cleo Earnest, Kendall; one son, George, Kendall; one sister, Mrs. Alta Wise, Winfield; nine grandchildren and 19 great grandchildren.

Funeral services were held at 2 p.m. Wednesday at Syracuse Methodist Church with the Rev. Evan Markley and the Rev. Burton Lovelady officiating. Burial was in the Kendall Cemetery.

TOPE, GEORGE H. - (Sec. 2) (The Lakin Independent, March 24, 1988) Funeral for George H. Tope, 77, was held at 10 a.m. MST Monday at the United Methodist Church, Syracuse, the Revs. Noel Bates and Steven Darr officiating. Burial at Kendall Cemetery.

He died March 18, 1988, at St. Catherine Hospital, Garden City. Born February 8, 1911, at Woodward, Oklahoma, he married Ethel Roberts, January 1, 1938, at Kendall.

A retired farmer and mill operator, he moved to Kendall in 1924 from Sylvia and moved to Syracuse in 1981.

Mr. Tope was a member of the Kendall United Methodist Church, was a 32nd Degree Mason and a member of the Masonic Lodge and Order of the Eastern Star, both of Syracuse.

Survivors include his wife, of the home; two sons, John, Syracuse, and Boone, Arkansas City; a daughter, Janet Loeppke, Lakin; sister, Cleo Earnest, Kendall; 10 grandchildren and two great grandchildren.

Greene Funeral Home, Syracuse, was in charge of arrangements.

TOPE, GRACIE MAY - (Sec. 2) (Lakin Independent, Thursday, Feb. 2, 1961) Gracie May Hiatt was born June 10, 1887, at Arlington, Kansas, and departed this life January 27, 1961, at her home in Kendall. Hers' was a lingering illness through which she remained most valiant.

Gracie was the second child of John and Flora Hiatt, now deceased. She was born on a farm near Arlington and spent her girlhood there. Mrs. Tope joined the church at an early age and later transferred her membership to the Methodist Church in Kendall.

KENDALL CEMETERY

On Sept 13, 1908, she was united in marriage to Eli Tope. To this union four children were born: Mrs. Elmer Elston of Hasty, Colorado; George Tope and Mrs. Ralph Earnest, both of Kendall; and John Leroy, who gave his life for his country in 1944.

Mr. and Mrs. Tope moved to Hamilton County in 1923 and lived on a farm south of Kendall until 1947 when they moved into town.

Grandma Tope, as she was affectionately known, was a devoted wife, mother and grandmother. She was a wonderful cheerful friend to all who knew her. Their home was always open to one and all.

She leaves to mourn her passing her good husband and the children; one sister, Mrs. Cora Clark of Kingman; one brother, Roy Hiatt of Hutchinson; nine grandchildren, 16 great grandchildren and a host of relatives and friends.

Funeral services were held from the First Methodist Church in Syracuse with Dr. Evan F. Markley, pastor of the Kendall church, officiating. Interment was in the Kendall Cemetery.

TOPE, JOHN - (Sec. 3) Buried in Belgium. This memorial marker is located near the flagpole under cedar trees.

(The Syracuse Journal, August 11, 1944) Last Tuesday Mr. and Mrs. E. H. Tope of Kendall received a message from the war department advising them that their son, Sgt. John Tope, was missing in action.

Saturday the following news release was received by the Journal from England.

An Eighth Air Force Bomber Station, England -- Joining the Eighth Air Force, as its latest all-out attack on German war-plants was thrown into high gear, Staff Sergeant John L. Tope, 20 year old B-17 Flying Fortress engineer and top turret gunner, of Kendall, Kansas, received his battle baptism in a recent assault on vital Nazi synthetic oil factories in central Germany.

Son of Mr. and Mrs. E. H. Tope, of Kendall, Kansas, S-Sgt. Tope graduated from Kendall High School in May 1942.

Conspicuous to the Kansan was the absence of Nazi fighter planes. According to Tope, little enemy resistance was encountered except for sporadic flak concentrations.

The Kansas flyer is on duty with a veteran group which holds a presidential citation for gallantry in action. His Fortress group has sent bombs falling on enemy targets, ranging from industrial objectives at Berlin to military installations along the French coast.

KENDALL CEMETERY

(Syracuse Journal, Oct. 1944) Mr. and Mrs. E. H. Tope of Kendall received a telegram Wednesday from the War Department advising them that they had received word through the American Red Cross that their son, S. Sgt. John L. Tope, was killed in action over Germany on July 19. Word had previously been received that he was missing in action.

S-Sgt. Tope was an engineer on a B-17.

TUTTLE, LAFAYETTE -

TUTTLIES, FRED - (Sec. 3) (Lakin Investigator, November 26, 1909) Died at his home ten miles north of Kendall, F. Tuttlies, Tuesday morning, November 23d, after several weeks sickness. Funeral services were held Thursday, the 25th, at the Kendall school house.

(Lakin Investigator, December 3, 1909) Fred Tuttlies, born in Insterburg, Germany, June 11th, 1844, died November 23d, 1909, age 65 years, five months and 12 days. November 30, 1872, he was married to Miss Mary Shagun; to this union ten children were born, five of whom preceded him to the better land. The others are still at home, except one daughter, Mrs. Richard Lehman, who lives near here. In 1886 he, with his family, came to America, settling at Dyersville, Iowa, where they resided until February 1895, when they came to Kearny County, taking a homestead. He leaves to mourn his loss, besides his children, a loving wife, and one sister. The funeral was held November 25th, from the Kendall church, and he was laid to rest in the cemetery there.

KENDALL CEMETERY

VALENTINE, JESSICA - (Sec. 2) 1988-1992

VALENTINE, STEWART DANIEL - (Sec. 2) (The Lakin Independent, March 2, 1995) Stewart Daniel "Dan" Valentine, 29, died Saturday, February 25, 1995, at the Hamilton County hospital, Syracuse. He was a truck driver and a Holcomb resident.

Dan was born October 18, 1965, at Syracuse, the son of Mary Foreman and Eugene Lease, Sr.

He grew up in the Kendall area and attended school at both Kendall and Lakin, graduating from Lakin High School in 1984. He attended Kansas State University, the Goodland Vo-Tech Automotive School and the Dodge City Vo-Tech School. Dan served in the Navy in 1986. He married Shauna Van Horn on March 12, 1988, in Syracuse.

For the past five years Dan has been a truck driver for both the MNX Trucking Co. and the C.F. McGraw Trucking.

Dan enjoyed music, motorcycles, collecting guns, electronics, writing and his family.

Survivors include: a daughter, Saraya Valentine, Syracuse; parents, Jerry and Mary Valentine, Eugene Lease, Sr., Walsh, Colorado; three brothers, Kent Bless, Dallas, Texas, Alan Valentine, Lakin, Eugene Lease, Jr., Charter Oak, Iowa; two sisters, Heather Burrows, Holcomb, Tammy Lease, Springfield, Colorado; grandparents, Steve and Pat Sharrock, Ulysses.

Funeral services were held Wednesday, March 1, at 2:00 p.m. at the United Methodist Church in Lakin with the Rev. Donald J. Koehn officiating. Burial was in Kendall Cemetery.

KENDALL CEMETERY

WARD, ELIJAH - (Sec. 3) (The Lakin Index, Feb. 11, 1898) Died, at his residence in the county, seven miles north of Kendall, February 4th, 1898, Elijah Ward, aged sixty-five years. He leaves a wife and four children, two sons and two daughters.

In the death of Mr. Ward, we have lost one of our best citizens. He was an old soldier, having served as a private for three years in Company A. Fourth Ohio Cavalry. As soldier, citizen, neighbor and friend, he was always loyal and true, a kind husband and father, and a man who was never blessed with much of the wealth of this world, but his strong hands was every ready to assist his neighbors in his hour of need. The word fear was not in his vocabulary. He acted and spoke as his good sense and conscience told him was right. His strong hand was ever ready to assist the weak, his unflinching courage and kindly word of advice gave courage to the timid and wavering. He died as he had lived, without fear. He answered his last roll call without a murmur, and passed on to join the mighty host of his old comrades who have gone before to take up their abode on that tentless field of the dead.

His wife, Mary Henrietta, died July 7, 1921, at Salt Lake City, Utah, and interment was made in Mt. Calvary Cemetery.

WASHBURN, MARY ALICE - (Kearny County Advocate, May 16, 1913) Mary Alice Washburn, second youngest daughter of Joseph W. and Isabella E. Washburn, from Flora, Clay County, Illinois, was born in Wakefield, Richland County, Illinois, on March 3, 1889, and died of consumption at the home of her brother and sister, Noah and Anna Washburn, near Hartland, Kansas, May 7, 1913, aged 24 years, two months and four days.

She united with the M. E. church in the year 1906, and was a faithful Christian until death. Her dying words were: "O, that crown, I know I am going to heaven."

Besides her grief stricken parents, she leaves two brothers and two sisters, together with a host of friends, to mourn her loss. The funeral services were conducted by Rev. Blair, pastor of the Kendall Methodist Church, and interment made in the Kendall Cemetery.

WELLS, GIRL - (Syracuse Journal, Nov. 1, 1901, Kendall Items) Four months ago the home of A. W. Wells was brightened by the birth of twins, a boy and a girl. Tuesday of this week the little girl died.

KENDALL CEMETERY

WELLS, FRANCES PEARL - (Sec. 3) Wife of Thomas Wells, Born March 3, 1886.

WELLS, MARY JANE - (Sec. 3) (Syracuse Journal, May 16, 1919) Mary Jane Turner was born in the state of Ohio, May 16th, 1846, and moved with her parents to Indiana in 1854, in which state she grew to womanhood.
 She was converted when young and joined the Bethel Baptist Church. She was married to Wm. Madison Wells, March 21, 1866. To this union seven children were born, six of whom survive her: Albert W. Wells of LeRoy, Minnesota, Thomas A. Wells and Lulu May Porter of Kendall, Kansas, Mrs. Belle Renshaw and Clement O. Wells of Denver, Colorado, and Lawrence E. Wells of Los Angeles, California. She is also survived by four sisters, all residing in Indiana and one brother, of Newton, Kansas. She came with her husband and children to Kendall, Kansas, in the fall of 1886 at which place she has since resided. There being no Baptist church at Kendall, she joined the Methodist Church, of which she was a member up until the time of her death.
 Her husband died April 24, 1918, at Kendall. She spent the past winter at Los Angeles, California, visiting her sons, Lawrence E. and Clement O. Wells. She returned to Denver, April 27th, her son Clement coming with her. She was stricken with paralysis of the left side May 8th, at 12:20 a.m. at the home of her daughter, Mrs. Belle Renshaw, Denver, Colorado. She was buried in the Kendall Cemetery, Monday afternoon, May 12th. All the children were present at the funeral, except Clarence E. Wells, of Los Angeles. Also her brother, Henry Turner of Newton, Kansas.

WELLS, TOM A. - (Sec. 3) (Lakin Independent, Dec. 14, 1934, Kendall News) We are sorry to hear of the death of an old friend and neighbor, Tom Wells, as yet we do not know the cause of death.
 (Lakin Independent, Dec. 21, 1934) Many people from the north Kendall flats attended the funeral of T. A. Wells at Kendall Thursday afternoon.

WELLS, WILLIAM M. - (Sec. 3) (Syracuse Journal, April 27, 1917) Mr. Wells dies. There will be no Kendall items in this weeks Journal because the faithful correspondent has laid down his pencil forever and has passed into the silent halls of death.

KENDALL CEMETERY

He passed away Tuesday evening of this week after suffering for years from the insidious disease, diabetes. During the last few weeks he was bedfast and even wrote under these trying conditions, he wrote his weekly letter with the assistance of his wife and daughter.

The simple funeral was held Wednesday afternoon from the little church where he was wont to worship. On the wall back of the sacred desk, was displayed the word "Welcome" a remnant of former decorations, but expressive of the sublime faith and fortitude with which our friend had met the death angel when he came to release him from his suffering. Rev. Frame, the new pastor, spoke feelingly of the times when he visited him and in a few fitting words told the simple story of the Christian's hope of a life beyond the grave. Then tender hands laid him to rest in the Kendall Cemetery and the long rays of the setting sun cast their parting beams on the little mound of earth with the benediction, "Well done, good and faithful servant, thou hast been faithful over a few things, I will make thee ruler over many things; enter thou into the joys of thy Lord."

(Syracuse Journal, May 4, 1917) William Madison Wells was born in Sullivan County, Indiana, on the 11th day of August 1845, and was converted and joined the Baptist church in 1865. He was united in marriage to Mary Jane Turner on March 21st, 1866. To this union were born seven children, five sons and two daughters, one dying at birth.

Those still living are: Albert W. Wells of Lime Springs, Iowa; Clement O. Wells and Lawrence E. Wells of Los Angeles, California; Mrs. Bell Renshaw, of Denver, Colorado; Thos A. Wells and Lulu May Porter of Kendall, Kansas.

He came to Kendall in 1886, joined the Methodist Episcopal Church in 1896. After suffering for seven years of diabetes he passed away April 24th, 1917, at 7 p.m. at the age of 77 years, 8 months and 11 days. He leaves a widow and six children. Among his last words, "I am only waiting my Master's call."

WHEELER, CALLIE - (Sec. 2) (The Lakin Independent, Oct. 5, 1951) Mrs. J. K. Wheeler passed away Wednesday, Sept. 26, 1951. Funeral services were held Monday afternoon.

WHEELER, JAMES KELLAM - (Sec. 2) (Lakin Independent, April 14, 1960) James Kellam (J. K) Wheeler, 83, died Saturday at Donahue Hospital in Syracuse. He was ill four days.

KENDALL CEMETERY

He was born May 3, 1876, at Huntsville, Arkansas, and lived here 41 years. He was a retired rancher and rural mail carrier.

He was a member of the Elks at Garden City.

Survivors are a daughter, Mrs. Thelma K. Amos, Granada, Colorado, and a sister, Mrs. Mattie Cisco, Detroit, Michigan.

Funeral at 2:30 p.m. Wednesday at the Kendall Methodist Church. Rev. E. F. Markley officiating. Burial was in Kendall Cemetery.

WILLIAMS, MRS. JOHN - (The Kendall Boomer, Wednesday, July 13, 1887) About a month ago John Williams left Clark County with his wife and one child in a covered wagon, enroute to some point in Colorado in the hope that his wife's health, which was bad, she being a subject of consumption, would be improved by the change. When the little company reached here, the poor woman, worn out by travel, gave up all hope and asked to be placed where she could rest in peace. A house was secured and the sufferer conveyed there and placed on a couch from which she never rose, her unfettered soul taking its leave of earth on Sunday evening (July 10, 1887). Her remains were interred here and the sad husband and father took his child and started back for Clark County.

WRIGHT, DORIS CHRISTINE - (Sec. 6) (The Lakin Independent, Dec. 29, 1983) Doris Christine Wright, 49, died December 25, 1983, at Lakin hospital after a short illness. Born Doris Christine Hulse, March 1, 1934, at Norton, she married Earnest Wright, June 4, 1964, at Lamar, Colorado. She had been a Kendall resident since 1966.

She was a member of the First Congregational Church, Arriba, Colorado.

Survivors: widower, of the home; sons, Cephas Clinton, Maryland, Virginia, Orren Ray, Cleveland, Texas; daughter, Phyllis Hendrickson, Gentry, Arkansas; brother, Harold Hodges, Westminister, Colorado; sisters, Maxine Warren, Grand Junction, Colorado, Dorothy Kelliher, Clifton, Colorado, Mildred Slancik, Cripple Creek, Colorado; nine grandchildren.

Funeral was at the United Methodist Church, Syracuse; the Rev. Don O'Hara. Burial at Kendall Cemetery. Greene Funeral Home, Syracuse, was in charge.

WRIGHT, EMMA L. - (Sec. 6) (The Lakin Independent, December 2, 1993) Emma L. Wright, 95, Kendall, died November 28, 1993, at the

KENDALL CEMETERY

Hamilton County Extended Care Facility in Syracuse.

She was born June 10, 1898, in Thayer, Kansas, the daughter of Arnold and Maud Mae Stipp Libertus. She came to this area with her parents as a young child and had been a resident of Hamilton County for 86 years.

She married Thomas William Wright Sr. on April 28, 1915, at Syracuse. He died March 29, 1984. To this union eight children were born. The family lived northeast of Coolidge on their homestead until 1928, moving from there to the Sunflower Ranch. They came to the Kendall area in 1938 where Mr. Wright worked at the Yingling elevator and farmed and ranched north of Kendall until 1961 when they moved to Kendall. Mrs. Wright continued to live there after her husband's death and still raised chickens.

Mrs. Wright was a member of Kendall United Methodist Church, Chatterbox Club, Pollyana EHU, and Loyal Neighbors Hall, all of Kendall.

Survivors include two daughters, Ellen Mae Kurz, and Ruby Lee Lohman, both of Kendall; a son, Earnest Wright, Kendall; a half brother, Clayborn Libertus, Casper, Wyoming; a half sister, Opal Cook, Phoenix; 22 grandchildren; 47 great grandchildren; nine great-great grandchildren; five step grandchildren; 20 step great grandchildren, and four step great-great grand-children.

She was preceded in death by two sons, Earl and Thomas William III, three daughters, Ona Louella, Golda Arlene and Loraine. Also two brothers, a sister, and a half sister.

Funeral was at 10 a.m. MST, Wednesday, at the First United Methodist Church, Syracuse, the Revs. Nathan Morgan and Jim Bush officiating. Burial was in Kendall Cemetery.

WRIGHT, THOMAS W. SR. - (Sec. 6) (The Lakin Independent, April 5, 1984) Funeral services for Thomas William Wright, Sr., 93, were held Saturday afternoon at the United Methodist Church in Syracuse with the Rev. Alvin Smith officiating. Burial was in the Kendall Cemetery.

Mr. Wright died Thursday, March 29, 1984, at his home in Kendall. He was born April 17, 1890, in Morgan, Ohio County, Kentucky, the son of Thomas William and Mary Ellen (Coleman) Wright.

He lived in Morehouse, Missouri, for 11 years, before coming to this area, December 2, 1913.

Tom married Emma Libertus, April 28, 1915, at Syracuse. To this

KENDALL CEMETERY

union eight children were born. The family lived northeast of Coolidge on their homestead until 1928, moving from there to the Sunflower Ranch. They came to the Kendall area in 1938, where he worked at the Yingling Elevator until 1948 and farmed and ranched north of Kendall until 1961 when they moved to Kendall.

He loved family gatherings and visiting people and enjoyed dancing, hunting and fishing, as well as all sports. Tom's home was always open to people. Several children stayed at his home while attending school.

Mr. Wright is survived by his wife of 68 years and 11 months, Emma; a son, Earnest of Kendall; two daughters, Ellen Kurz and Ruby Lohman of Kendall; two sisters, Ena Haney of Concord, California, and Ona Libertus of Coolidge, 22 grandchildren, 47 great grandchildren.

Also his son-in-law, LeRoy Lohman, Ralph Jury and Roy Kurz, and a daughter-in-law, Alice Wright, and a host of relatives and friends.

He was preceded in death by two sons, Earl and Thomas William Jr.; three daughters, Ona Louella, Golda Arlene and Loraine; one brother, Dee Wright; four sisters, Debbie Cauthon, Maris Graham, Ida Glover and Ersie England.

KENDALL CEMETERY

YINGLING, EFFIE R. - (Sec. 5) (The Lakin Independent, March 7, 1963) Mrs. Ira (Effie R.) Yingling, a resident of Kendall for 35 years, died Sunday at Donahue Memorial Hospital, where she had been a patient for the past six weeks. Mrs. Yingling, 82, had been in ill health for two years.

Funeral services were held at 2:30 p.m. Wednesday at the Syracuse Methodist Church with Rev. Paul Brooks. pastor of the Kendall Methodist Church, and Rev. Harry Walz, pastor of the Syracuse Methodist Church, officiating. Interment was in the Kendall Cemetery.

Mrs. Yingling was born October 21, 1880, in Ohio and was married at Thayer, Kansas, in September of 1912. The couple celebrated their 50th wedding anniversary last year.

Mrs. Yingling was a member of the Methodist Church, the Women's Society of Christian Service of the Kendall Methodist Church, the Lieurance Music Club, the Business and Profession Woman's Club and the Hamilton County Republican Women's Club.

She is survived by her husband, Ira, of the home; two sisters, Mrs. Irma Sutton of Salmyr, California, and Mrs. Ethel Adams of Boulder, Colorado, and one brother, Ernest L. Sinclair of Sylvia.

YINGLING, IRA - (Sec. 5) (The Lakin Independent, Dec. 8, 1966) Ira R. Yingling, 87, died early Thursday morning in the Greeley County Hospital after a four day illness.

He was born March 23, 1879, in Coffey County. He married Effie Sinclair in September 1912, at Thayer. She died in 1963. He moved to Kendall in 1927, and established the Yingling Grain Elevator there. Mr. Yingling was a member of the Methodist Church and a past member of the Syracuse Hospital Board.

Surviving are a sister-in-law, Mrs. Ethel Adams, and several nieces and nephews.

Funeral was held Tuesday at the First Methodist Church, Syracuse, the Rev. Harry Walz officiating.

LYDIA GERMAN LUTHERAN CEMETERY

(German Lutheran Church Records, Lydia, Wichita County, Kansas, 1906-1916, copied from the original register by Mrs. Alberta V. Dennis, 510 Eugene Place, Garden City, Kansas) The Lydia German Lutheran Cemetery is located in the NW corner of the NE/4 of Section 27, Township 20, Range 36, and we find this indenture made this 28th day of January 1905, Page 555 in volume number 15 made by Tamme Rewerts and Frances Rewerts where they gave the German Lutheran Church a strip of land in the NW corner of the NE/4, Section 27-20-36 containing six acres more or less. Eighty rods east and west by twelve rods north and south with one acre to be used for cemetery purposes. Hugh Glenn was Register of Deeds at this time.

The big prairie fire that swept through this community in the spring of 1916 burned the church to the ground, never to be rebuilt. Some of the people that had relatives buried there wished that all should not be lost, sent money to fence the cemetery and the local people built the fence as requested. For the lack of interest very little care was taken. Fences filled with weeds, all the land was cultivated around the cemetery. Along came the dirty thirties with the dusters that filled the fence inclosure and left nothing but a big dust pile. With the organizing of the Wichita County Cemetery District this became one of the Boards responsibilities. The fence had been bulldozed into a pile so that the dirt would blow away. At this time or soon after, while Arthur Kuhlman was County Commissioner, he asked the County Road Department to come down and scrape the dirt to the side in order that the graves might be located as there were only three graves with markers.

By moving about twelve inches of dirt to the side the graves were easily distinguished and we located fifteen more unmarked graves. To be an abandoned cemetery all graves would have to be moved to some other place. The Cemetery Board had a cable fence built around the portion where the graves were located. They bought stones to mark each grave.

In the Church Register we find the record of deaths has the following, listed on page 197. (Some of the writing is hard to make out as it is written in German:)

Henis Fischer died July 24, 1907
Elisabeth Langlitz died June 21, 1907
Hanna Krom died August 4, 1907
Edmond Winick died June 18, 1907
Samuel Scheuermann died August 26, 1908

LYDIA GERMAN LUTHERAN CEMETERY

David Scheuermann died July 5, 1908
Elma Holstein died May 30, 1909 (moved to Leoti Cemetery)
Heinrich Hartman died February 15, 1911
Scheuermann baby died April 10, 1911
Elsa Hannemann (twin) died May 10, 1911
Lea Hannemann (twin) died December 17, 1911
Adam Lautensclaeger died August 21, 1913
Mattie Lisbeth Holstein died November 26, 1916 (moved to Leoti Cemetery.

This still leaves 5 graves unaccounted for and we hope we haven't made too many mistakes in our translations.

This was two typed pages loose in the church register.

Information furnished to me by Nellie Jane Scheuerman. My thanks to her.

LYDIA GERMAN LUTHERAN CEMETERY

FISCHER, HENRY - Date of death, July 24, 1907, age 1 yr., 20 days. Parents: Heinr and Maria E. Fischer.
(East Hibbard Township Record, ending March 1, 1908) Henry Fischer died of whooping cough, July 24, 1907, 1 year old.

HANNEMANN. ELSA - Date of death May 23, 1911, 13 days. Parents: Conrad and Anna Kath. Hannemann.

HANNEMANN. LEA - Date of death December 17, 1911, date of birth May 10, 1911.

HARTMAN, HEINRICH - Date of death February 15, 1911, 55 years, 23 days.
(The Leoti Standard, Thursday, Feb. 16, 1911) Henry Hartman, a farmer living in the southeast part of the county, died at his home last night. Cancer of the stomach or liver and heart trouble was the cause of his death. Mr. Hartman was 55 years old and leaves a wife and three sons, two of whom are married, to mourn his death. The funeral services will be held tomorrow afternoon at the German Lutheran Church two miles east of Lydia.

HOLSTEIN, ELMA - Date of death May 30, 1909, date of birth February 15, 1909. Parents Johannes and Maria Elizabetha Holstein. (Church records show date of birth as February 25, 1909) (Moved to Leoti Cemetery)

HOLSTEIN, MARIE ELIZABETH - (The Leoti Standard, Nov. 30, 1916) Mrs. John Holstine died Monday at the hospital in Great Bend as the result of an operation. Mrs. Holstine has been a great sufferer for a long time and has been through several operations which they hoped would cure her. She leaves a husband and a large family of children who have the heart felt sympathy of the whole community.
(The Leoti Standard, Dec. 7, 1916) Marie Elizabeth Gorlitz was born in Schventhal, Russia, February 4th, 1871. She lost her parents in early childhood. She united in marriage to John Holstein in 1890. To this union twelve children were born, some of whom are living, three sons and six daughters. In 1898 she came to Rush County, Kansas, where the family resided five years. She then moved with her family to Wichita County, which was her home until her death. Two years ago she became

LYDIA GERMAN LUTHERAN CEMETERY

very ill with inflammation of the gall bladder and gallstones. She underwent three operations at the Garden City hospital within the two years. She suffered greatly at times and failing to regain her health her husband finally decided to take her to the hospital at Great Bend. There another operation was performed, but the result was not the one hoped for. She passed peacefully away Sunday evening November the 26th at the hospital in Great Bend. The remains were brought home and funeral services held from the house conducted by Rev. Bischoff of Otis, Kansas. A large concourse of friends and neighbors followed the body to its resting in the Lutheran Cemetery, showing the esteem in which she was held in the community.

Mrs. Holstein was a devout Christian, a good neighbor and a loving and devoted wife and mother. Her daughter, Mrs. J. J. Scheuermann, was a patient at the hospital in Great Bend at the time of her mother's death.

Besides her immediate family here she leaves three brothers in Russia.

Date of death November 26, 1916, 45 years, 9 months, 23 days. (Church records show date of birth as July 4, 1871)

Later moved to the cemetery at Leoti.

KROM, HANNA - Date of birth July 15, 1907 and died August 4, 1907. Parents, Conrad and Maria Kath. Krom.

LANGLITZ, ELISABELLA - Date of birth May 15, 1906 and died June 21, 1907.

LAUTENSCHLAGER, ADAM - (The Leoti Standard, Aug. 28, 1913) Last Thursday morning a peculiar accident happened to the 10 year old son of Adam Lautenschlager, who lives in the southeast part of this county. The boy was walking across the floor of the haymow when a board broke, causing him to fall to the floor below. He fell on the broken end of the board and was disemboweled. Dr. Smith was called and after a thorough examination hurried the boy to the Garden City hospital where he died on the operating table. The remains were brought home and buried in the cemetery near Lydia.

Date of death, August 21, 1913, age 7 years, 8 months and 28 days.

SCHEUERMAN, BABY - Died April 10, 1911, age 4 days. Parents: Heinrich Scheuerman.

LYDIA GERMAN LUTHERAN CEMETERY

SCHEUERMAN, DAVID - Died July 5, 1908, age 10 years and 4 months. Parents: Gottlieb and Wilhelamine Scheuerman.

SCHEUERMAN, SAMUEL - (The Leoti Standard, August 27, 1908) Samuel Scheuerman, the fifteen year old son of Mr. and Mrs. J. P. Scheuerman of this city, died at the home of his parents yesterday afternoon, August 26, 1908, at 4 o'clock, after an illness of five weeks with typhoid fever.

Sammy, as he was familiarly known, was one of the best boys in town, industrious and of a quiet nature that made all who knew him a friend. Through these weeks of sickness the boy made a desperate struggle for life and was conscious to the last and during the last few hours of life talked to the family of school and his desire to get started with his lessons. But during the afternoon Sammy realized that the struggle was about over and told those about him that he would soon have to leave them.

Funeral services were held at the M. E. Church this morning at 9:30, Rev. R. S. Rutledge preaching the sermon. The body was then taken to the Lutheran Church near Lydia where another service was held by Rev. Vanangle and the remains laid to rest in the cemetery near that church.

Mr. and Mrs. Peter Scheuerman and Miss Julia Scheuerman, father, mother and sister of J. P. Scheuerman, arrived this morning from Rush County to attend the funeral.

The family have the sympathy of the community in the loss of their oldest son who was honest and kind and had many friends. His associates all have a kind word for Sammy which expressed better than anything else the true life of the boy.

He was born February 8, 1894, in Rush County, Kansas.

WINICK, EDMUND - Born April 14, 1907, and died June 18, 1907. Parents: Friedr. and Katherina Winick. (Church records show born April 15, 1907)

LYDIA LUTHERAN CEMETERY

Lydia Lutheran Cemetery (Evangelical) is located in the northwest corner of the northeast quarter of Section 32, Township 20, Range 36, in Wichita County, Kansas. The cemetery is located on Highway 25 at Milepost 101.

William H. Kuhlmann and wife Minnie deeded it to the Evangelical Lutheran Church, an area of some fifteen acres to be used for church purposes, with the stipulation that the land should revert to the owner if it ceased to be used. This instrument was dated December 21, 1906, and recorded in Wichita County.

It is also recorded that the trustees of the church gave this tract back to Leona P. Sonderegger on August 26, 1961. Also dated that day, Leona P. Sonderegger and husband, Paul, deeded a tract of land 490 feet by 460 feet in the northwest corner of the above quarter to the Wichita County Cemetery District.

LYDIA LUTHERAN CEMETERY

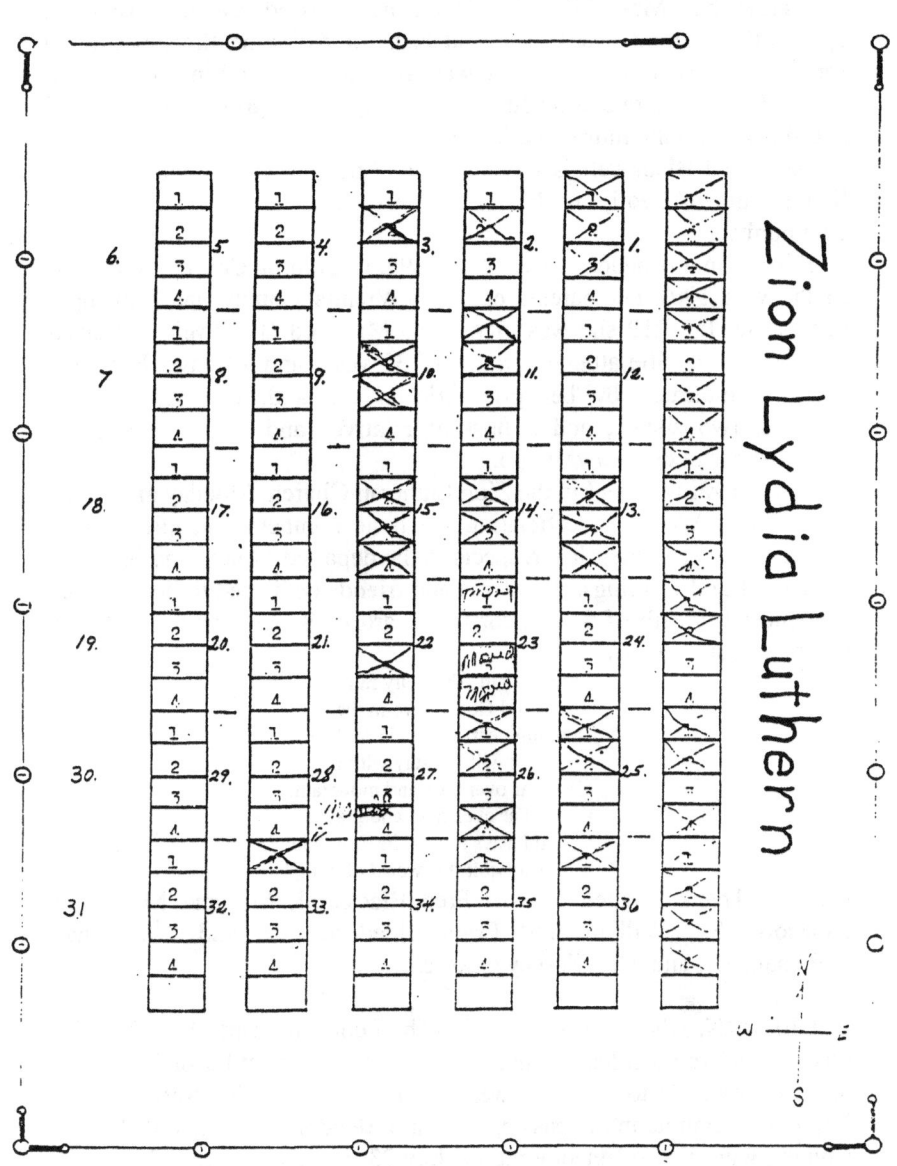

LYDIA LUTHERAN CEMETERY

BLACKWELL, ELISE EMMA - (Plot 2) (Leoti Standard, Aug. 1, 1929) It was a shock to the entire community when it became known last Thursday that Mrs. Elise Blackwell had passed away. Although apparently in good health, she had been ill for some time, becoming seriously ill two weeks ago. She was taken to a hospital in Kansas City, and underwent an operation July 23. The operation proved unsuccessful and she died on the morning of July 25.

Mrs. Fred Blackwell is a daughter of Mr. and Mrs. Wm. Bloedorn, living south of Leoti, and has spent the greater part of her life in this community.

Elise Emma Bloedorn was July 2, 1892, in Cuming County, Nebraska. In the year 1901 her parents came of Wichita County and took up a homestead. In 1919 she was married to Mr. Fred Blackwell of Kansas City, Missouri. She attained an age of 37 years and 23 days. Her early death is mourned by her grief-stricken husband, her parents, two brothers, two sisters, and a host of relatives and friends. A sister preceded her in death a year ago.

The funeral was held in the Zion Lutheran Church, Monday afternoon, Rev. Walter Wehmeier officiating. A large number of people were in attendance, to pay their last respects to the departed. Many and beautiful were the floral offerings. Relatives and friends dedicated to her memory a memorial wreath of $16.00 for the Board of Support of the Lutheran Church. (Contributed)

"Jerusalem, thou city fair and high,
Would God I were in thee!
My longing heart fain, fain to thee would fly,
It will not stay with me;
Far over vale and mountain,
Far over field and plain,
It hastes to seek its Fountain,
And quit this world of pain,"

Card of Thanks signed by Mr. Fred Blackwell, Mr. and Mrs. Wm. Bloedorn, Sr., William and Erich Bloedorn, Mr. and Mrs. Chas. Kuhlman, Mr. and Mrs. Harvey Graves.

BLOEDORN, ANNA A. - (Plot 13) (The Leoti Standard, Aug. 2, 1928) One by one we must leave this earth and enter the great beyond. The call to return extends to youth as well as to the aged. This truth is again impressed upon us in the passing of Anna Bloedorn, a citizen of Wichita County, who died of pneumonia on July 23, in Los Angeles, California.

LYDIA LUTHERAN CEMETERY

Anna Auguste Martha Bloedorn was born June 21, 1896, in Cuming County, Nebraska. At the age of four her parents removed to Wichita County, and have lived here since. Anna spent practically all of her life in this community. After having received instructions in the Christian faith she was confirmed on March 26, 1911. She was always a member of the Lutheran Church. In the early part of 1927, she left for Los Angeles, California, and has worked there till her death, with the exception of a brief visit with home folks last fall. She attained an age of 32 years, 1 month, 2 days.

Funeral services were conducted on Friday afternoon at the home of her parents and at the Zion Lutheran Church, Rev, Wehmeier officiating. Interment was made in the Zion Lutheran Cemetery. A host of friends had gathered to pay their last respects. In her memory two memorial wreaths were made. One by the relatives, and one by the Lydia Lutheran Ladies Aid. Many and beautiful were the floral offerings. Pallbearers were Henry Holstein, Fred Sommers, Fred Kuhlmann, Ben Goken, Aleck Holstein, and Theodore Sommers.

She leaves to mourn her early death her grief stricken parents; two brothers, William and Erich; three sisters, Mrs. F. Blackwell, of Kansas City, Mrs. Charles Kuhlmann of Lydia, and Mrs. Harvey Graves of Garden City; a host of relatives and friends.

"A slumber I know in Jesus' name,
A rest from all toil and sorrow'
Earth tenderly takes my weary frame,
To sleep till the blissful morrow;
In heaven my soul with God abides,
Forgotten are cares and trials."

BLOEDORN, EMMA - (Plot 24) (The Leoti Standard, Sept. 30, 1960) Funeral services for Mrs. Emma Bloedorn were held at 2:00 p.m., Wednesday at the Zion Lutheran Church in the Lydia community of south Wichita County. Rev. Clarence Born officiated at the services.

Rev. Born delivered the funeral sermon for the respected elderly woman who had so many friends in this community.

Mrs. Emma Bloedorn, 86, died at 3:20 a.m. Monday at the hospital in Leoti, following a short illness.

She was born October 15, 1873, at Brandenburg, Germany, and came to the United States in 1891.

Emma Therese Bloedorn was the daughter of Mr. and Mrs. John Brietkreutz, of New Knestrinchen, province of Brandenburg, Germany.

LYDIA LUTHERAN CEMETERY

She came to America with her brother John and his wife, and her sister Elise.

She was married to Wilhelm Bloedorn July 28, 1891, at Wisner, Nebraska. To this union were born two sons and four daughters.

Later they moved to Wichita County in 1901 where they lived on a farm during the days of the early settlers in the community.

Mrs. Bloedorn was a member of the Zion Lutheran Church of Leoti.

In 1934 she and her husband moved to Leoti. He passed away April 15, 1935.

Also preceding her in death was one son, Wm. Jr., and three daughters, Elise, Minna, and Anna.

Survivors are a son, Erich, Leoti; a daughter, Mrs. Charles Kuhlman, Kearny County; two brothers, Frank Breitkreutz, Germany, and Richard Breitkreutz, Leoti; 12 grandchildren, 30 great grandchildren and two great-great grandchildren.

The casket bearers were LeRoy Bloedorn, Marvin Bloedorn, Wallace Kuhlman, Warren Graves, and Lee Ballinger.

Interment was in the Zion Lutheran Church Cemetery. The Weinmann Funeral Home was in charge of arrangements.

(The Leoti Standard, Oct, 6, 1960) Out of town relatives attending the last rites of Emma Bloedorn were the following: Mr. and Mrs. Warren Graves, Jane, Ruth and Susan of Canon City, Colorado; Mr. and Mrs. Lee Ballinger, Judy, Janet, Jean, Jimmy, Jerry and Johnny, of Garden City; Mrs. Dean Reid, Diana and Dennis and Miss Carol Bloedorn, all of Denver, Colorado; Mrs. Emma Breitkreutz of Janesville, Ohio; Mrs. Donald Johnson and Jenny of Firstview, Colorado; Mr. and Mrs. Chas Kuhlman, Mr. and Mrs. Erwin Kuhlman, Pamela and Dennis, Mr. and Mrs. Wallace Kuhlman, Sherri, Trudy, Kathy, Sandy, Mark and Becky, all of Lakin.

Included among friends attending the funeral services, held from the Zion Lutheran Church, Lydia, were the following: Mr. and Mrs. H. W. Kuhlman, and Otto Ballinger of Garden City; Mrs. Preston Kysar, Mrs. Dick Litton, Mrs. Jack Miller, Mrs. Frank Phillips, Mr. and Mrs. Ede Wilken, Mr. and Mrs. Arthur Joiner, all of Lakin, and Mrs. Leonard Harms and Mrs. Clyde Logan of Scott City.

BLOEDORN, OLGA E. - (Plot 2) (Garden City Telegram, Jan. 2, 1992) Funeral for Olga E. Bloedorn, 87, was held at 1 p.m. January 2, 1992, at Price and Sons Funeral Home, Leoti. The Rev. Kenneth Haskall

LYDIA LUTHERAN CEMETERY

officiating. Burial at Lydia Cemetery, Leoti. She died December 25, 1991, at Great Bend.

Born Olga E. Brack, December 10, 1904, at Walla Walla, Washington, she married William Bloedorn, September 1, 1929, at Leoti. He died September 26, 1952.

Mrs. Bloedorn was a homemaker and baker at Concordia College and Hamline University, both at St. Paul, Minnesota, retiring in 1986. She had been a Great Bend resident since 1990, moving from St. Paul.

She was a member of the Trinity Lutheran Church, Great Bend.

Survivors include a son, Richard, St. Paul; two daughters, Vivian Bushman, Dallas, and Carol Braun, Denver; five sisters, Agnes Johnson, St Paul, Esther Scheck, Great Bend, Viola Gross, Hays, Dorothy Frisch, Merrill, Wisconsin, and Angelina Miro, Vero Beach, California; eight grandchildren; and seven great grandchildren.

Memorials to the Great Bend Manor in care of the funeral home.

BLOEDORN, WILHELM LUDWIN - (Plot 24) (The Lakin Independent, April 26, 1935) Wilhelm Ludwin Bloedorn was born in Naugard, Province Pommern, Germany, January 31, 1857, and passed away on April 15, 1935, at his home in Leoti. In 1881 he immigrated to America with his parents and located in Cuming County, Nebraska. In 1891 he was united in marriage with Emma Breitkreutz, and this union was blessed with six children, two sons and four daughters. In 1901 he moved to Wichita County, Kansas, and settled southwest of Leoti, where he farmed until he moved to Leoti in September 1934. He was a communicant and voting member of the Zion Lutheran Church.

Two daughters, Anna and Elise, have preceded him in death. He leaves to mourn his death his wife, Mrs. Emma Bloedorn; sons, William Jr. and Erich of Leoti; two daughters, Mrs. Chas. Kuhlman of Lakin and Mrs. Harvey Graves of Garden City; ten grandchildren; three sisters; and one brother. Two brothers have preceded him in death. Funeral services were conducted on Thursday afternoon at the home in Leoti; from there to the Zion Lutheran Church, Rev. J. R. Weber officiating. Interment was made in the Zion Lutheran Cemetery. A host of friends gathered to pay their last respects. In his memory a memorial wreath was made by the family and relatives. Pallbearers were Wm. Kuhlman, Henry Kuhlman, Aleck Apple, Fred Apple, Conrad Hartman, and R.D. Smith.

LYDIA LUTHERAN CEMETERY

A slumber I know in Jesus' name,
A rest from all toil and sorrow;
Earth tenderly takes my weary frame,
To sleep till the blissful morrow;
In heaven my soul with God abides,
Forgotten are cares and trials."

BLOEDORN, WILLIAM - (Plot 2) (The Leoti Standard, Oct. 2, 1952) William Ernest Richard Bloedorn, son of William and Emma Bloedorn, was born September 30, 1899, near Wisner, Nebraska. He was received into God's Kingdom of Grace by Holy Baptism at St. John's Lutheran Church, Wisner, Nebraska, November 5, 1899. On April 5, 1914, he was received into communican membership by Rite of Confirmation at Zion Lutheran Church, Leoti. In 1929 he was united in holy wedlock to Miss Olga Brack. To this union was born two girls, Vivian and Carrol.

On Sept. 18-19, he was in a hospital in Minneapolis. Thereafter he stayed at the home of a sister, and went daily for treatments until Friday, September 26, the day he passed away, at the age of 52 years, 11 months and 26 days.

Two sisters and his father preceded him in death.

Services were held last Sunday afternoon at Mt. Calvary Lutheran Church, Miltona, Minnesota. During the services in Minnesota, Harold Ochs of La Crosse sang the Lord's Prayer.

The departed leaves to mourn his bereaved wife, Mrs. Olga Bloedorn; two daughters, Mrs. Vivian Marmholz of Merril, Wisconsin, Carrol Bloedorn of Minneapolis, Minnesota; one son, Richard Bloedorn; his mother, Mrs. Emma Bloedorn; of Leoti; one brother, Eric Bloedorn of Leoti; two sisters, Mrs. Minnie Graves, Garden City, and Mrs. Charles Kuhlman, Lakin; other relatives and a host of friends.

BOHL, ADAM - (Plot 36) (The Lakin Independent, July 28 1950) Adam Bohl was born in Aerenfeld, Russia, on June 25, 1874.

Soon after his birth he was received into the Covenant of God through the Holy Sacrament of Baptism; later he was also instructed in the chief parts of Christian doctrine and was received into communicant membership in the Lutheran Church through the rite of confirmation.

In 1891 he entered into the Holy Estate of matrimony with Marie Madeline Knaus. This union was blessed with 12 children. His wife and six children have preceded him into eternity.

LYDIA LUTHERAN CEMETERY

He came to this country in 1900, and in 1908 the Bohls settled in Kearny County, Kansas.

After an illness of three days he passed away on July 22, 1950. He is survived by his children: Mrs. Fred Kleeman and Fred Bohl of Lakin, Mrs. Ben Giesick and Mrs. Sam Giesick of Leoti, Mrs. Emanuel Mai of Tribune and Henry Bohl, Sharon Springs; by 20 grandchildren and 4 great grandchildren; by four sons-in-law and two daughters-in-law, as well as by other relatives and friend.

He reached the age of 76 years and 27 days.

Funeral services were held at Lydia Lutheran Church on Tuesday afternoon Pastor Paul H. C. Stengel of Deerfield in charge. Interment was made in the congregation's cemetery.

BOHL, ADAM - (Plot 36) Born in 1842 and died in 1924. (Fred Bohl told me his grandfather died in the winter time and his body was taken to the grave on a sled.)

BOHL, MARIE MADELINE - (Plot 36) (The Lakin Independent, June 27, 1947) Funeral services were held Saturday, June 28, at the Lydia Lutheran Church at 2:30 o'clock for Mrs. Adam Bohl, who died at her home Wednesday. Rev. Paul H. Stengel of Deerfield conducted the services and burial was in the Lydia Cemetery.

Mrs. Bohl had been ill for a considerable time and had been in the Kearny County Hospital from December 3, 1946, to May 25, when she was dismissed to go to her home.

Mrs. Bohl was 72 years of age and had lived in Kearny Country for 39 years. She is survived by her husband; two sons, Fred of Lakin and Henry of Sharon Springs; and four daughters, Mrs. Fred Kleeman of Lakin, Mrs. Sam Geisick and Mrs. Ben Geisick, both of Leoti and Mrs. Emanuel Mai of Tribune.

(The Lakin Independent, July 4, 1947) Marie Madeline Knaus Bohl was born in Awrenfeld, Russia, on July 18, 1874. Soon after her birth she was received into the Covenant of God through the Holy Sacrament of Baptism, later she was also instructed in the chief parts of Christian doctrine and was received into communicant membership in the Lutheran Church through the rite of confirmation.

In 1891 she entered into the Holy estate of matrimony with Adam Bohl. This union was blessed with 12 children; six of whom have preceded their mother into eternity.

LYDIA LUTHERAN CEMETERY

She came to this country in 1900, and in 1908 the Bohls settled in Kearny County, Kansas.

After a lingering illness she passed away peacefully on June 25, 1947.

She is survived by husband, Adam Bohl; by her children: Mrs. Fred Kleeman of Lakin, Mrs. Ben Geisick of Leoti, Mrs. Emanuel Mai, of Tribune, Henry Bohl of Wallace and Fred Bohl of Lakin; by 19 grandchildren and two great grandchildren; by 4 sons-in-law and two daughters-in-law and one brother, Henry Knaus of Wakeeney, Kansas; as well as other relatives and friends.

Funeral services were held at Lydia Church on Saturday afternoon with Pastor Paul H. C. Stengel of Deerfield in charge. Interment was made in the congregation's cemetery.

BOHL, SOPHIE - (Plot 36) Born in 1842 and died in 1918.

BREITKREUTZ, BERNICE- (Plot 12) (The Lakin Independent, Oanica News, Sept. 30, 1921) The little daughter of Mr. & Mrs. Earnest Breitgridtz of Lydia died late Saturday. The funeral services were held last Monday afternoon.
Born in 1920.

BREITKREUTZ, ELDA - (Plot 1) (The Lakin Independent, Fairview News, April 24, 1931) This neighborhood extends sympathy to Mr. and Mrs. Earnest Breitkreutz. The death angel claimed their baby girl after a very brief illness.

BREITKREUTZ, EMMA - (Plot 1) Born in 1895 and died in 1979. (Buried in Ohio)

BREITKREUTZ, EMMALINE - (Plot 1) (The Lakin Independent, Sept. 21, 1928) The week old baby girl of Mr. and Mrs. Ernest Breitkreutz died at the Cottage Hospital at Garden City last Thursday and was buried in the Lutheran Cemetery at Lydia, Friday. We extend our sympathy. Date of birth September 5 and died September 13, 1928.

BREITKREUTZ, ERNST GUSTAVE - (Plot 1) (The Lakin Independent, June 21, 1946) Ernest Gustave Breitkreutz, son of Mr. and Mrs. John Breitkreutz, was born June 27, 1882, at Neu Keustrinchen, province of Bradenburg, Germany. He passed away at his home near Leoti, Kansas,

LYDIA LUTHERAN CEMETERY

on June 14, 1946, after an illness of two months.

He came to America with his parents at the age of eleven years and lived with them at Wisner, Nebraska, for eight years before the family moved to Wichita County, Kansas, in 1901.

Mr. Breitkreutz was a resident of Wichita County for nearly a half a century and was active in the many pioneering enterprises of the county. He was reared in the Lutheran Church and became affiliated with Zion Lutheran Church of Lydia, Kansas, and maintained his membership there for forty-five years.

He was married to Miss Emma Kuhlman on November 18, 1918, at Ellsworth, Kansas. To this union were born twelve children, seven of whom preceded their father in death.

He leaves to mourn: his grief stricken wife, Emma; one son, Robert; four daughters, Ona, Elda and Wilma, all of Leoti, Kansas, and Mrs. Dorothy Reed, Zanesville, Ohio.

He is also survived by two brothers and four sisters: his twin brother, Richard, of this community and one brother living in Germany; Mrs. Emma Bloedorn of Leoti, Kansas; Mrs. Morton Cox of Phoenix, Arizonia; Mrs. Anna Arsdale of the State of Washington; and Miss Martha Breitkreutz of Los Angeles, California. One brother, of Wisner, Nebraska, preceded him in death several years ago.

The funeral services were held Monday afternoon, June 17. After a short service in his home, the mortal remains of deceased were taken to Zion Lutheran Church where he so often and so joyfully had gone to hear the living, saving word of the Gospel of Salvation. His pastor, the Rev. H. Stengemann, addressed the audience and comforted the bereaved on the basis of John 11. 25-26, where we read the words of our Savior: " I am the Resurrection and the Life: he that believeth in me, though he were dead, yet shall he live: And whosoever liveth and believeth in Me shall never die." A quartet sang, " Nearer My God to Thee," "Asleep in Jesus," and "What a Friend We Have in Jesus." His mortal body was then laid to rest in the church cemetery, there to await the coming of Him who is the Resurrection and the Life.

> His trials and his griefs are past;
> A blessed end is his at last;
> He bore Christ's yoke and did His will;
> And tho he died, he liveth still.

The sympathy of the entire community, especially of his Christian brethren of Zion Lutheran Church, goes out to the bereaved families of our beloved brother in the Lord.

LYDIA LUTHERAN CEMETERY

BREITKREUTZ, ERNST RICHARD - (Plot 13) (The Lakin Independent, Fairview News, March 13, 1925) The infant son of Mr. and Mrs. E. G. Breitkreutz passed away Tuesday. Funeral was held at the Lutheran Church Wednesday afternoon. The bereaved parents have the sympathy of the entire community.

(Lydia News) Friends and relatives were shocked to hear the death of little Earnest Richard Breitkreutz last Tuesday morning. Funeral services were held Wednesday and the remains were laid to rest in Lydia Lutheran cemetery. The parents, Mr. and Mrs. E. G. Breitkreutz, have the sympathy of the entire community.

BREITKREUTZ, KARL ELTON - (Plot 12) (The Leoti Standard, Feb. 2, 1933) Baby boy Karl Elton Breitkreutz, infant son of Mr. and Mrs. E. G. Breitkreutz, was born Sunday, January 29, and passed away January 31. Funeral services were held at the Zion Evangelical Church by Rev. J. R. Webber, and interment was made in The Lutheran Cemetery at Lydia.

BREITKREUTZ, MARTHA E. - (Plot 12) Born April 27, 1880 and died July 17, 1953.

BREITKREUTZ, VELMA - (Plot 13) Born and died in 1924.

BREITKREUTZ, WILHELMINE - (Plot 12) (Kearny Country Advocate Eureka News, Oct. 9, 1914) Mrs. Breitkreitz died at her home Thursday evening, October 8, at 6:30, and was buried Sunday P.M. at the Lutheran Cemetery at Lydia. She was born November 25, 1839.

BREITKREUTZ, TWIN - (The Lakin Independent, Jan. 4, 1935) Twin babies were born to Mr. and Mrs. Ernest Breitkreutz Christmas Day at St. Catherine's Hospital at Garden City. One of the babies was still born, and the other one is so delicate it was necessary to place it in an incubator. Fairview folks extend sympathy to Mr. and Mrs. Breitkreutz and are hoping that Mrs. Breitkeutz and infant will soon be able to come home.

BRUCE, HENRY CHRISTOPHER - (Plot 26) (The Leoti Standard, Feb. 3, 1927) The grim reaper Death has again visited a Wichita county home, and cut off the life of a well know old resident in the person of Mr. Bruce.

LYDIA LUTHERAN CEMETERY

Mr. Bruce had not been well for some time. About a week and a half prior to his death he became bedfast. His death was caused by a hemorrhage of an ulcer of the stomach. He died January 27, 1927, at his home in the southern part of the county.

Henry Christopher Bruce was born in Germany, October 11, 1877. He came to this country about five years later with his parents and located in Ackley, Iowa. When about fifteen years old the family moved to Parker, South Dakota, and in 1901 came to Wichita County, where he lived the rest of his life. He attained the age of 49 years, 3 months, and 16 days. His father, mother, and one brother have preceded him in death. He received instructions in the Christian faith and became a member of the Zion Lutheran Church in the year 1918. He was married to Loma Long, December 7, 1918. To this union two children were born, Genevieve, aged seven, and Eugene, aged four. He leaves his grief stricken family, two brothers, John and Adolph; three sisters, Mrs. Grace Rhodes, Mrs. Lena Gortemaker and Miss Anna, to mourn his death.

His mortal remains were laid to their last resting place Sunday afternoon, January 30th. At funeral service his pastor delivered a consoling sermon on Ps. 119. 76. The large attendance at the funeral gave evidence of a large circle of friends.

> "His trials and his grief are past;
> A blessed end is his at last;
> He lived where none do mourn and weep,
> And calmly shall his body sleep."

BRUCE, JOHN F. - (Plot 26) (The Lakin Independent, Fairview Items, August 13, 1926) Grandpa Bruce, one of the pioneer settlers of this neighborhood, passed away last week and was buried in the Lutheran Cemetery at Lydia.

John Bruce and wife, of Lennox, South Dakota, Miss Grace Rhodes and son, Warren of Eagle Bend, Miss Anna Bruce of Chicago, Illinois, are here visiting, having been called home to attend the funeral of their father, John F. Bruce.

LYDIA LUTHERAN CEMETERY

GOERLITZ, JOHN - (Plot 21) (The Leoti Standard, April 11, 1929) John Goerlitz, an old resident of this county, died Friday afternoon at the home of his son, Alex Goerlitz, southeast of Leoti.

The funeral was held at 2 p.m., Monday, at the Goerlitz home, and interment was made in Lydia Cemetery. The services were conducted by Rev. Mueller of the Lydia Lutheran Church.

At his own request, there were no flowers at his funeral. The Lydia folks, in his memory, raised a sum of money instead, and sent it to an orphan's home in Wichita.

John Goerlitz, was born on February 25, 1866, and on March 10th was baptized into the Evangelical Lutheran faith. Fifteen years later he was confirmed in the same faith. His native land was Russia. In 1890 he came to America and settled in New York. Later, after residing in Kansas for some time, he returned to New York where he married Miss Emilie Scheuermann. They resided at different times in Kansas, Washington, and in that state his wife preceded him in death, 19 years ago. He later moved to Wisconsin, after another stay in Kansas, and lived in that state until about a year ago, when he came to make his home with his son, Alexander. His health has been failing for many months, and last Friday he passed away quietly to the rest of the children of God, at the age of 63 years, one month and eleven days.

John Goerlitz leaves eight children, four sons and four daughters. Alexander and Henry live near Leoti; William and David Goerlitz, and Mrs. Lydia Heid, Mrs. Rosa Weber, and Mrs. Mollie Schlegel, and Mrs. Elsie Feimen. Three sisters also survive him, still in Russia; several sons-in-law and daughters-in-law and seven grandchildren.

"Blessed are the dead which die in the Lord
from henceforth."

GOKEN, BEN - (Plot 4) (The Garden City Telegram, Dec. 26, 1989) Funeral for Ben J. Goken, 88, was at 2 p.m. December 26, at the First Baptist Church, Scott City, the Rev. Lynn Smith officiating. Burial at the Lydia Lutheran Cemetery, Lydia, in Wichita County.

He died December 23, 1989, at Scott County Hospital, Scott City.

Born March 9, 1901, in Wichita County, he married Charlotte Strickert, April 25, 1940, at Scott City.

Mr. Goken was a retired farmer and stockman and had been a Scott City resident since 1960.

He was a member of the Zion Evangelical Lutheran Church, Lydia,

LYDIA LUTHERAN CEMETERY

and eternal partner of the Oral Roberts ministry, and a member of the V.I.P. Senior Citizens Center, Scott City.

Survivors include his wife of the home, and one brother, Gerhard Goken, Goodland.

Memorials to the First Baptist Church, Scott City, in care of Price and Sons Funeral Home, Scott City.

GOKEN, LAMMART J. - (Plot 3) (The Leoti Standard, March 2, 1933) Lammert Goken died suddenly on Tuesday evening, at his home southwest of Leoti. Death was due to heart trouble. He was at the supper table, just beginning to eat, when he was stricken.

Mr. Goken was one of our oldest residents, having spent over 40 years in this county. He was nearly eighty years of age. Mr. Goken leaves his wife, one daughter, two sons and one step-son, and many other relatives.

Services were held March 2 at Lydia, with Rev. Weber conducting.

Born in 1853.

GOKEN, MELVIN AND BROTHER - (Plot 4) (Brother may have been Elvin Russel Goken.)

LYDIA LUTHERAN CEMETERY

HEMPLER, ALFRED - (Plot 14) (The Leoti Standard, July 26, 1945) Alfred Hempler, long time resident of Wichita County, was killed instantly Wednesday night a few minutes before seven o'clock, when he stepped in front of a big grain truck on Highway 96 east of Leoti.

The information that we gathered is that Alfred was talking to the driver of an Iowa truck with trailer that was stalled on Highway 96 east of Leoti, in front of his home at the roadside. He started across to the house and stepped directly in front of the truck driven by Alva Idhe, of Elmo, Kansas.

Mr. Hempler came to this county, from Phillips County, a number of years ago. He was a good man who always attended strictly to his own business. He was single and at this time details as to relatives are meagre.

(The Leoti Standard, August 2, 1945) Again the hand of death has claimed for its' charge one of our pioneer citizens, Gustave Alfred Hempler, son of Rev. and Mrs. Herman Hempler, born March 28, 1881, at Helena, Nebraska.

He was killed in a tragic accident on Highway 96, at 6:45 p.m., July 25, at the age of 64 years, 3 months and 27 days.

He was one of a family of twelve children, has been preceded in death by his parents, four sisters and two brothers. Those left to mourn his loss are three brothers, Chris and Herman Hempler, of Phillipsburg, Kansas, Otto Hempler, of Almena, Kansas and two sisters, Mrs. Freda Veeh and Mrs. Josie Imm, of Orange, California, besides a host of other relatives and friends.

He was laid to rest with graveside services by Rev. Stegmann in the Lutheran Cemetery, Friday afternoon, July 27. Dr. Geo Abel, of Scott City, in charge of the burial.

LYDIA LUTHERAN CEMETERY

KUHLMAN, A. REINHART - (Plot 27) (The Garden City Telegram, March 10, 2001) A Reinhart Kuhlman, 90, of Lead, S.D. died Wednesday, March 7, 2001, at Dorsett Health Care Center in Spearfish, South Dakota.

He was born June 22, 1910, at Lydia, the son of August and Clara (Prousch) Kuhlman. He graduated from the University of Nebraska with a master's degree.

On April 4, 1970, he married Della M. James at Lakin. They moved to the Black Hills of South Dakota in 1973 following his retirement from the United States Department of Agriculture after more than 33 years as service as an agronomist.

Mr. Kuhlman was a member of Shepherd of the Hills Lutheran Church in Lead, was a 60 year member of the Lions Club and the Boy Scouts, received the "Top Hand Award" from the Society of Range Management, and received the Silver Beaver and Llama Award in Boy Scouts.

He is survived by his wife; two sons, Myron Kuhlman, Houston, and Armine Kuhlman, San Diego; a stepson, Fred Anschutz, Tonto Verde, Arizona; a stepdaughter, Nancy Robinson, Marion, Illinois; a brother, Elton Kuhlman, Great Bend; a sister, Violet Joiner; Lakin; five grandchildren; and two great grandchildren. He was preceded in death by his parents; his first wife in 1968; and a sister.

Graveside service will be 11:30 a.m. Tuesday in Lydia Cemetery. Friends are invited to Garnand Funeral Home, Lakin, from 9 to 11 a.m. Tuesday before leaving for the cemetery.

Memorials are suggested to the Sight and Sound Project of the Lions Club, in care of Garnand Funeral Home, Garden City.

KUHLMAN, AUGUST - (Plot 27) (The Lakin Independent, Feb. 18, 1944) August Kuhlman, 58, well known and substantial farmer from north Kearny County met his death Saturday evening, when attacked by an infuriated bull. The trampled and bruised body was found late that night in the lane about 200 yards from the coral.

Mr. Kuhlman had gone after the cows on foot and when he failed to return for supper, Mrs. Kuhlman searched the premises. Not finding him, she drove the car to the Ede Wilken home and got Ede to help search for Mr. Kuhlman. They passed near the body but failed to discover it in the darkness.

They then went out to secure help and practically the entire

LYDIA LUTHERAN CEMETERY

community came out to make an extensive search for the missing man, their friend and neighbor. The body was found by Ede Wilken and Herman Kuhlman by the time other help arrived, at about 10 o'clock.

Mr. Kuhlman came in 1887 with his parents, Mr. and Mrs. Wm. Kuhlman, from Warden, Illinois, when two years old and has lived in Lydia community since that time. He was married to Miss Clara Preusch of Healy, Kansas, and there are four children, Reinhart of Nelson, Nebraska, Elton of Wichita, Mrs. Ellen Wilken of Lydia, and Mrs. Violet Joiner of Uniontown, Kansas. All the family was present at the funeral. The service was held at the home, Tuesday afternoon, and interment made in Lydia Lutheran Cemetery, Rev. H. Stegemann, Lutheran pastor, was in charge of the services. Pallbearers were: Wm. Wilken, G. C. Whitaker, Ed Grusing, Tom Rewerts, John Holstein, Jr., Ernest Breitkreutz.

August William Herman Kuhlman, son of Mr. and Mrs. William H. Kuhlman, was born in Worden, Illinois, on May 20, 1885. He was baptized on June 7, 1885, and came to this community with his parents in the spring of 1887. He grew to manhood in this community as a member of a family of eight children.

He attended the local grade school, and also received instruction in the chief doctrines of religious faith during his childhood. He was confirmed as a member of Zion Lutheran Church on May 26, 1901. He attended the academy of St. John's College at Winfield, Kansas, for one semester.

On June 2, 1909, he was married to Miss Clara D.M. Preusch of Healy, Kansas. To this union were born four children, all of whom survive to mourn his death.

As a young man he took up a homestead in northern Kearny County, where he built a home and resided with his family. He was deeply interested in nature, and spent much time beautifying the general surroundings of his home.

He was also interested in school and community building improvements, and in the general development of church projects. For a number of years he served as treasurer of Zion Lutheran Church of this community, and he was a member of the board of trustees at the time of his death.

He died at his home on the afternoon of February 12, 1944, as the result of a farm tragedy, at the age of 58 years, 8 months, and 22 days.

He is survived by his wife, Mrs. Clara Kuhlman, two sons, and two daughters. They are: Armin Reinhart Kuhlman of Nelson, Nebraska; Elton Lawrence Kuhlman of Wichita; Ellen Louise (Mrs. Ede Wilken) of this community; and Violet Irene (Mrs. Arthur Joiner) of Uniontown, Kansas; also four grandchildren.

Living to mourn their loss are five brothers and one sister. They are: Henry Kuhlman, Charles Kuhlman, Herman Kuhlman, Fred Kuhlman, and Mrs. R. J. Breitkreutz, all in this community; and Prof. G. A. Kuhlman of Winfield, Kansas.

KUHLMAN, CHARLES - (Plot 9) (The Lakin Independent, April 4, 1974) Charles L. Kuhlman, 91, died at his home March 29, 1974. Born December 23, 1882, in Dielmissen, Germany, the son of William and Wilhelmina Lohman Kuhlman. They came to the United States in 1884, settling in Staunton, Illinois, then to western Kansas in 1887, where they lived in south Wichita County. He moved to Kearny County in 1910. He was married to Marie Bloedorn, November 12, 1913, at Lydia Lutheran Church. She died September 7, 1969.

He was a member of the Lutheran Church.

He lived alone at his farm home, 20 miles north of Lakin, after the death of his wife and was still active in his farming activities.

Surviving him are three sons, Erwin and Wallace of Lakin and Earl of Marshfield, Missouri; two brothers, Gustave of Winfield, Kansas, and Henry of Garden City. Also surviving him are 15 grandchildren and seven great grandchildren.

Funeral services were held Tuesday afternoon at the Immanuel Lutheran Church in Deerfield with the Reverent Norman Heironimus officiating. Burial in Lydia Cemetery.

KUHLMAN, CLARA DOROTHEA MARGARET - (Plot 27) (The Garden City Telegram, May 11, 1967) Mrs. Clara Dorothea Margaret Kuhlman, 79, of Garden City, died Thursday, May 11, 1967, at St. Catherine Hospital following a lengthy illness.

Born August 8, 1887, in Lane County, she was married to August Kuhlman on June 2, 1909, at Healy. They homesteaded a farm north of Lakin in 1909 where they lived for many years. Mr. Kuhlman died February 12, 1944, and she moved to Garden City in 1945.

She was a member of the Trinity Lutheran Church.

Surviving are two daughters, Mrs. Ellen Wilken, Garden City, Mrs. Violet Joiner, Lakin; two sons, Armine R., Newell, South Dakota, and

LYDIA LUTHERAN CEMETERY

Elton L., Great Bend; a brother, Henry J. Preusch, Healy; a sister, Mrs. Louisa Settles, Dighton; 12 grandchildren and eight great grandchildren.

Funeral services were held May 13 at the Trinity Lutheran Church, the Rev. Walter Schmidt officiating. Burial was in the Lydia Cemetery, in Wichita County.

KUHLMAN, EDNA ROWENA - (Plot 22) (The Lakin Independent, Fairview News, April 24, 1925) The little infant daughter of Mr. and Mrs. Wm. Kuhlman was buried in Lydia, Wednesday afternoon. They have the sympathy of the entire community. Moved to the Lakin Cemetery.

KUHLMANN, HARLAN DUANE - (Plot 10) (The Leoti Standard, Feb. 23, 1933) Baby boy Harlan Duane Kuhlmann, infant son of Mr. and Mrs. Fred Kuhlmann was born January 22, 1933, and passed away on February 20th, at the age of 4 weeks and one day.

Baby Harland Duane was a twin, preceded in death by his sister who died when one day old.

The funeral took place Tuesday afternoon and was conducted by Mr. Vet Coates. Services were held in Zion Evangelical Lutheran Church in the English and German languages. Interment followed in the Lutheran Cemetery. Rev. John R. Weber officiated.

KUHLMANN, HERMAN - (Plot 16) (The Lakin Independent, April 14, 1950) Herman William John Kuhlmann was born January 5, 1891, at Lydia, Kansas, and died in Wichita after a brief illness on April 6, 1950, at the age of 59 years, three months and one day.

He was the son of Mr. and Mrs. William Kuhlman Sr., who were pioneer settlers in Wichita County. In early infancy he was baptized and upon completion of the grade school, he was confirmed as a member of Zion Lutheran Church on May 6, 1907. On January 1, 1914, he became a voting member of this church, in which he served for many years as trustee and treasurer.

On August 26, 1925, he was united in marriage to Miss Olga Kettler of Deerfield, Kansas. To this union were born four children: Alma Louise, Verna Jeane, Valeria Joyce and Norma Lorene. Norma Lorene passed away in infancy.

He established a home in northern Kearny County, where he lived with his family as a farmer and stockman. At various times he served in

LYDIA LUTHERAN CEMETERY

community projects.

In January of this year he became seriously ill and was taken to a Garden City hospital, where he was in the care of specialists at the time of his death.

Two brothers, William and August, preceded him in death.

Surviving to mourn his death are his wife and two daughters, Verna and Joyce, in the family home; a married daughter, Alma Louise, and her husband, Charles Campos, and a granddaughter, Priscilla, living near Leoti. Also mourning his loss are four brothers, Henry Kuhlmann of Garden City, Charles and Fred of this community, and Gustave of Winfield; and one sister, Mrs. R. J. Breitkreutz, of this community.

Funeral services were held at the Lydia Lutheran Church, Monday afternoon. The afternoon was windy and dusty but the church was almost inadequate for the large crowd.

KUHLMAN, IVY AILEEN - (Plot 27) (The Lakin Independent, May 16, 1968) Funeral services for Ivy Aileen Kuhlman, 55, Newell, South Dakota, wife of Armine Reinhart Kuhlman, former Kearny County resident was held Saturday morning at 10 o'clock at the Trinity Lutheran Church, Garden City, with the Rev. Walter G. Schmidt officiating. Burial was in the Lydia Cemetery.

Mrs. Kuhlman was born May 26, 1912, in Belleview. She was married to Reinhart Kuhlman in 1938 in Milo, Missouri. She had lived in Newell the past 11 years, moving there from Hebron, Nebraska.

She was a member of the Lutheran Church in Newell.

Survivors include the widower, two sons, Armine, Columbia, Missouri, and Myron, LaFayette, Indiana, three brothers and one sister.

KUHLMAN, MARIE - (Plot 9) (The Garden City Telegram, Sept. 8, 1969) Mrs. Marie O. Kuhlman, 76, died September 7, at Kearny County Hospital.

Born June 21, 1893, at Weisner, Nebraska, she moved to Wichita County in 1901 with her parents. She was married to Charles Kuhlman, November 12, 1913.

She was a member of the Zion Lutheran Church, Lydia.

Survivors include the widower; three sons, Erwin and Wallace, both of Lakin; and Earl, Clarkston, Georgia; 15 grandchildren and one great grandchild.

Funeral was held at the Immanuel Lutheran Church, Deerfield, the

LYDIA LUTHERAN CEMETERY

Rev. Norman Heironimus officiating. Burial in Lydia Cemetery.
She was the daughter of Wilhelm and Emma Bloedorn and moved to Wichita County with her parents in 1901.

KUHLMAN, NORMA LORENE - (Plot 16) (The Lakin Independent, Jan. 18, 1935) Norma Lorene Kuhlman was born at Lakin, Kansas, on November 9th and departed this life on January 10, 1935; having reached the age of 2 months and 1 day. A brief illness of bronchial pneumonia caused her death. On December 9th she was baptized in the Lutheran faith. She leaves to mourn her passing her father and mother, Mrs. and Mrs. Herman Kuhlman, and three sisters, Alma, Verna, and Valeria, and a host of relatives.
The body was laid to rest in the Lydia Lutheran Cemetery on January 11, at 2 p.m. Rev. J. R. Weber conducted the funeral service.
"Give place, the maid is not dead, but sleepeth." Matt.9:24

KUHLMAN, OLGA - (Plot 16) (The Lakin Independent, Feb. 25, 1982) Olga A. Kuhlman, 78, died February 20, at Wichita County Hospital, Leoti, after a long illness. Born Olga Kettler, October 15, 1903, at Block, she was married to Herman Kuhlman, August 26, 1925, at Tiffany, Colorado. He died April 6, 1950, at Wichita. She had lived in the Lydia community and Leoti for 55 years.
She was a member of Holy Cross Lutheran Church, Scott City, Happy Hour Club, Leoti Anns EHU, and Senior Citizens Club, all of Leoti.
Survivors: daughters, Joyce Miller, Golden, Colorado, Alma Campos, Leoti; sister, Helen Schultz, San Antonio, Texas; 13 grandchildren; nine great grandchildren.
Funeral was at 2 p.m. Tuesday at First Presbyterian Church, Leoti; the Rev. Richard Kaczor. Burial in Lydia Cemetery, Wichita County.

KUHLMAN, VERA LUCILLE - (Plot 22) (Kearny County Advocate, Feb. 4, 1921) Vera Lucille, infant daughter of Mr. and Mrs. William Kuhlman was born September 13th, 1920, and died January 29th, aged four months and sixteen days. Death was due to complications incident to whooping cough followed by pneumonia, and after eleven days of intense suffering, during which time all that human hands could do but to no avail, its soul returned to God who gave it. Funeral services conducted by Rev. Heike, Pastor of the Lutheran Church and were

LYDIA LUTHERAN CEMETERY

attended by a large number of sympathizing friends. She leaves to mourn father, mother, and sister, Leona, and other relatives. The sympathy of the entire community is with the grief stricken parents in the time of sorrow.
Moved to the Lakin Cemetery.

KUHLMANN, WM. SR. - (Plot 15) (The Leoti Standard, Mar. 23, 1916) Again the hand of death has crowded into our midst and claimed for its charge one of our pioneer citizens. In its mysterious and silent manner, death has taken from us Mr. Wm. Kuhlman Sr.
The life of Mr. Kuhlmann has been simple, honest and Christian. He was born on November 20th, 1848, in Dielmissen, Germany, a small village in the province of Brounschweig. From early childhood he showed himself to be honest and hardworking.
On July 22nd. 1876, he was married to Miss Wilhelminne Lohman, also of the same province. This union was blessed with eight children, one daughter and seven sons, all of which remain to mourn his loss.
In the spring of 1884 he sailed with his family across the Atlantic, that they might together enjoy the advantages of the United States, and upon arrival, he at once settled in Warden, Illinois. After living there three years, however, he became interested in Western Kansas, and accordingly filed on a homestead in the southern part of Wichita County, where he moved with his family in the pioneer days of March 1887. Since this time he has been a constant resident of Wichita County. He was robust and healthy, until in the spring of 1915, when he became ill with appendicitis, and was taken to Minnaqua Hospital, Pueblo, Colorado, for an operation. At this operation, however it was found that he was suffering from a cancer of the bowels. After his return home, it seemed for a time that his recovery would be permanent, but with the coming of winter, he was taken abed with sickness, since then he slowly dwindled down, becoming constantly weaker, until he quietly passed away at 3:30 p.m. on March 13th. He was aged 67 years, 4 months and 11 days.
Mr. Kuhlmann has shown himself to be a sincere friend, a devoted husband, a loving father, and a devout Christian. All those who have made his acquaintance have recognized in him an honest, open hearted, and sympathetic man in all his dealings, a man, who contributed greatly to the progress of the neighborhood, a man, who kept his word and stood by his friends with true sympathy in time of need.

LYDIA LUTHERAN CEMETERY

To his wife and children, he has always shown himself to be exceptionally kind and well meaning. His first thought and care was apparently always for his wife and family. He has been to them a model husband and father.

Mr. Kuhlmann was a faithful member of the Evangelical Lutheran Church, and earnestly strove to live a true Christian life in both word and deed. He constantly endeavored to follow onward in the footprints of his Lord and Savior, Jesus Christ, in whom, when finally the last hour of trial came, he still gladly confessed his hope and faith for eternal life.

Besides a great host of friends, Mr. Kuhlmann leaves a devoted wife, eight children, three brothers, one sister and seven grandchildren to mourn his death.

The funeral was conducted by Rev. A. T. Merkel, the services being held at 12:45 in the home, and at 1:45 in the Lutheran Church at Lydia. The body was then laid to rest in the Lutheran Cemetery.

(The Leoti Standard, March 16, 1916) William Kuhlmann died Monday afternoon, March 13th, and the funeral was held yesterday at the Lutheran Church at Lydia and the remains buried in the Lutheran Cemetery. The services were conducted by Rev. A. T. Markel.

Death was the result of a cancer of the stomach, and he had been confined to his bed for about three months. Mr. Kuhlmann was one of our pioneers who had prospered because he knew the value of work and had faith in the country. He was a Christian man who loved his God and his fellowman. We were only slightly acquainted with the deceased but the first time we met him we were impressed with the fact that he was a man of noble character with a big generous heart.

KUHLMAN, W.H.C. - (Plot 22) (The Lakin Independent, Jan. 8, 1943) Mr. William H. C. Kuhlman was born in Brunswick, Germany, on August 20, 1877, and died of a heart ailment at his home south of Leoti, Kansas, at 4:45 o'clock on Saturday afternoon, December 26, 1942, at the age of 65 years, 4 months and 6 days.

He was the oldest son of the late William Kuhlman, Sr., and came with them to America at the age of seven in April 1884. For a period of three years the family lived in Worden, Illinois.

Mr. Kuhlman was a resident of Wichita County for more than 55 years, having come here with his parents in March 1887. He grew to manhood in this community and was active in many enterprises of the community. His voting membership in Zion Lutheran Church extended

LYDIA LUTHERAN CEMETERY

over a period of 37 years; and his service as an elder in the church extended over a period of more than 20 years.

On February 14, 1907, he was married to Miss Katherine H. Coerber of Deerfield, Kansas. This union was blessed with three daughters, two of whom, Vera Lucille, and Edna Rowena, died in early infancy.

He is survived by his wife, Mrs. W. H. C. Kuhlman, and his daughter, Leona, Mrs. Paul Sonderegger and her son, Raymond, of Philadelphia, Pennsylvania. Also six brothers and one sister survive to mourn his loss. They are: Henry, Charles, August, Herman, and Fred of this community, and Gustave of Winfield; and Mrs. R. J. Breitkreutz, also of this community.

"There is an hour of peaceful rest
To mourning wand'rers giv'n;
There is a joy for souls distrest,
A balm for ev'ry wounded breast;
Tis found above-in heav'n."

Relatives and friends who came to attend the William Kuhlman funeral were Oscar Schaaf, a nephew in the service, from Chicago; Gustave Kuhlman, a brother, from Winfield; Mrs. Fred Schaaf, of Wichita; Mrs. Frank Schubert, of Tulsa, Oklahoma; Mrs. Paul Sonderegger, a daughter, and Mr. Sonderegger, of Philadelphia, Pennsylvania; John Marquardt, Otto Sonderegger and Miss Martha Marquardt, all of Garden City.

Moved to the Lakin Cemetery.

KUHLMAN, WILHELMINA - (Plot 15) (The Lakin Independent, Nov. 1, 1935) Grandma Kuhlman passed away Tuesday evening at the home of her daughter, Mrs. Richard Breitkreutz, at Lydia; her husband, Wm. Kuhlman, Sr., having preceded her in death several years ago. The Kuhlmans came here as pioneer settlers near the north county line. A German Lutheran Church was built, a post office established and Lydia became a community center. Six of her sons and a daughter settled on surrounding farms, built substantial improvements, and raised a high grade of live stock. Trees were planted at their homes and they raised fruits and gardens. The children took advantage of school privileges and became well informed and substantial men of affairs. While Grandma Kuhlman could not have the modern conveniences and entertainment because of the pioneer stage of development, hers was the more sublime satisfaction of seeing her life's work build up and develop a substantial community of honest and honorable citizens.

LYDIA LUTHERAN CEMETERY

(The Lakin Independent, Nov. 8, 1935) Mrs. Wilhelmina Kuhlmann, nee Wilhelmina Lohmann, was born in Wangelnstedt, Braunschweig, Germany, on March 27, 1855, and died at the home of her daughter, Mrs. R. J. Breitkreutz, near Lydia, Kansas, at 7:00 o'clock on Tuesday evening, October 29, 1935, at the age of 80 years, 7 months, and 2 days.

Her parents, Henry and Wilhelmina Lohmann, having passed away while she was yet a small child, she grew up in the home of relatives in the village in which she was born.

On July 22, 1876, she was married to Mr. Wilhelm Kuhlmann, a young man from a neighboring village. This union was blessed with eight children, one daughter and seven sons, all of whom are living and were present to mourn her death.

On April 24, 1884, she, together with her husband and three children, set sail for America. The family first settled in Worden, Illinois, where they remained for a period of three years.

In March 1887, the family came to western Kansas, settling with the early pioneers in the south part of Wichita County. In the struggle for a livelihood during the pioneer days especially, she proved herself a most faithful helpmeet and made many sacrifices for husband and children. Her desire to rear her children in the fear and admonition of the Lord was manifested in the many sacrifices which she and her husband made in order to arrange for the preaching of the Gospel of Christ in the home community, and finally to bring about the organization of Zion Lutheran Church at Lydia, Kansas. She retained a deep interest in church activities throughout her life.

Her husband preceded her in death twenty years ago, having passed away in March 1916.

For several years Mrs. Kuhlmann had been in failing health. After a brief illness of a little more than a week, she passed away quietly at the home of her daughter, Mrs. R. J. Breitkreutz, with whom she had been living for several months.

Her children, all of whom were present at her bedside at the time of her death, are: Mr. William Kuhlmann; Mr. Henry Kuhlmann; Mr. Charles Kuhlmann; Mr. August Kuhlmann; Mrs. R. J. Breitkreutz; Mr. Herman Kuhlmann; Mr. Fred Kuhlmann, all of this community; and Prof. G. A. Kuhlmann of Winfield, Kansas. In addition she is survived by 25 grandchildren and 2 great grandchildren.

"Blessed are the dead which died in the Lord henceforth; yea, saith the Spirit, that they

LYDIA LUTHERAN CEMETERY

may rest from their labors; and their works do follow them." Rev. 14:13

KUHLMANN, WILMA JEANNE - (Plot 10) (The Leoti Standard, Jan. 26, 1933) Baby girl, Wilma Jeanne Kuhlmann, one day old twin baby daughter of Mr. and Mrs. Fred Kuhlman passed away on Monday, January 23rd. Funeral services were held at the Zion Evangelical Church on Tuesday, January 24th. Interment followed in the Lutheran Cemetery. Rev. J. R. Weber officiated.

LYDIA LUTHERAN CEMETERY

MICHEL, GEORGE - (Plot 34) 1828-1916 (The Lakin Independent, October 29, 1916) Geo. W. Michel, one of the oldest residents of North Kearny County, died Monday evening. The funeral was held Tuesday with interment in the family block near his late home. He had reached the ripe old age of 88 years. He was the father of Chris Michel.

LYDIA LUTHERAN CEMETERY

SCHAUER, PHILIP - (Plot 32) (The Lakin Independent, April 26, 1935) Philip Schauer, 55, of Tribune died April 15th of pneumonia. He was born in Russia and came to America with the family at the age of 19, settling in North Dakota. Mr. Schauer came to Kansas in 1925. Funeral services were held in the Lutheran Church at Lydia and interment followed in the Zion Lutheran Cemetery.

(The Leoti Standard, April 1935) Philip Schauer, second son of Jake and Katherine Schauer, was born in Russia, November 15, 1879, and died at his home in Greeley County, on April 15, 1935, at the age of 55 years and 5 months.

Death was caused from pneumonia. He also suffered from Diabetes for the past 15 years. His father died when he was a young boy. At the age of 19 he came to America with his mother, one sister and three brothers. They settled at Harvey, North Dakota. Soon he took a homestead at Underwood, North Dakota, on which place he lived for 28 years. On December 22, 1901, he was united in marriage to Mathilda Schimke. This union was blessed with eleven children, one infant and a little girl, 8 years of age, preceding him in death.

He leaves to mourn his passing, his loving wife, four daughters and five sons: Emma Fredrick, Marie, Martha, and Elsie Schauer, Reinhold, Tafiel, Ervin, Hilbert and Reuben, all of the home. Three brothers, Jake, Louis, and Adolph all of North Dakota; his sister having preceded him in death in 1932.

He, with his family, came to Greeley County, Kansas, in 1925, moving there for his health. He was a member of St. John's Lutheran congregation, Tribune. He was a kind and loving husband and father; loved by all who knew him. Funeral services were held in the Lutheran Church at Lydia and interment followed in the Zion Lutheran Cemetery.

"Blessed are the dead that died in the Lord
from henceforth."

(moved from this cemetery)

SOMMERS, LOUIS - (Plot 14) (The Leoti Standard, July 18, 1940) Louis Sommers, a pioneer resident and respected citizen of Wichita County passed away Tuesday, July 16, in a Scott City hospital where he had been ill for some time. Mr. Sommers was a prominent farmer in the Lydia community for a number of years and was also postmaster there at one time.

He moved to Leoti when his health began to fail and has since made

LYDIA LUTHERAN CEMETERY

this his home.

Surviving are his two sons, Fred of Leoti, and Ted of Manhattan; two daughters, Mrs. Elmer Hartman of the Lydia community and Mrs. W. S. Akers, of Orange, California.

The sympathy of a wide circle of friends is extended to the bereaved in their sorrow.

Funeral services were held from the Lutheran Church at Lydia, Friday afternoon at two o'clock.

(The Leoti Standard, July 25, 1940) Funeral services were held at two o'clock Friday afternoon for Louis Sommers, pioneer of Wichita County, Kansas, who was nearly 78 years of age.

Interment followed at the Lydia Cemetery, near the site where he was a homesteader in 1905.

Since 1929, when he disposed of his property at Lydia he has lived in Leoti with the exception of 9 months he was in California operating a store. His health caused his return to west Kansas. For the past several months he had been in failing health, with heart attacks.

Prior to his arrival in Wichita County, Mr. Sommers operated a first class bakery at Russell, Kansas, for several years. That was his original trade.

He was a quiet, reserved man who made scores of friends by always being friendly. His way of life was getting something to do and to do it without interfering with other peoples' business. He was a good citizen and will be greatly missed by the people of this community.

Obituary: Louis Sommers was born July 20, 1862, at Wittenberg, Brackenheim, Germany, and died July 16, 1940, at Scott City, Kansas, at the age of 77 yrs, 11 mos., and 26 days. The cause of his death was the complications of old age.

When about 16 years of age he came to America. In 1905 he settled in Wichita County on a homestead near the site of the old town of Lydia. In this town he also operated a store until 1918.

On August 5, 1896, Mr. Sommers was united in marriage with Mathilda Hempler at Stuttgart, Kansas. She preceded him in death in 1922. To this union four children were born, all of whom survive their parents.

Mr. Sommers was baptized and confirmed in the Lutheran Church, in which church he also held membership all his life. He was a charter member of this congregation, Zion Lutheran, south Wichita County, Kansas.

LYDIA LUTHERAN CEMETERY

He leaves to mourn his passing two sons, Fred of Leoti, and Theodore of Topeka, Kansas; two daughters, Mrs. Elmer Hartman of Leoti, and Mrs. W. S. Akers of Orange, California; five grandchildren; and a host of friends and acquaintances.

SOMMERS, MATILDA - (Plot 14) (The Lakin Independent, July 14, 1922) Matilda Hempler was a native of Nebraska. She was married in 1896 to Mrs. Louis Sommers in Phillips County and they moved to the Lydia neighborhood about 15 years ago. They formerly conducted a store but when automobiles became numerous the trade went to the larger towns on the railroads and they abandoned the store but have been keeping the post office ever since.

Mrs. Sommers died in the hospital at Garden City, July 7, at the age of 51 years, 5 months and 2 days. The funeral services were held Monday, July 10, and the body was laid to rest in the Lutheran Cemetery at Lydia. Her husband and four children survive her.

She will be greatly missed by the people of her neighborhood and a large number of friends and neighbors came out to the funeral to pay their last respects.

LYDIA LUTHERAN CEMETERY

WAGNER, BOY - (The Leoti Standard, Dec. 12, 1907) The little seven months old boy of Mr. and Mrs. Conrad Wagner, who live seventeen miles Southeast died on Wednesday of last week. The remains were buried in the Lutheran Cemetery near Lydia.

WEIDMER, EMMA L. - (Plot 25) (The Leoti Standard, Jan. 20, 1916) Mrs. Weidmer was buried at the cemetery of the Zion Evan. Lutheran Church on January 12.

(The Leoti Standard, Jan. 13, 1916) Last Monday morning the sad news was brought to town that the aged wife and mother had passed away. Mrs. Weidmer was born in Lotzwyn, Hanton Bern, Switzerland, November 28, 1846.

In 1867 she was united in marriage to John Weidmer. To this union ten children were born, five of whom are living. She came to this county with her husband and family in the year 1887, having been a resident in this county for twenty-nine years. Mrs. Weidmer was a sweet spirited Christian woman. She was a devout member of the Lutheran Church.

Funeral services were held in the Lutheran Church at Lydia on yesterday afternoon, after which all that was mortal of this sainted mother and wife was laid to rest in the Lydia Cemetery. Buried January 12.

WEIDMER, JOHN - (Plot 25) (The Advocate, Lydia News, Oct. 1, 1920) The body of Mr. Weidmer, who died at Chanute, Kansas, arrived here Friday morning. Funeral services were held at the Lutheran Church near here and interment was made in the cemetery near the church.

Born November 20, 1838 and died September 21, 1920.

WENICK, FREDRICK - (Plot 36) 1841-1927

LYDIA METHODIST CEMETERY

The Lydia Methodist Cemetery, also known as Eden Methodist Church Cemetery, is located in Wichita County, Kansas. on the Southeast Quarter of Section 36, Township 20, Range 36. It was organized and chartered in May 1907. They started building their church, and on September 25, 1907, before it was finished, one of their members died (Mary Hartman). The cemetery was begun eighty rods west of the church, which stands in the southeast corner of the section. A child, Cristina Wittman, was buried there on September 15, 1907.

LYDIA METHODIST CEMETERY

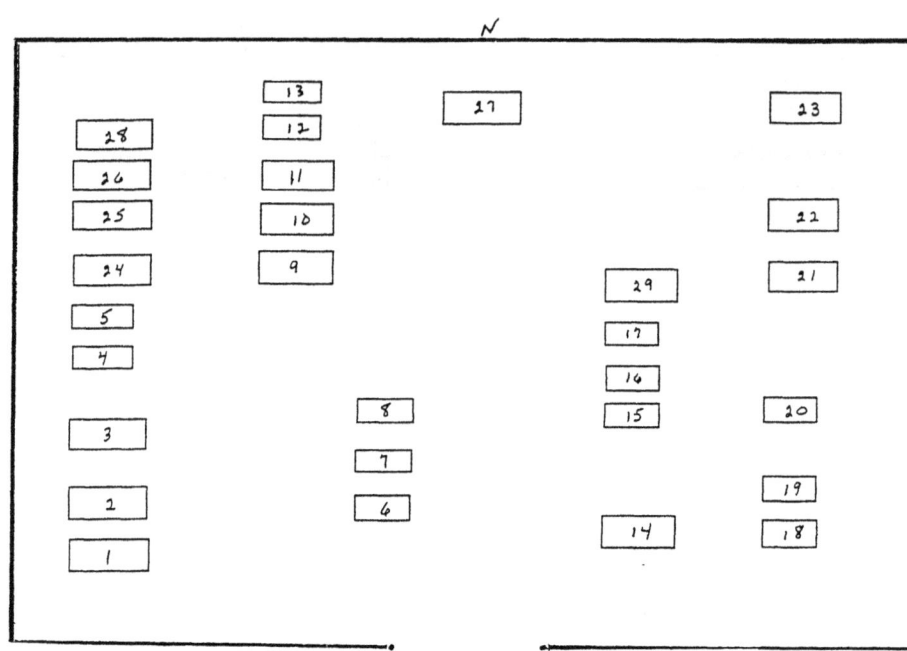

1. JOHN GRUSING
2. ANNA GRUSING
3. GRACE L. GRUSING
4. RONALD A. WARRINGTON
5. DARREL K. WARRINGTON
6. FLOYD MCQUILLIAM
7. GERTRUDE MCQUILLIAM
8. ORLANDO MCQUILLIAM
9. L. E. POSEY
10. HENRY YAKEL
11. GEORGE YAKEL
12. RUBY ANN YAKEL
13. ALICE MAE YAKEL
14. SOPHIA BENDER
15. WILLIAM LAUTENSCHLAGER
16. BENDER INFANT
17. TRELLA IONE PENNINGTON
18. WITTMAN INFANT
19. WITTMAN INFANT
20. ALVINA GIDEON
21. IRENA BOTTS
22. JOHN BOTTS
23. MARY HARTMAN
24. LESLIE WARRINGTON
25. DAVID GRUSING
26. MARY GRUSING
27. DICK LITTON
28. BEN GRUSING
29. JOHN WESLEY GRUSING

LYDIA METHODIST CEMETERY

BENDER, SOPHIA - (Lakin Investigator, April 8, 1910) The funeral of Mrs. H. O. Bender was held in the German Methodist Church, Friday of last week.
    Born in 1860 and died April 1910.
    Church records show born August 8, 1858, and died March 3, 1910.

BENDER, INFANT - Infant of John Bender died 2/10/1912.

BOTTS, IRENA VIOLA - 1871-1929

BOTTS, JOHN R. - 1870-1943

LYDIA METHODIST CEMETERY

GIDEON, ALVINA - Born March 10, 1906 and died February 10, 1908.

GRUSING, ANNA - (The Lakin Independent, Jan. 29, 1959) Anna Dorothy, daughter of Herman and Grace de Vries, was born in Germany, December 17, 1878. She came, with her parents to Macon, Nebraska, in 1884, where she became an active member of the Methodist Church at the age of 13, which activity was a major part of her life until the end. She was a charter member of the Macon Church and was active in Sunday school, Epworth League and Women's Society wherever she lived.

On March 2, 1899, she was united in marriage to John Grusing. To this union 14 children were born, seven sons and seven daughters. The first child, a daughter, died in infancy. One other child was born in Nebraska and then the family moved to Oregon in March 1902. There four members of the family were added. Then, in early September of 1908, the Grusing family moved from Oregon to Western Kansas. The principal factor in this move were two: first, there was a German Methodist Church close by and second: there was land adjacent to the church which could be homesteaded. And on September 7, 1908, the family moved onto the farm which has since been their home. Eight more sons, and daughters were born in this family, all raised in the strength of a Christian spirit, so strong that it has literally been carried to the far places of the earth.

Anna Grusing is survived by her husband, John, of the home; seven sons, David of Colby, Kansas, Herman of Western Grove, Arkansas, Louis of Byers, Colorado, Edward of Leoti, Henry of Isabel, Ben of Leoti, and Wesley of Lakin; six daughters, Grace Grusing of Hutchinson, Helen Kysar of Lakin, Martha Brown of Nigeria, West Africa, Alice Geyer of WaKeeney, Kansas, Clara Warrington of Rich Hill, Missouri, and Edith Litton of Lakin; one sister, Mrs. Oliver Brunkow of Manzanita, Oregon; and one brother, William de Vries of Salem, Oregon; 39 grandchildren and 12 great grandchildren and other relatives and friends.

Anna Grusing passed away quietly at her home Friday morning, January 23, 1959. Funeral services were held at the Lydia Methodist Church, Monday afternoon with the Rev. F. A. O'Kelley officiating. A male quartet from Leoti sang the songs which she had requested. Six grandsons, Johnny Grusing, Robert Grusing, Kenneth Kysar, Melvin Grusing, Ray Grusing and Galen Geyer were pallbearers. Interment was

LYDIA METHODIST CEMETERY

in the Lydia Methodist Cemetery.

GRUSING, B. R. 'BEN' - (The Lakin Independent, April 13, 2000) Leoti--Funeral for B. R. "Ben" Grusing, 80, was held at 10 a.m. Friday at Christ Covenant Church, Leoti, with the Rev. Dave Brogren officiating. Burial was in Lydia Cemetery in Wichita County.

Mr. Grusing died Tuesday, April 4, 2000, at Swedish Hospital in Englewood, Colorado.

He was born June 13, 1919, in Kearny County, the son of John and Anna (DeVries) Grusing. A lifetime resident of western Kansas, he was a cowboy and belonged to Christ Covenant Church.

On December 3, 1939, he married Vandella Moore in Wichita County. She survives. He is also survived by three sons, Ray Grusing, Glenwood Springs, Colorado, Dale Grusing, Lubbock, Texas, and Butch Grusing, Colorado Springs, Colorado; a daughter, Judy Woods, Leoti; three brothers, Bill Grusing, Byers, Colorado, Henry Grusing, Hutchinson, and Wesley Grusing, Lakin; four sisters, Helen Kysar and Edith Litton, both of Lakin, Alice Geyer, WaKeeney, and Clara Warrington, Manzanola, Colorado; nine grand-children; and five great grandchildren. He was preceded in death by three brothers and two sisters.

Memorials are suggested to Christ Covenant Church, Lydia Church or the Leoti Emergency Medical Technicians, all in care of Price & Sons Funeral Home of Leoti.

GRUSING, DAVID F. - (The Lakin Independent, Oct. 17, 1985) Funeral for David F. Grusing, 84, was at 10:30 a.m., Tuesday, at the Harrison Funeral Chapel, Colby. There was a short service at 3 p.m. Tuesday at the Lydia Methodist Church in southern Wichita County, the Rev. Nellie Holmes officiating. Burial at the church cemetery. He died Saturday, October 12, 1985, at the Citizen's Medical Center, Colby.

Born January 28, 1901, at Macon, Nebraska, he moved with his family from Oregon to the Lydia community in 1908. He married Mary Hendrix, September 16, 1934, in Hutchinson. She died January 14, 1985. The couple moved to Colby in 1934.

A retired farmer-rancher, Mr. Grusing was a member of the First Methodist Church in Colby, the Thomas County Historical Society, the Sod House Society and the Butterfield Trail Association.

Surviving are six brothers, Herman, Hilbre, Manitoba, Canada, Louis,

LYDIA METHODIST CEMETERY

Byers, Colorado, Ed, Lakin, Henry, Hutchinson, Ben, Leoti, and Wesley, Lydia; four sisters, Helen Kysar, Lakin, Alice Geyer, WaKeeney, Clara Warrington, Ordway, Colorado, and Edith Litton, Lydia.
Burial at Lydia Methodist Cemetery.

GRUSING, GRACE L. - (The Lakin Independent, Dec. 1967) Grace Louisa Grusing, daughter of John and Anna Grusing, was born in Salem, Oregon, on October 17, 1904, and departed this life at the Grace Hospital in Hutchinson, Kansas, on December 10, 1967. Early in her childhood she came with her parents to Western Kansas, where she grew up and received her grade and high school education. After she completed her normal training she taught rural grade schools in Kearny and Wichita counties for ten years.

She had a deep conviction in her Christian faith, and from early in life she dedicated herself to the mission field in China. She served as a missionary in the China Inland Missions until her health forced her to return to the homeland. As a continued service for her church and her master she served as a minister in the following churches of the Central Kansas conference of the Methodist Church: Maple Leaf and Zion of the Hugoton circuit, Rolla, Richfield, Moscow, Manter and Radium. She moved to Hutchinson in 1951 and became active in the First Methodist Church. After several years she became the parish visitor of First Methodist Church and served in this capacity until her death.

Grace joins her parents in her home-going. She is survived by 12 brothers and sisters: David Grusing of Colby, Kansas; Herman Grusing, Western Grove, Arkansas; Helen Kysar, Lakin, Kansas; Martha Brown, Nigeria, West Africa; William Grusing, Byers, Colorado; Ed Grusing, Leoti, Kansas; Alice Geyer, WaKeeney, Kansas; Clara Warrington, Rich Hill, Missouri; Henry Grusing, Haddam, Kansas; Ben Grusing, Leoti, Kansas; Edith Litton and Wesley Grusing, both of Lakin, Kansas. Besides these there are many other relatives and friends who will remember Grace as a determined and dedicated worker.

Funeral was held at Hutchinson, 10 a.m., Tuesday, in the First Methodist Church, Rev. Lyman Johnson and 2 p.m., Wednesday, Lydia Methodist Church, Leoti; Rev. Lyman Johnson. Burial at Lydia Methodist Cemetery.

GRUSING, JOHN - (The Lakin Independent, April 6, 1961) John Grusing was born in Germany, August 22, 1873; he passed from this life

LYDIA METHODIST CEMETERY

on March 30, 1961.

He came to the United States at the age of 19, and settled at Macon, Nebraska. Here he met, and in 1899 married Anna de Vries. Their first child died in infancy. Mrs. Grusing passed away in January of 1959.

The Grusing family moved from Nebraska to Oregon in 1901 and from Oregon to Kansas in 1908, where they settled on the homestead which has since been their home.

Mr. Grusing is survived by seven sons: David, Colby, Kansas; Herman, Western Grove, Arkansas; Louis, Byers, Colorado; Ed and Ben, Leoti, Kansas; Henry, Natoma, Kansas; Wesley, Lakin, Kansas; and six daughters: Grace of Hutchinson, Kansas, Helen Kysar, Lakin, Kansas; Martha Brown, Nigeria, Africa; Alice Geyer, WaKeeney, Kansas; Clara Warrington, Rich Hill, Missouri; and Edith Litton, Lakin, Kansas.

There are 39 grandchildren and 19 great grandchildren and a number of nieces and nephews. Also left to mourn his passing are the many neighbors and friends with whom he has worked for so many years.

Mr. Grusing was a life long member of the Methodist Church and it must be said that his family and his church were his life.

A tribute paid by a neighbor: "If every man in the world were like John Grusing, we would need no armies and no policemen."

Buried in the Lydia Methodist Cemetery.

GRUSING, JOHN WESLEY - (The Garden City Telegram, January 15, 2001) Funeral for John Wesley Grusing, 77, was held at 10:30 a.m. Tuesday at Lydia United Methodist Church, with the Rev. Warren Hett officiating. Burial in Lydia Cemetery.

Mr. Grusing died Saturday, January 13, 2001, at the Kearny County Hospital in Lakin.

He was born May 10, 1923, in northern Kearny County, the son of John and Anna (DeVries) Grusing. He attended Eureka Rural School in Kearny County and graduated from Lakin Rural High School in 1940.

A lifelong farmer and stockman in northern Kearny County, he was very involved with different species of poultry and gave many tours of his farm to school children, showing the various kinds of birds and animals. He also had a special interest in horticulture, growing different kinds of plants in his garden and yard.

Mr. Grusing was a member of the United Methodist Church of Lydia, belonged to the Southwest Kansas Feather Fanciers, was a founder and leader of Highlanders 4-H Club and a former member of the Kearny

LYDIA METHODIST CEMETERY

County Fair Board.

On Aug. 21, 1946, he married Mabel Pennington at Liberal. She survives. He is also survived by two sons, Steve Grusing, Syracuse, and Damon Grusing, Lakin; two daughters, Linda Beth Doubrava, Durant, Oklahoma, and Margaret Jennings, Lakin; two brothers, Bill Grusing, Denver, and Henry Grusing, Hutchinson; four sisters, Helen Kysar and Edith Litton both of Lakin, Alice Geyer, WaKeeney, and Clara Warrington, Manzanola, Colorado; and 11 grandchildren. He was preceded in death by his parents; four brothers, Dave Grusing, Herman Grusing, Ed Grusing and Ben Grusing; and two sisters, Grace Grusing and Martha Brown.

Memorials to the United Methodist Church, the National Parkinson Foundation or Kearny County Hospital, all in care of Garnand Funeral Home, Lakin.

GRUSING, MARY MYRTLE - (The Lakin Independent, Jan. 31, 1985) Mary Myrtle Grusing was born November 22, 1904, in Fairburg, Nebraska, to Mr. and Mrs. William Hendrix. She came to Colby, Kansas, in the spring of 1908. She died in Colby on January 14, 1985.

She received her elementary schooling in a sod school house and attended high school in Colby and then attended college in Hutchinson.

After her college graduation she worked in an office in Hutchinson until her marriage to David Grusing on September 16, 1934. After their marriage Dave and Mary made their home on a farm south of Colby where she spent the rest of her life. She gave her life to the Lord early in life and remained faithful to her Master.

From December 10, 1951, to December 30, 1969, she worked for the High Plains Co-op in Colby. She also was a member of the Farm and Fireside Extension Homemakers Unit for over 50 years. She was a member of the Colby United Methodist Church.

Services were held at the Harrison Chapel in Colby, January 17, at 10:30 a.m. with the Rev. John Saville, Guy Rendoff and Henry Grusing officiating. Soloist was Leon Woofter and organist was Kay Carl.

Pallbearers were Galen Geyer, Dick Grusing, Don Litton, Kenneth Kysar, Damon Grusing, Steve Grusing, Butch Grusing, Duane Woods and Scott Sheets.

Burial was in the Lydia Methodist Cemetery in south Wichita County. Services were conducted by the Rev. Nellie Holmes, minister of the Lydia and Deerfield Methodist Churches.

LYDIA METHODIST CEMETERY

HARTMAN, MARIA ELIZABETH - (Leoti Standard, Leoti, Wichita Co., Oct. 3, 1907) Maria Elizabeth Hartman, oldest daughter of Mr. and Mrs. William Hartman died at their home near Lydia on the 25th of this month. She was thirteen years of age and a favorite among her friends. Appendicitis was the principal cause of her death.

Born September 25, 1893, and died September 25, 1907.

LYDIA METHODIST CEMETERY

LAUTENSCHLAGER, WILLIAM - Born 9/15/1912, died 9/25/1912.

LITTON, DICK - (The Lakin Independent, October 19, 1995) Dick Litton, 94, a longtime resident of Kearny County, died October 11, 1995, at the Kearny County Hospital in Lakin. He was a retired farmer and stockman.

Dick was born December 16, 1900, in Gove County, the son of William Day and Viola Wrighter Litton. He grew up and attended schools in Gove County.

Mr. Litton was a member of Lydia United Methodist Church.

On May 22, 1949, he married Edith Grusing at Lakin. They have lived in Kearny County since their marriage.

He is survived by his wife; a son, Don Litton, Garden City; a daughter, Susan Litton, Lakin; and one grandson.

Funeral services were held Saturday, October 14, at 2 p.m. at the Lydia United Methodist Church in north Kearny County. The Rev. Donald J. Koehn officiated. Burial was in Lydia Cemetery.

Memorials may be made to the church or the Alzheimer's Foundation, both in care of Garnand Funeral Home, Lakin.

LYDIA METHODIST CEMETERY

MCQUILLIAM, FLOYD - (The Standard, Leoti, Kansas, Sept. 3, 1914) Twin boys were born to Mr. and Mrs. D. P. McQuilliam, Tuesday, August 25. One of the babies died and was laid to rest in the M.E. cemetery, last Friday. In this hour of bereavement we live in hopes to meet this deserted one in heaven.

MCQUILLIAM, GERTRUDE - 1/10/1922 - 7/6/1922

MCQUILLIAM, ORLANDO - 5/22/1923 - 3/12/1925

LYDIA METHODIST CEMETERY

PENNINGTON, TRELLA IONE - Infant of A. E. Pennington's. Born and died June 27, 1934.

POSEY, LOUIS E. - (Funeral Records) Died Oct. 3, 1916, farmer & stockman, killed in auto by Santa Fe train at Deerfield, buried in cemetery north part of Kearny County.
 (The Lakin Independent, Oct. 6, 1916) While L. E. Posey, of the north eastern part of the county, and a neighbor, were crossing the Santa Fe tracks at Deerfield, Tuesday in an automobile on their way to Lakin, the car was struck by train No. 8, which leaves Lakin about three o'clock in the afternoon. It is the supposition that when they saw the train they wanted to put more speed on the car and used the emergency lever which stopped the car on the tracks. Mr. Posey was instantly killed and the other man in the car was bruised on the head. Mr. Posey was picked up and removed to Dr. Foster's office where Justice Wells held the inquest, Ralph Thorpe, Undertaker Nash and L. P. Kimball being present. The funeral of the unfortunate man will be held Sunday, and the remains interred in the family plot near his home. He was aged 47 years and was resident of this county eleven years. He was born in Philadelphia, Pennsylvania.
 (The Lakin Independent, Oct. 13, 1916) The remains of Lewis Posey, who met such an untimely death on the tracks at Deerfield, were laid to rest in the family block in cemetery near their home in the northeastern part of the county. The funeral was largely attended by friends and acquaintances who came from far and near to pay their last respects. J. J. Nash had charge of the funeral arrangements.
 Louis E. Posey was born in LaSalle County, Illinois, July 25th, 1869. At the age of 13 years he moved with his parents to Pennsylvania, where he grew to manhood. In 1904 he moved to Reno County, and from there in 1906 to his farm about twenty miles north of Deerfield. On October 3d he met death in the city of Deerfield while crossing the Santa Fe railroad track in an automobile in company with J. R. Clamphill. On October 3d, 1889, while living in Pennsylvania, he was married to Minnie Moser, from which union six children were born, six of whom are living, five having passed to the great beyond in childhood. He is survived by his aged parents, who reside in Indiana, his wife and children, Mrs. Edith Newhouse, living in Oregon, Ellsworth, John Wesley, Idaho, Jacob and Alice at home, besides other relatives, neighbors and friends to mourn his early demise. In May 1896, he was

converted, joining the M. E. Church, of which he ever remained a member. He was a sincere Christian, doing the will of God at all times. Although denied the privilege of church services, he used the means of Grace at hand being a zealous reader of the bible and conducting family worship in his home. During the last few years a Sabbath school was conducted in the neighborhood; in which he took a great interest. Arrangements had been made to have regular preaching services at that place, to which he looked forward with great joy, mentioning the work and minister in family prayer the morning before his departure. He was a good neighbor, never refusing to help in any possible way. He will be sadly missed by his wife and children, being ever mindful of their comfort and happiness. What is their loss is heaven's gain. Funeral services were held Monday, October 9th, at the home, and at the German M.E. Church on the southern boundary of Wichita County, conducted by Rev. W. Berg, of Kinsley, Kansas, and interment made in the cemetery nearby.

LYDIA METHODIST CEMETERY

WARRINGTON, DARREL K. - 12/15/1941 - 12/15/1941

WARRINGTON, LESLIE ALLEN - (The Lakin Independent, March 4, 1982) Leslie Allen Warrington, was born February 7, 1916, at Oak Valley, Kansas, to Alvin and Cora Warrington. He died February 23, 1982, at La Junta, Colorado, following a heart attack. When he was a young child his parents moved to Wichita County where Leslie grew to manhood. On May 2, 1927, he was married to Clara Grusing. To this union two sons were born, who preceded him in death.

Leslie was a retired farmer and rancher having lived in Missouri, Deerfield and most recently near Rocky Ford, Colorado.

He was an active member of the Rocky Ford United Methodist Church. He was a loving husband, a helpful friend and neighbor.

He is survived by his wife, Clara, of the home, one sister, Nellora Holstein of Leoti, nieces and nephews and many other relatives and friends.

Funeral services were held Thursday, February 25, in the United Methodist Church of Rocky Ford and in the Weinmann-Price Funeral Home in Leoti. Burial was in Lydia Methodist Cemetery.

WARRINGTON, RONALD ALLEN - (The Lakin Independent, July 4, 1947) Ronald Allen, infant son of Mr. and Mrs. Leslie Warrington, was born June 29, in Denver, Colorado, and passed away only a few hours after his birth.

He leaves to mourn his early departure his bereaved parents, four grandparents, besides his uncles, aunts and cousins. A brother preceded him in death.

Interment was made in the Lydia Methodist Cemetery, Rev. Leonard Cowan of Lakin officiated.

WITTMAN, CRISTINA - (Birth and Death Records, East Hibbard Twp, Kearny County, Kansas, ending March 1, 1908) Eight month old female, born in Colorado, died September 13, 1907. Lydia Methodist Cemetery.

WITTMAN, INFANT - Infant of Mr. and Mrs. Carl Wittman died July 20, 1909.

LYDIA METHODIST CEMETERY

YAKEL, ALICE MAY - (The Lakin Independent, Dec. 1939) Alice May, daughter of Mr. and Mrs. Fred Yakel, was born October 5, 1939, and after two months and three days stay in this home the little life winged its way back to the Heavenly Father on December 8, 1939.

Her stay was not long but she had won a place in the hearts of her family, and heaven holds a treasure for each of them.

She leaves to mourn her going, besides her father and mother; four brothers, Lewis, Melvin, Marvin, and Merle; and one sister Fredia, as well as other relatives.

The funeral service was held December 11, at Lydia Methodist Church, conducted by the Rev. J. M. Jones of Leoti. Interment was made in the Lydia Methodist Cemetery.

YAKEL, GEORGE - (The Kearny County Advocate, Jan. 30, 1920) George Yakel was born July 14th, 1898, and died January 23rd, 1920, at the age of 21 years, 6 months and 9 days. He came here with his parents in 1902 from Otis as a small boy and grew to young manhood. He was well liked by all who knew him. He united with the M.E. Church here on July 13, 1918, and was an active member both in Church and Sunday school work. Funeral services were conducted by the Rev. W. Berg of Kinsley at the M.E. Church here Sunday afternoon and was one of the largest ever held in this vicinity. He leaves to mourn his departure, his mother, three brothers and two sisters. The sympathy of the entire community is extended to the bereaved family in their sad hour.

Buried in Lydia Methodist Cemetery.

Fred Yakel came in from Coaldale, Colorado, Wednesday morning to attend the funeral of his brother.

YAKEL, HENRY - (The Lakin Independent, Mar. 22, 1918) Henry Yakel, living in Wichita County, was killed in Rocky Ford, Colorado, March 14, by being run over by a train. He was on his way to visit a daughter and family in Trinidad. Mr. Yakel was born in Wiesenmuller, Russia, in 1854, coming to this country in 1902, settling in Rush County. He moved to Wichita County in 1904, taking up a claim upon which he prospered and built up a nice home. He leaves to mourn his loss his wife, six children and his aged mother, four brothers and one sister. Burial services were held at the home and in the German M.E Church last Monday. Rev. Besy of Kinsley officiated.

LYDIA METHODIST CEMETERY

YAKEL, RUBY ANN - (The Lakin Independent, June 26, 1942) Funeral services for Ruby Ann Yakel was held at Lydia Methodist Church, on Thursday afternoon, at 2:30 o'clock.

The 19 month old daughter of Mr. and Mrs. Fred Yakel, who lived 13 miles north of Lakin, was drowned in a stock tank Tuesday afternoon. She had been missing from the house about ten minutes, and during that short time had wandered to the water tank and fell in.

(The Lakin Independent, July 3, 1942) Ruby Ann, the little daughter of Mr. and Mrs. Fred Yakel, was born November 18, 1940. Her little life brought joy and gladness to that home. But her stay was not long, for on June 23rd, 1942, all unexpectedly and accidentally, her little life ended in this world, and her spirit winged its way back to the Father, who gave it one year, seven months and twenty-five days ago, to join the little sister who preceded her in death less than three years ago.

She leaves to mourn her going her father and mother, two sisters and three brothers: Louis, Melvin, Freda, Marvin and Merle, and other relatives and friends.

Funeral services were held at the home and at the Lydia Methodist Church with Rev. J. W. Jones of Leoti in charge. Pallbearers were Doris Williams, Shirley Wray, and Dorothy and Marjorie Kysar. Burial in Lydia Methodist Cemetery.

SHOCKEY CEMETERY

Shockey Cemetery is located in Grant County, Kansas, seven miles north of Ulysses on Highway 25, 7 miles west and 1/2 mile south and 1/2 mile east.

(Ulysses News, April 10, 1942) Shockey is located on Section 29, Twp. 27, Range 28, in the northwestern part of Grant County. It was established in 1888 and grew to a thriving town of 50 inhabitants. The Shockey Plainsman was published weekly. The post office was installed in a farmhouse and served the people of the community many years. Citizens were Mid Shockey after whom the town was named, T. R. Horniday, J. W. Plunkett, Davis Holmes, A. W. Snider, F. W. Rider, George Rider, Karl Gall, T. W. Swinney, whose daughter was Mrs. Annie L. Hoffman, A. W. Anderson, Peter Kiistner, Peter Molz, L. Binney and Judge Wm. E. Hutchinson.

(Shockeyville Eagle, June 1, 1886) We have heard it mentioned that a cemetery should be laid off near the city, not that is has been needed heretofore; but as the country settles up there will be more or less deaths and it will save going to the railroad to bury them.

(Golden Gazette, May 11, 1887) The name of LaPorte has been changed to Shockey, to take effect July 1.

(Shockey Independent, Dec. 14, 1887) Let all who feel themselves interested agitate the subject of a cemetery at this place. This is a matter which can be arranged for now, cheaper and easier than at any future time. Let us organize.

(Shockey Ind., Dec. 21, 1887) A new cemetery site has been selected on A. W. Nixon's claim adjoining town.

(Hartland Herald, Jan. 28, 1888) The Maple Grove Cemetery Association of Shockeyville have filed a charter with the Secretary of State. The incorporators are J. N. Plunkett, A. W. Nixon, T. M. Divine, G. A. Anderson, and Wm. Shockey.

(Shockeyville Plainsman, Jan. 4, 1889) The attention of the officials of Maple Grove cemetery is called to the fact that although the grounds have been fenced and otherwise improved, there are still two very important matters overlooked - a survey and plat and the filing of a copy of the same with the county clerk, and of procuring a suitable book for a registry. These matters ought not to be neglected.

(The Shockey Plainsman, Feb. 16, 1889) The directors and all others interested in Maple Grove Cemetery, are hereby notified that a meeting will be held in Shockeyville, Saturday, the 16th inst., at 1 o'clock p.m., to transact very important business for the association, signed W. P.

SHOCKEY CEMETERY

Struthers, Secy. M.G.C. Ass'n., Shockeyville, Kans., Feb. 9, 1889.

(Ulysses Tribune and Grant County Register, June 5, 1891) Mid Shockey and family attended the Decoration Day exercises at this place Saturday. Mr. Shockey informs us that the old soldier's grave in the cemetry at Shockeyville was not neglected. His family with one or two others went to the cemetry in the early morning before starting for Ulysses and strewed the grave with flowers. (Fielding Pope?)

(April 10, 1941) William Shockey helped to establish, survey and lay out the first cemetery in Grant County. The Shockey cemetery still is used. Two surveyors Jessie Correy and Mr. Small helped in developing the new country, surveying thousand of acres of land and townsites. They were assisted by Wm. Shockey and his young daughters.

Following are excerpts from a letter received by Mrs. R. R. Wilson from Mrs. Jane Shockey Fulk of Winfield. "Mrs. Fulk's father and others laid out the townsite of Shockeyville. They lived there about two years when they sold to Mid Shockey. This place joined the townsite on the west." Mrs. Wilson explained: "I'm again picking up the thread of old times. I'm the youngest daughter of Wm. (Bill) Shockey. There were two of we girls. Minnie lives in Colorado, mother of two boys and two girls. My father passed away several years ago. Yes, I remember the Molz family. My father met them at the railroad, brought them out and located them. Lena Molz carried the mail from Shockey to Cincinnati and Ulysses in an old buggy. I also remember Mr. and Mrs. Struthers, also Yetta, she died and I am sure was the first white child buried in the Shockey cemetery. Mr. Pope was the first person to die near us. He was buried on his claim. (Mr. Pope was the father of Mrs. Tom Tuggle who resided in Scott City). My father was deeply touched and felt the need of a cemetery. He and others had the Shockey Cemetery surveyed.

SHOCKEY CEMETERY

ALLER, MARGARET - (Grant County Republican, New Ulysses, Kansas, Jan. 8, 1910) Mrs. Aller was buried at Shockey Cemetery on Friday of last week. A large crowd of friends and relatives were present. Born August 19, 1844 and died December 29, 1909.

ALLER, RICHARD - (The Kearny County Advocate, Feb. 11, 1897) Died on Tuesday, February 9, 1897, Richard Ohler, aged 74 years. He was resident of Stanton County for the past ten years, and came here about three months ago in search of employment, and made his home at the residency of Thos. Tuggle, one mile west of town, and was sick but a few days. He leaves a wife, three daughters and a son. His remains were taken to Stanton County for interment.
Born June 8, 1824 and died February 9, 1897.

ANDERSON, ALLEN S. - (The Ulysses News, Jan. 2, 1991) Allen S. Anderson, 77, died December 27, 1990, at Bob Wilson Memorial Hospital, Ulysses, Kansas. He was born April 11, 1913, the son of Alonzo and Hattie Staples Anderson. A retired farmer, he was a lifetime resident of Ulysses.

He was a member of the Shelton Memorial Christian Church.

On November 29, 1934, he married Norma Nichols at Lakin, Kansas. She survives.

Other survivors include a daughter, Mary R. Anderson, Washington, D.C.; a brother, J. J. Anderson, Lakin; and a sister, Mary S. Davis, California.

Funeral services were at the Shelton Memorial Christian Church with Rev. Bill Harrold presiding. Burial in Shockey Cemetery.

ANDERSON, ALONZO W. - (Lakin Independent, July 27, 1920) A. W. Anderson was born in Indiana, February 13th, 1868, died at his home in Grant County, Kansas, July 22nd, 1920, aged 51 years, 5 months and 9 days. He was the son of G. M. and Margaret Anderson. On January 1st, 1889, he was married to Miss H. E. Staples and to this union were born seven children, three sons and four daughters, all of whom survive him, besides his father, sister, six grandchildren and a host of friends. Mr. Anderson was one of the early settlers of Grant County and became a successful farmer. While in the flow of health he was interviewed by friends to accept a county office but declined for a time, but afterward concented and was elected. During his term he attended to his official

SHOCKEY CEMETERY

duties in such manner that it won him many friends. His family lost a kind, affectionate husband and father and the community loses a noble citizen. The funeral was held at the family home, conducted by W. S. Prather of Lakin.

ANDERSON CHILD - (Ulysses Tribune, Sept. 27, 1888) Diphtheria prevails in the vicinity of Shockeyville. A child of G. A. Anderson's died of that dread disease last week.

ANDERSON, HATTIE E. - (The Lakin Independent, Jan. 9, 1953) Hattie Eudora Staples, daughter of George and Allie Staples, was born August 30, 1870, in Brown County, Indiana, where she grew to womanhood.

On January 1, 1889, she was united in marriage to Alonzo W. Anderson. To this union seven children were born.

She moved with her husband and family to a ranch in Grant County, Kansas, in 1907, where she lived for 20 years.

Besides performing her duties as a wife and mother during these pioneer days, she was active in community affairs such as church, school and health programs, and was never too busy to assist a neighbor.

In early girlhood she dedicated her life to her Savior and remained a faithful Christian to the end. For the past 25 years, she had been an active member in the Church of God at Ulysses.

In 1920 her husband passed away.

In 1927 she moved to Ulysses where she made her home until failing health made it necessary for her to live with her children.

On December 29, 1952, she passed this life at the home of her daughter, Mrs. Ora Carter, Lakin, Kansas, at the age of 82 years and 4 months.

She is survived by 6 of her children: Charlie, of Lamar, Colorado; Bertha Carter, of Lakin; Joe, of Ulysses; Alta Ogilvie, La Canada, California; Mary Davis, of Fair Oaks, California; Allen of Ulysses, and one brother, John Staples, of Indianapolis, Indiana.

She is also survived by 20 grandchildren, 16 great grandchildren, and three great-great grandchildren, and host of other relatives and friends.

ANDES, CHARLES R. - (The Garden City Telegram, June 13, 1991) Funeral for Charles R. Andes, 97, was held at 10 a.m., June 14, 1991, at the Shelton Memorial Christian Church, the Rev. Bill Harrold

SHOCKEY CEMETERY

officiating. Burial at the Shockey Cemetery, Ulysses.

He died June 12, 1991, at Bob Wilson Memorial Hospital, Ulysses.

Born December 12, 1893, (headstone reads Nov. 3, 1893) in Shelby County, Illinois, he married Flossie Rider, November 3, 1925, at Dodge City. She died February 18, 1981.

Mr. Andes was a retired jockey and farmer and had been a Ulysses resident since 1972.

He was a member of the Shelton Memorial Christian Church, Ulysses.

Survivors include two nephews. He was preceded in death by two brothers and two sisters.

Friends may call at Phillips Mortuary, Ulysses. Memorials to the Western Prairie Nursing Home, in care of the mortuary.

ANDES, FLOSSIE J. - (The Ulysses, News, March 5, 1981) Flossie Jane Andes, 80, died Saturday, February 28, 1981, at Bob Wilson Memorial Hospital, Ulysses, following a lengthy illness. Born Flossie Jane Rider, June 1, 1900, in Grant County, she married Charles R. Andes, November 3, 1925, at Dodge City.

Survivors include the widower, of the home, brothers, Ralph Rider and C. D. Rider, both of Ulysses, sisters, Dove Rexroat, and Thelma Frazee, both of Ulysses.

Funeral Tuesday at Phillips Mortuary Chapel, Ulysses, with the Rev. Harry Hubbard. Burial at Shockey Cemetery, Ulysses.

SHOCKEY CEMETERY

BANNISTER, C. W. - (Grant County Republican, July 10, 1897) C. W. Bannister after and illness of but a few days died last Monday evening, at the residence of C. S. Scott. Mr. Bannister has long been a resident of this county, but has always been in poor health. He was ruptured years ago and this was the immediate cause of his death. The doctor made several unsuccessful attempts to reduce the rupture, mortification set in and death soon claimed him as a victim. His remains were interred at Shockey at 4 o'clock p.m., July 6th.

BANNISTER, W. H. - (The Kearny County Advocate, Mar. 5, 1915) The remains of W. H. Bannister, who departed this life some eighteen years ago, and laid to rest in the Shockeyville cemetery in Grant County, was disinterred last week by H. B. Young, a relative, and taken to Kansas City for final interment.

BLOOM, DAVID - Born March 6, 1847 and died December 24, 1904.

BORDINE, JACOB - (Ulysses Tribune, Oct. 31, 1890) Died on Monday, October 27, 1890, at his home near the Baker schoolhouse, Jacob Bordine, aged 58 years, of Sciatic Rheumatism. The following day the funeral services, conducted by Rev. R. Farguson, were attended by a large concourse of friends and neighbors.

    Mr. Bordine was one of the old settlers of Grant County, and was honored and respected by all who knew him. He died just 5 years and 2 months after coming into the county, and was buried just that long after taking the land where he proved up. In all those years none of his acquaintances can point to a single mean act. He lived the life of a noble citizen and after a long illness, died as the good man dieth, with the assurance of a better life beyond the grave. He leaves a widow and two small children at home, and other married children. The bereaved family has the sincere sympathy of the entire community.

    He was born June 10, 1832.

SHOCKEY CEMETERY

CALDWELL, HARRY H. JR. - (The Garden City Telegram, February 5, 2001) Harry H. Caldwell, Jr. 90, of Ulysses, died Sunday, February 4, 2001, at Stanton County Long Term Care Unit in Johnson City where he had been a resident since May 1997.

He was born April 19, 1910, in Ford County, the son of Harry H. and Tessey (Halstead) Caldwell, Sr. When he was 5, the family moved from Ford County to Grant County by covered wagon.

A farmer and rancher, Mr. Caldwell was a member of Shelton Memorial Christian Church at Ulysses, the Southwest Kansas Irrigation Association and the Ulysses Co-op.

On February 7, 1942, he married Betty L. Livesay at Garden City. She survives. He is also survived by two sons, Jerry K. Caldwell and Randall L. Caldwell, both of Ulysses; two daughters Wanda J. Holland, Oktaha, Oklahoma, and Janet E. Rolick, Anaheim, California; a brother, Hubert Caldwell, Johnson City; a sister, Ellen Barber, Ulysses; seven grandchildren; and six great grandchildren. He was preceded in death by his parents; a grandson; a brother, Mitchell Caldwell; two infant brothers; and two sisters, Agnes Cox and Marie Oliver.

Funeral was held Thursday at Shelton Memorial Christian Church, Ulysses, with the Rev. Bill Harrold officiating. Burial in Shockey Cemetery, Ulysses.

Memorials to the Diabetes Association or the Stanton Long Term Care Unit, both in care of Grant County Funeral, Ulysses.

CAMP, EDWARD - (Kearny County Advocate, Sept. 1, 1888) Died Edward Camp, at Shockyville, on Sunday morning, August 26, at the residence of his daughter, Mrs. T. R. Hornaday, in his 78th year, of general debility, and was interred in the Shockyville Cemetery, Monday. He was the father of D. H. Camp, now of this place. He leaves one other daughter in Chase County, Kansas.

CAMP, ROWENA - (Shockeyville Eagle, Mar. 31, 1887) Mrs. Camp, mother-in-law of T. R. Hornaday, living three miles north of town is reported seriously ill.

(Shockeyville Eagle, April 14, 1887) Died on April 10th, Easter Sunday, of pneumonia, Mrs. Rowena Camp, aged 77 years. Her illness lasted four weeks, and a bereaved husband is left in his 77th year, to mourn the departure of a loved wife, after 55 years of married life.

(Shockeyville Eagle, April 28, 1887) Rowena Gard Camp, wife of

SHOCKEY CEMETERY

Edward Camp, was born in Washington County, Ohio, December 10th, 1810, and died April 10th, 1887. She was married to Edward Camp in 1832, living together as husband and wife nearly 55 years, most of that time in Washington Co., Ohio. In 1885, though aged as they were, they came of Western Kansas, seeking a home in this new country. About one year ago they settled on a quarter section of government land, three miles north of this place, near the claims of two of their daughters. Through the kindness of their children they were provided with a comfortable house, and spent the past year very pleasantly. Mother Camp was one of the nobles of women, possessed of an extraordinary mind a sweet temperament. She possessed those qualities which made all who came into her presence feel the gently, elevating and cheering influences of her nature. She was a consistent member of the M. E. Church from childhood. The fatal sickness had its inception in a severe cold contracted about one year ago, from the effects of which she never entirely recovered. She retained her mental faculties to within a few hours of her death. She leaves two sons, three daughters, besides a host of dear friends here in Kansas and in Ohio, to mourn. The influences of her noble character will last forever, to which all who knew her will bear testimony. We hope to meet her ere long in a brighter land. A.C.H.

COOPER, MRS. JOHN - (Shockeyville Eagle, Shockeyville, Hamilton County, Ks., May 18, 1886) The wife of Mr. John Cooper is dangerously ill.
(Shockeyville Eagle, May 25, 1886) We regret to announce the death of Mrs. John Cooper which occurred Friday morning.

CORLEY, BESSIE - (The Lakin Independent, Feb. 10, 1977) Private graveside services were conducted Friday morning at Shockey Cemetery in northwest Grant County for Bessie M. Corley, a pioneer Garden City resident.
Mrs. Corley died Wednesday afternoon, February 2, 1977, at her home. She was 82.
Born near the now non-existent town of Hartland in Kearny County on July 1, 1894, she moved to Grant County in 1895. Her parents, her parent's families and her husband's family all homesteaded in Grant County as ranchers and farmers.
She attended Grant County schools and Mount Carmel Girls Academy in Wichita and returned to Grant County where she taught in rural

SHOCKEY CEMETERY

schools.

She was married to Harry H. Corley on December 8, 1915, and in 1921 they moved to Garden City where he founded what is thought to be the first tire shop and filling station in the city. Her husband died October 12, 1923.

In 1924, Mrs. Corley returned to the farm in Grant County with her three children. In 1926 they moved to Lakin where she served as register of deeds. In 1932 she returned with her family to Garden City.

She is survived by three children, Carmen Campbell, Dale Corley and Erdene Corley, of Garden City; six grandchildren and two great grandchildren.

She was preceded in death by her parents, Mr. and Mrs. Charles Hoffman; two brothers, Thomas R. Hoffman (1915) and C. E. (Babe) Hoffman (1971).

Mrs. Corley requested that no announcement of her death be made until after her burial. A private family funeral was conducted at Garnand Chapel, the Rev. Ronald Cebik officiating. Burial was in the Shockey Cemetery near the now extinct town of Shockey in northwest Grant County.

CORLEY, HARRY - (The Lakin Independent, Oct. 19, 1923) The funeral of Harry Corley was held Tuesday and interment made in the Shockey Cemetery. Mr. Corley was 32 years of age; he was formerly a resident of Grant County and son-in-law of Chas. Huffman, but during the last year he has been operating a battery station in Garden City. He attended the Lakin Fair and then went for treatment to the Dodge City hospital where he died. The remains were taken to Garden City where funeral services were held; then shipped to Lakin and taken to the Shockey Cemetery where services were conducted by the Odd Fellows Lodge of Ulysses.

He was born January 29, 1889 and died October 14, 1923.

COX, ETTA - (Lakin Investigator, May 18, 1906) It is with great sorrow that we announce the death of Mrs. Horace Cox at her home near Shockey. She leaves a devoted husband and three loving children. We extend to the family our heartfelt sympathy. Mr. Cox and family formerly lived on the Lake place on the South-side.

She died May 15, 1906, at the age of 32 years and 20 days.

SHOCKEY CEMETERY

COX, INFANT -

CRARY, INFANT OF ROBERT - Died in December 1889.

SHOCKEY CEMETERY

DAVIS, LEE CHARLES - (Grant County Republican, Ulysses, Kansas, June 7, 1928) Ulysses and community was deeply shocked Friday afternoon when report of the death of Lee Davis came to them. Mr. Davis had been ill but a few days when his condition suddenly took a turn for the worse, bringing about his death. The immediate cause of his death was double pneumonia.

Uncle Lee was another of the old citizens of this county who had spent his life in the upbuilding of the country. Coming here in 1885, he has lived here since that time and has seen the changes come over this country from the barren plains of the early days to the fruitful soil of today. He, like all those who have gone before him, or who are still living, gave his time and energy to this change.

For years he has followed the carpenter trade in Ulysses and was actively engaged in it, until a few days of his death. He contracted influenza a few days prior to his death, which rapidly run into pneumonia.

Uncle Lee had many friends. He was quiet and unassuming, but withal one of the finest men in the country, and had the respect and love of his fellowmen.

Burial was made in Shockey Cemetery last Sunday. Rev. R. T. Powell, of the Methodist Church, had charge of the services.

Lee Charles Davis was born January 17th, 1865, at Moston, Wisconsin. Died June 1, 1928, at the home of his sister, Mrs. Amy Rider, at the age of 63 years.

In 1875 he moved to Council Grove, Kansas, with his parents, and from there to Kiowa, Kansas. In 1885 he moved to Grant County, where he has made his home until his death.

Mr. Davis is survived by a sister, Mrs. Amy Rider, of Ulysses, Kansas, a brother, H. W. Davis, of Clayton, New Mexico, and a host of relatives and friends.

Card of Thanks signed by Mrs. Amy Rider and Family, Mr. H. W. Davis and Family and Mr. C. S. Terrill and Family.

DEAL, DANIEL - (Ulysses Tribune, Dec. 26, 1890) Died at his home, three miles northwest of Surprise, on December 19th, Daniel Deal, aged 63 years. The funeral was conducted from the residence, by Rev. Farguson, on the 20th inst., and the remains laid to rest in the cemetery at Shockey. Mr. Deal leaves a wife and several children, who have the sympathy of the community. Born November 9, 1827.

SHOCKEY CEMETERY

ELWOOD, HARRY - (Grant County Republican, New Ulysses, Kansas, Sat., Oct. 19, 1918) J. B. Elwood was summoned to La Junta the first of the week by a telegram announcing the serious illness of his brother, Harry, who has pneumonia.
On Thursday his body arrived for burial after an illness lasting only a few days. He was taken with influenza which quickly developed pneumonia and this soon took him off. He was laid to rest in Shockey Cemetery near his mother who died two years ago. He leaves a wife and child besides his father and several brothers and sisters. He had spent his whole life except the last four years in Grant County where he had many friends.
Harry was born in Grant County, Kansas, January 10th, 1889, and died at La Junta, Colorado, October 15, 1918.

ELWOOD, INFANT SON - (The Ulysses Tribune, Aug. 12, 1893) Sad news reached us recently, of the death of the infant son of Mr. and Mrs. Elwood, Monday. The sorrowing parents have the heartfelt sympathy of the community in their sad bereavement.

ELWOOD, CATHERINE - (Grant County Republican, New Ulysses, Kansas, Sat., Sept. 30, 1916) Mrs. J. N. Elwood died Thursday morning at 9:30 after a short illness, following a paralytic stroke last week. She suffered her first stroke in 1910 from which she never recovered and she was almost helpless during the last six years of her life. She was laid to rest in Shockey Cemetery Friday afternoon, after a short funeral sermon by Rev. Davis. She was one of the earliest settlers of Grant County and had many friends who mourn her loss.

EYMAN, DELLA O. - Born in 1875 and died in 1907. Wife of Monte E. Eyman.

EYMAN, INFANT -

SHOCKEY CEMETERY

FRAZEE, DALE - (The Ulysses News, Oct. 7, 1954) Funeral services for Stephen Dale Frazee, 55, were held Saturday afternoon at 2 o'clock at the Assembly of God Church. The services were conducted by D. C. Branha, pastor of the Ulysses church, assisted by R. F. McAdams, pastor of the Assembly of God in Garden City.

Mr. Frazee died Wednesday afternoon, September 29, after an illness of several months.

A resident of Grant County since 1927, he had spent his entire adult life in farming. He moved to Stevens County at the age of 18, then came to this county where he was engaged in farming in the northwest part of Grant.

Music at the funeral services was by Mr. and Mrs. McAdams, who sang, "Beyond the Sunset", "God's Tomorrow", and "A Home Up In Heaven".

Pallbearers were nephews of Mr. Frazee.

Burial was in the Shockey Cemetery, with the Phillips Mortuary in charge of arrangements.

Survivors include his wife and four children, Ada Jane, Leona Fern, Ralph Stephen and Wilma Love, all of the home; two brothers, William of Eads, Colorado, and Dorr of Walsh, Colorado; six sisters, Eda Nolder of Dodge City, Zepha Lowery of Hugoton, Mina John of Spring Dale, Arkansas, Rena Strait of Hooker, Oklahoma, Estell Johnson of Byers, Kansas, and Ester Henderson of Garden City.

He was born in 1899.

FRITZ, JOHANNA - (Grant County Register, Feb. 13, 1897) Died at her home near Shocky on February 7th, Mrs. Johanna Fritz. Mrs. Fritz was the mother of Mrs. Karl Gall and was at an advanced age at the time of her death.

She was born November 8, 1818.

SHOCKEY CEMETERY

GALL, CAROLINE - (Grant County Republican, Sat., Dec. 17, 1921) Caroline R. Fritz, daughter of Frederick and Johanna Fritz, was born in Wurttemberg, Germany, July 30th, 1840, and grew to womanhood in that same community. She was married to Karl E. Gall in the fall of 1864. They settled down at Affaltrach, Wurttemberg, and remained there for the next twenty years. Mr. Gall being in business there during this time. In the year 1883 the oldest son, Charles, came to American, and the oldest daughter, Lizzie, and her grandmother, came about one year later. The rest of the family decided to follow, so came over with the remaining five children. They first settled near Lincoln, Nebraska, some of their relatives having settled there before. They did not like that part of the country very well, so decided to come to Kansas. The family arrived in Grant County in April 1886, and settled on a homestead about 18 miles northwest of Ulysses. They remained in that community, followed farming and stock raising until Mr. Gall's death, which occurred on March 2nd, 1905. Since that time Mrs. Gall had made her home with her daughter, Augusta and son, Earnest. They remained on the farm until the year 1917, when they moved to Ulysses.

Nine children were born to this union, four boys and five girls. The husband and three of the children having passed to the spirit world, two of them died in infancy and one at the age of 14 years.

Mrs. Gall grew up in the faith and was confirmed in the German-Lutheran Church at the age of 14 years, and remained true to the faith until she was called to her reward on December 7th, 1921, at the age of 81 years, 4 months and 8 days.

She leaves three sons, three daughters, thirteen grandchildren and six great grandchildren, together with a host of friends to mourn her departure. The surviving children are: Mrs. William Simshauser of Calhan, Colorado; August W. Gall of Washington, D.C. Mrs. Charles Hoffman, Charles C. Gall, Augusta W. Gall and Ernest H. Gall of Ulysses, Kansas. Three of them were with her during her last hours, the other three and five of the grandchildren arrived for the funeral.

Funeral services were held in Ulysses on Sunday, December 11, in charge of Rev. Ramsay and the body was placed in the Shockey Cemetery beside that of her husband.

GALL, FRIEDERIEKA C. - (Ulysses Tribune, Dec. 12, 1891) We learn of the sad death of little Rica Gall, which occurred Tuesday evening, after ten days severe suffering. The trouble was lock-jaw. The child's

SHOCKEY CEMETERY

jaws had been locked for over a week, and she had suffered untold misery. The trouble was probably caused by severe tooth ache. The family has the sympathy of all in their affliction.

She was born March 18, 1877.

GALL, KARL E. - (Grant County Republican, March 4, 1905) Died Karl Gall of Shockey, Kansas, at 2 o'clock on the morning of March 1st, 1905. He was 68 years of age, an old settler of the county and a highly respected citizen. He leaves a wife and seven children to mourn his death. The bereaved family has the sympathy of the entire community.

He was born May 25, 1839.

(Lakin Investigator, March 3, 1905) We are very sorry to announce the death of Karl Gall, of Grant County, who died on his farm Thursday a.m. at two o'clock, at the age of 66 years. Mr. Gall was born in Germany and came to the United States about nineteen years ago. He stopped in Iowa for about two months and then moved to Grant County and filed on his homestead where he has resided ever since. Mr. Gall has passed through all the vicissitude of which we western people only know, but had by thrift, industry and perseverance, accumulated a comfortable amount of this world's goods. He leaves a widow, three sons and three daughters to mourn his death and we extend them our heartfelt sympathy in their bereavement.

GLASSER, GOTLEIB - (Lakin Investigator, April 19, 1907) Gotleib Glasser, an old and respected citizen of Kearny County, committed suicide Sunday p.m. by hanging. Mr. Glasser was a German, sixty-four years of age and had resided in Kearny County nearly twenty years, and accumulated considerable property. For some time he had been despondent, and Sunday afternoon told his wife he would not be here much longer and immediately went to the barn, and standing on a large box tied the rope over a beam, kicked the box from under him. Within fifteen minutes his wife followed and told the son he better watch his father. The boy went at once to the barn and found him dead. Coroner Chas. H. Waterman summoned a jury and the verdict rendered was: "Death by hanging, caused by his own hand, account despondency."

(The Kearny County Advocate, April 18, 1907) Gotlieb Glasser, a German, about 60 years of age, long a resident of Kearny County, who lived about 20 miles south and west of Lakin, about 4 o'clock last Sunday afternoon, committed suicide by hanging himself by a lasso

SHOCKEY CEMETERY

attached to a rafter in his own barn, while in a fit of despondency caused by domestic infelicity. Mrs. Glasser was his second wife, with whom he had more or less frequent quarrels. He decided to end all bickerings by effacing himself from the world, and had been missed only ten minutes when his son went to the barn and found him lifeless.

In that short time his father had taken the rope off the saddle, the usual place, attached it to a rafter, tied it around his neck, mounted a box, and then kicked the box aside, and was already dead.

Coroner Waterman accompanied by Justice Kimball and other citizens went up to the Glasser homestead Monday morning, and rendered a verdict of suicide, which was in accordance with the facts developed.

The victim was buried Monday afternoon.

The disagreeing couple were comfortably situated, and but for an incompatibility of temper ought to have been contented and happy. Their old, original dug-out, which still stands near a modern home, and necessary outbuildings attest their industry and frugality in conquering a home from the desert. They understood how to build the semblance of a home, but love was absent, and they did not care to bridle their ungovernably tempers, and what they might have made a Heaven on earth, they easily converted into an amateur t'other place. So true is it that mutual affection, respect, and forbearance can make a happy home, while mutual distrust, ill-will, and recrimination can produce only the most poignant misery.

Headstone reads 1848-1906.

GORDON, ROBERT A. - (The Lakin Independent, March 20, 1931) Robert A. Gordon was born April 3rd, 1848, near Palmira, Missouri. He departed this life March 12th, 1931, at the age of 82 years, 11 months, and 9 days.

When a young man he united with the Baptist Church. For a number of years he has made his home with his nephew, Billy McRae.

He leaves to mourn his death three sons, one grandson, two granddaughters, and five great grandchildren, beside a host of other relatives and friends. His wife and two daughters preceded him in death.

The funeral service was held last Friday afternoon at the home of his nephew, J. W. McRae, and was conducted by Dr. Honsaker, pastor of the Presbyterian Church. The body was laid to rest in the Shockey Cemetery.

SHOCKEY CEMETERY

GREVES, GIRL - (Shockey Plainsman, Jan. 4, 1889) A nine year old of Mr. and Mrs. Greves, who live a few miles west of Shockeyville, died of diphtheria on the 21st ult. and was buried here in Maple Grove Cemetery on the 22d. The bereaved parents have the sympathies of the whole community. A parent's sorrow cannot be assuaged by the commonplace expressions of sympathy, but there is one thing that ought to soften the sharpness of a parent's agony under such bereavement. It is the reflection that "little children are pure, and of such is the kingdom of heaven." "It is well with the child."

GUTSCHE, HERMAN - (Grant County Republican, New Ulysses, Kansas, Mar. 22, 1919) Herman Gutsche, who lived on the Henthorn place in the north part of this county, was found dead in his room last Sunday about noon. His health had been very poor for several months past and it is thought that this caused him to take his own life, which he did by hanging. He was laid to rest in the Shockey Cemetery on Monday.

SHOCKEY CEMETERY

HILL, EMILY - (Shockey Plainsman, Aug. 27, 1889) Mrs. Hill of north Grant, aged 71 years, died yesterday of paralysis, after an illness of but a few days. The burial will take place at 11 a.m. today at Maple Grove Cemetery, Shockeyville.

(Ulysses Tribune, Aug. 19, 1889) Died: Hill - at her home eleven miles North of Ulysses, on Sunday night, August 24, 1889, of paralysis, Emily, wife of Alanson Hill, aged 70 years, 4 months and 18 days.

Mrs. Emily Hill was born in Hamilton County, Ohio, April 7th, 1889 (date as in paper), and was married to Alanson Hill on June 13, 1842. She lived with her husband in Hamilton County, Ohio, until the year of 1867, when they moved to Shelby County, Illinois, where they resided until coming to Grant County early in the spring of 1886. They settled upon a claim in Sherman Township, which has since been their home.

Mrs. Hill was a loving wife and mother, a kind neighbor and was universally loved and respected by all who knew her. She was a member of the M. E. Church. Nine children have been born to Mr. and Mrs. Hill, seven of whom are now living.

Although she had been sick but a few days, death's grim reaper had come to garner her to that great beyond from whence none ever return. We should shed no tears of regret; we should rejoice that she lived so long. She had lived her life. In nature's course her time has come, the four seasons were complete. The spring could never return again. She had taken life's seven steps, the measure of her life was full. When the gold of evening meets the dusk of night beneath the silent stars, the tired laborer should fall asleep.

The remains were borne to their last resting place in Maple Grove Cemetery at Shockey, accompanied by a number of friends and relatives. The sorrowing father and children have the sympathy of the entire community.

HOFFMAN, ANNIE LAURA - (The Ulysses News, June 3, 1965) Mrs. Annie L. Hoffman, 97, a Grant County resident since 1886, died Tuesday morning at 8:30 o'clock in Bethel Home at Montezuma, where she had been a patient since 1961.

Since she still was enumerated in the census here, she was Grant County's oldest resident. Of four daughters born to her, only Mrs. P.M. Hampton survives, and among her grandchildren here are the Cantrells, children of the late Mrs. Robert O. Cantrell.

Mrs. Hoffman was the daughter of Thomas and Hannah Swinney,

SHOCKEY CEMETERY

who homesteaded in the Shockey community northwest of Ulysses, in 1886. She was a school teacher there, and after her marriage to Isaac Hoffman, she lived in the Ulysses community. Mr. Hoffman died in 1913.

Funeral services were at 2 o'clock Friday at the Church of God, the Rev. Harold Taves officiating. Burial in the old Shockey Cemetery, directed by Phillips Mortuary.

She was born November 27, 1867.

HOFFMAN, GLADYS- (Grant County Republican, July 16, 1898) Died Friday, July 8th, 1898, the five months old child of Mr. and Mrs. Isaac Hoffman.

She was born February 10, 1898.

HOFFMAN, ISAAC - (Kearny County Advocate, Feb. 7, 1913) Isaac Hoffman, of Grant County of the firm of Hoffman Bros., died at three p.m., Tuesday, February 4, 1913, at Wm McRae's restaurant on Main Street. Mr. Hoffman had been brought here from his home only a couple of hours before in an auto, intending to take him to Kansas City for an operation. It was a complication of bowel trouble that caused his death. His remains were taken to Shockey for interment. Mr. Hoffman was 51 years old, and leaves a family and his brother, Charles. He has been one of Grant County's prominent cattlemen for many years, and a highly respected citizen.

He was born January 7, 1862.

HOFFMAN, MARGARET - (Funeral Record) Died January 12, 1922, age 78 years. Died of nephritis, northeast of Ulysses. Single. Buried at Shockey Cemetery.

Headstone reads born in 1843.

HOFFMAN, NANCY - (Kansas State Census, Grant County, 1895) 73 years old prior to March 1, 1895, born in Indiana.

Headstone reads born September 15, 1822, died December 7, 1901.

HOFFMAN, THOMAS RAYMOND - (The Kearny County Advocate, Nov. 17, 1915) After an illness of a little more than twenty four hours, Thomas Raymond Hoffman died at his home about 15 miles south of Lakin of a complication of diseases. He was a promising youth of 16

SHOCKEY CEMETERY

years and had a bright future. The funeral was held today with interment at Shocky. E. S. Snow, a local funeral director furnished a pretty casket.
  Headstone reads born August 24, 1899, and died November 16, 1916.

HUNT, JESSIE - (Grant County Republican, March. 6, 1920) Jessie Hunt, one of Chris Molz's hired hands died Sunday morning. He was just getting over the flu and went to help dip cattle and took a chill. The next morning Mr. Molz called him and he didn't answer so he went to him and found him dead. He was buried in the Shockey Cemetery, Monday.

HURT, INFANT - (Shockeyville Eagle, Shockeyville, Grant County, Kansas, June 23, 1887) An infant child of Mr. and Mrs. Hurt, who reside a few miles west of town, died on the 16th, and was buried the next day.

SHOCKEY CEMETERY

JARVIS, THELMA NORA - (Grant County Republican, Ulysses, Kansas, Saturday, July 26, 1924) A baby girl was born to Mr. and Mrs. Claude Jarvis, July 17, but died Sunday morning at 7 o'clock. Burial was in Shockey Cemetery, Monday at 10 o'clock.

SHOCKEY CEMETERY

KASH, RAY WILLIAM - (Paper of June 10, 1909) The little three year old boy of Mr. and Mrs. John Kash was buried last Saturday at old Shockeyville, in Grant County. Mr. Kash moved into the south part of Kearny County, last March from Marion. It was their oldest child and they felt the loss very deeply.
Died June 4, 1909, of diphtheria.

KIISTNER, AUGUST - (The Ulysses News, Sept. 22, 1960) August Kiistner, 81, spent 72 years of his life in Grant County preceding his death last week. Funeral services were conducted Friday afternoon, September 16, in the Methodist Church with Rev. Robert Peters officiating.
Mr. Kiistner was born in Edar, Germany, in 1878, and came with his parents and family directly to Grant County in 1888. His father, Peter Kiistner, was one of the original settlers of the county.
The son, August, grew to manhood here and homesteaded in the Shockey community. In 1914 he married Miss Myrtle Miller of Chanute, who was teaching the Shockey School. She taught there for several years after their marriage. Her death occurred in 1934 and in 1937 Mr. Kiistner sold his land and moved to Ulysses, where he had lived since.
Survivors include two brothers, W. A. Kiistner of Tulsa and P. C. Kiistner of Ulysses; and three sisters, Mrs. C. H. Binney and Mrs. R. R. Bechtelheimer of Ulysses, and Mrs. Earl H. Moore of Johnson.
Pallbearers at his service were his nephews, Harold Binney, L. E. Annis, Wendell Cheek, Merle Rider, Floyd Kiistner and Robert Moore. Music was by Mrs. Robert Gilger, organist and Richard Mason, soloist.
Burial in the Ulysses Cemetery was directed by Phillips Mortuary.

KIISTNER, MAGGIE ELMIRA - (The Lakin Independent, March 16, 1923) Maggie Elmira Anderson, the oldest daughter of Mr. and Mrs. A. W. Anderson was born in Brown County, Indiana, and departed this life at the age of 31 years, 7 months, and 23 days.
She was united in marriage to Pete C. Kiistner, May 23, 1914. In 1910 she united with the Church of Christ and lived faithful to her God.
She leaves to mourn her loss a loving husband, two children, a mother, three brothers, three sisters, and a host of friends.
Deceased contracted the influenza and died Tuesday at noon as a result of heart failure. Every one loved her, and her loss is keenly felt by all who knew her.

SHOCKEY CEMETERY

Born in 1891 and died in 1923.

KIISTNER, MYRTLE BELLE - (Grant County Republican, January 3, 1935) Word was received in Ulysses early Sunday morning that Mrs. Myrtle Kiistner, wife of August Kiistner, had passed away at their home in the northwest part of Grant County.

Mrs. Kiistner had been in poor health for the past three years and continued to grow worse from the first signs of her illness, having lost her eyesight about a year ago and been in a helpless condition since that time. She leaves to mourn her loss, her husband and a host of relatives and friends. Funeral services were held Monday afternoon and interment was made in the Shockey Cemetery.

Myrtle Belle Miller, daughter of Mr. and Mrs. Wm Miller was born in Neosho County, Kansas, August 18, 1888, and passed from this life at her home in Grant County, December 30, 1934, at the age of 46 years, 4 months and 12 days.

She was married at Chanute, Kansas, May 31, 1914, to August Kiistner of Ulysses, Kansas.

Besides her husband, she leaves two brothers and two sisters, Clyde C. Miller, Wm. Miller, Mattie Vance and Alice Schomer, all of Chanute.

She has been a member of the Christian Church since her girlhood days. Twenty years of her life was spent as a public school teacher, fifteen of which were in Grant and neighboring counties.

Her labors have ceased, but her influence lives on.

Funeral services were conducted by Roxie T. Powell, Methodist minister of Ulysses at the Shockey School House and the body laid to rest in the Shockey Cemetery.

KIISTNER, PETE C. - Name is on headstone but is buried in the Lakin Cemetery. Born December 31, 1889, and died May 15, 1981.

KINSMAN, INFANT - Infant child of Mr. and Mrs. Tom Kinsman.

SHOCKEY CEMETERY

LEIGH, ALFRED - Son of Samuel and Mary Leigh, born February 28, 1839, in Clinton, New Jersey, died May 27, 1930, of diabetes.

(Grant County Republican, Ulysses, Kansas, Thursday, May 29, 1930) Grandpa Leigh, who has practically been an invalid for the past three years, has passed on, according to word received here Tuesday. The obituary will be printed in next week's issue.

(Grant County Republican, Thursday, June 5, 1930) On Tuesday, May 27, 1930, at 3:30 o'clock, at the age of 93 years, 2 months, and 27 days, Alfred Leigh passed out of this life of much suffering and pain at the home of his son, W. H. Leigh, where he had been very carefully and lovingly cared for for several years. For the last two years his son had done nothing but wait upon his aged father with his own hands. Twenty years ago a doctor told Mr. Leigh he could live but a few days longer, but with a great amount of reserve strength he fought thru that and many other afflictions until three strokes within two weeks made the brave warrior at last give up the battle.

He came to this part of the country in 1885 from New Jersey, where he had been in the machine business and has been a farmer since then as long as he was able to work. His wife died in 1892. Five children survive him: Mrs. Ruby Waterman, of Blain, Colorado, A. B. Leigh, of Hutchinson, Charles E., Roe B. and W. H. Leigh, all of Grant County.

Funeral services were held in the Shockey school house Wednesday, May 28. Mrs. Asa Ratliff sang two solos and Gerald G. Bentley, minister of the Church of Christ, read the scripture and brought a short message on the resurrection. A great many of the old settlers were there to pay their last respects to this old pioneer of western Kansas. He was laid to rest by the side of his wife in the cemetery near the Shockey school house.

He was a life long member of the Methodist Church.

He came from a family who lived long lives, his father living to the age of 105 years and 5 days, and his aunt to the age of 107 years and 7 days.

Our heartfelt sympathy goes out to the bereaved during this hour of deep grief.

Card of Thanks. We wish to thank the friends and neighbors who so kindly assisted us in the care of our dear father, during his sickness and burial, and for the beautiful floral offerings.--William H. Leigh, Chas, E. Leigh, A. B. Leigh, Mr. and Mrs. R. B. Leigh and family and Mr. and Mrs. Chas Waterman and family.

SHOCKEY CEMETERY

LEIGH, CHARLES EMERY - (The Ulysses News, February 2, 1961) Members of pioneer families of Grant County Friday attended funeral services for Charles E. Leigh, 97, last of one of the original families who settled here in 1885.

Rev. A. Gerald Whittier officiated at the services at Shelton Memorial Christian Church.

Music was by Lyle Morris, soloist, who and 'Near to the Heard of God' and 'In The Garden'. He was accompanied by Mr. H. C. Snodgrass, organist.

Pallbearers were Harold Binney, David Sullivan, Phillip Shorter, Arthur Williams, Ralph Rider and Eugene Lozar.

Mr. Leigh died Wednesday, January 25, at Bob Wilson Memorial Hospital, where he had been a patient since May. For the last 12 years he had made his home with Mr. and Mrs. W. A. Leigh.

He was born December 5, 1863, in Allertown, New Jersey, and was 97 years, one month and 20 days old. He came with his parents, Alfred and Susan Leigh to Grant County in the fall of 1885, where they homesteaded and later he and three brothers also homesteaded.

He was preceded in death by his parents, four brothers and one sister.

Among the survivors are five nieces, Mrs. Oleta Ross of Centerville, Kansas, Mrs. Nona Mackey of Pueblo, Mrs. Betty Clark of Sedgwick, Mrs. Blanche Streeter of Monte Vista, Colorado, and Mrs. Herma Snodgrass of Las Animas, Colorado; seven nephews, Harry Wartman of Holly, Tom Wartman of Monte Vista, Dr. Calvin Wartman of Bremerton, Wash., Alvin Wartman, Delmar Wartman and John Wartman, all of Pierceville and W. A. Leigh of Ulysses; and a sister-in-law, Mrs. A. B. Leigh of Keswick, Virginia.

LEIGH, LEONA FRANCIS - Born April 27, 1907, and died September 18, 1907, of cholera infantum.

(Grant County Republican, Sept. 21, 1907) Died on Wednesday night, the infant child of Mr. and Mrs. R. B. Leigh. The bereaved parents have the sympathy of the entire community.

LEIGH, MARGARET - (The Ulysses News, April 21, 1960) Mrs. Margaret Leigh, 71, long time resident of Grant County, passed away about noon Tuesday, in St. Catherine's Hospital in Garden City. She had been in a Garden City rest home for several months until Friday, when she entered the hospital for treatment.

SHOCKEY CEMETERY

Mrs. Leigh came to Grant County as a bride, nearly fifty years ago. Her husband, Roland Leigh, preceded her in death in 1949. She had been an active member of the Shelton Memorial Christian Church, as well as a member of a farm bureau unit and the Happy Hour Club.

She is survived by a son, W. A. Leigh of Ulysses, and a daughter, Mrs. Oleta Ross of Centerville, Kansas.

Funeral services were conducted by Rev. A. Gerald Whittier at the Shelton Memorial Christian Church, Friday afternoon at 2:00 p.m. Burial at Shockey Cemetery.

(The Ulysses News, Apr. 28, 1960) Funeral services Friday, April 22, at Shelton Memorial Christian Church drew a large crowd, especially of pioneers who had been friends and neighbors of Mrs. Margaret Leigh nearly 50 years.

She came here as a bride and previously had lived with her mother and family on a homestead in Stanton County.

Mrs. Leigh died Tuesday, April 19, at a Garden City hospital. She was 72.

Memorial services Friday were conducted by Rev. A. Gerald Whittier. Music was by the Spring Valley quartet, H. D. Kliewer, A. P. Kliewer, Alvin Harms and Ike Harms.

Pallbearers were Ray Fogleman, Keith and Cecil Pucket, Merle Nickerson, Jr., Charles Smith and Philip Shorter.

Burial at Shockey Cemetery was directed by Phillips Mortuary.

Mrs. Leigh is survived by two children, Oleta Ross and W. A. Leigh, and a brother, E. H. Friend of Grand Junction, Colorado.

LEIGH, ROLAND BERRYHILL - (The Ulysses News, July 27, 1950) Roland B. Leigh, a lifetime resident of Grant County died suddenly at his home at 9 a.m. Tuesday morning. Mr. Leigh was riding a horse at his farm when stricken with a heart attack. He was 69 years of age.

Funeral services were held at the Christian Church Friday afternoon at 2:30. Rev. Alfred E. Webb officiated. Burial in the family plot at Shockey Cemetery.

Surviving are his wife, Margaret, a son, W. A. Leigh of Ulysses, a daughter, Mrs. Oleta Ross of Centerville, Kansas, two brothers, C. E. Leigh of Ulysses and A. B. Leigh of Hutchinson, and five grandchildren.

(The Ulysses News, August 3, 1950) Roland B. Leigh, son of Alfred and Susan Emery Leigh, was born in Newton, Kansas, September 27, 1880. He moved to Grant County with his parents in 1885, where he

SHOCKEY CEMETERY

lived ever since and passed away July 25, 1950, at the age of 69 years, 7 months and 25 days.

On May 28, 1906, he was united in marriage to Margaret L. Friend of Johnson, Kansas, and to this union three children were born. Leona Francis preceded her father in death at the age of four months and twenty-two days. Oleta Leigh Ross of Centerville, Kansas, and William A. Leigh of Ulysses remain.

A kind and loving father and husband from us has gone to his last resting place and reward after having lived a very useful and kindly life toward all his neighbors, friends and relatives.

LEIGH, SUSAN - Susan Fairchild Emery, daughter of Charles and Lavinnah Emery of Scottish ancestry, was born September 30, 1839, in New Jersey of English and Holland Dutch descent. Married Alfred Leigh, died September 28, 1892, of cancer.

LEIGH, WILLIAM "BILL" ALFRED - (Garden City Telegram, Jan. 9, 1998) Funeral for William "Bill" Alfred Leigh, 81, lifetime resident of Ulysses, was held at 10 a.m. Saturday at Ulysses Mennonite Brethren Church. Loyal Martin, pastor, and the Rev. Bill Harrold officiating. Burial in Shockey Cemetery, rural Ulysses.

Mr. Leigh, a farmer and rancher, died Wednesday, January 7, 1998, at Columbia Wesley Medical Center, Wichita.

He was born September 26, 1916, on the family farm in Grant County, the son of Roland Berryhill and Margaret Lena (Friend) Leigh.

Mr. Leigh was a member of Odd Fellow, National Rifle Association, Southwest Kansas Irrigation Association, Modoc Gun Club and Grant County Farm Bureau.

On December 8, 1939, he married Helen Robinson in Baca County, Colorado. She survives.

Other survivors are four children, George Leigh, Ulysses, Charles Leigh, Copperas Cove, Texas, Susan Siebert, Garden City, and Etta Friesen, Lynden, Washington; a sister, Oleta Ross, Louisburg; 11 grandchildren and seven great grandchildren.

Visitation hours are at Phillips Mortuary, Ulysses. Memorials to the Grant County Senior Center, Ulysses.

LEIGH, WILLIAM HENRY - Born March 8, 1877, at Newton and died October 21, 1937, of coronary thrombosis.

SHOCKEY CEMETERY

(The Ulysses News, November 4, 1937) Funeral services for William Henry Leigh, 60, Grant County pioneer, were held Tuesday afternoon at the Methodist Church and interment was in the Shockey Cemetery. He died of a heart attack in his yard Sunday morning about 11 o'clock. He was returning from Johnson and had stepped out of the car to open a gate when he was stricken.

Mr. Leigh, who had been in the county 51 years, lived five miles west of Ulysses with a bachelor brother, C. E. Leigh. The deceased was also a bachelor. He was a farmer and had worked in Ulysses as a blacksmith. He had been in poor health about two years. Rev. Roxie Powell conducted the funeral services and the Phillips Mortuary was in charge of the burial.

Mr. Leigh is survived by three brothers, D. W., Ulysses, R. B., Ulysses, and A. B., Hutchinson and by a sister, Mrs. Charles Warman of Pierceville.

SHOCKEY CEMETERY

MAIN, LOREN P. - (Grant County Republican, New Ulysses, Kansas, Sat. Jan. 30, 1915) Loren P. Main died at about nine o'clock Tuesday morning after an illness lasting ten days and was buried on Wednesday in Shockey Cemetery.

(Grant County Republican, Jan. 23, 1915) L. P. Main was found on his cabin floor Monday morning in an unconscious condition, with cuts on his face where he had struck his head when he fell. He had lain so long in his night clothes that he was badly chilled and could not talk. He is better now and in a good way to recover.

He was born in 1858.

MAIN, MINNIE - (Grant County Republican, New Ulysses, Kansas, Sat., Dec. 30, 1911) Mrs. L. P. Main who lived in the northwest part of the county, died at 11 o'clock on Saturday night of last week and was buried at Shockey Cemetery on Monday afternoon. She had not been in good health for some time but for the past few weeks she grew worse and passed away on December 24, of dropsy. She had many relatives and friends in the community who sympathize with Mr. Main in his bereavement.

(Headstone may read born in 1866)

MCGOWN, BABY - (History Book) Child of Frank Silvis' second wife, probably buried at Shockey Cemetery.

MCRAE, JAMES WILLIAM - (The Lakin Independent, February 26, 1932) James William McRae, son of William Fee and Margaret Gordon McRae, was born August 20th, 1854, in Adams County, Illinois; departed this life February 22, 1932, at the age of 77 years, 6 months and 2 days.

He was united in marriage to Miss Josie M. Simma, July 8th, 1889. To this union five children were born, three daughters and two sons. One son, William Floyd, preceded him in death.

Those left to mourn this loss are his loving wife, Mrs. Josie McRae; a son, Geo. McRae of Lakin; the daughters, Mrs. E. R. Kemper of Liberal, Mrs. Fred Rogers of Ulysses, Mrs. Oren Humphreys of Ulysses; one sister, Mrs. Ella Ward of Camp Point, Illinois; two brothers, Arch McRae of San Diego and Sanford McRae of Geyeserville, California; also a host of relatives and friends.

At the time of his death Billy McRae was the oldest "old settler" in

SHOCKEY CEMETERY

Grant County. He came to this country in 1882 and homesteaded while it was still a part of Seward County. He was a real pioneer, a successful farmer and stockman, and was still going strong when the end came.

These "old timers" are fast passing away, as they come to the end of the trail. The funeral service was conducted by Dr. Honsaker, pastor of the Presbyterian Church, assisted by the choir of the church, and was held in the McRae home Wednesday afternoon, February 24th, at two o'clock. Burial was made in the Shockey Cemetery.

It was one of the largest funerals ever held in Grant County. Friends from far and near gathered to pay their sad tribute to their old friend, Billy McRae, whom they had loved and honored in the many years of their friendship.

MCRAE, JOSIE - (The Lakin Independent, May 26, 1960) Josephine Marie Simma, a daughter of Willebald and Anna Marie Simma, was born October 2, 1866, in Wertenberg, Germany. She departed this life May 18, 1960, at the age of 93 years, 7 months and 15 days.

She was united in marriage to James William McRae July 8, 1889. To this union five children were born, three daughters and two sons. One son, William Floyd, preceded her in death.

Those left to mourn this loss are her children, George McRae of Lakin, Agnes Kemper of Dodge City, Alice Rogers and Margaret Humphreys of Ulysses. One sister of Burbank, California, 21 grandchildren and 20 great grandchildren.

She was the oldest old settler in Grant County and one of the oldest in Kearny County.

MCRAE, WILLIAM FLOYD - (Grant County Republican, April 15, 1905) Card of Thanks: To the many friends that helped us in time of need during the time our son lived after the accident he met with, we wish to express our sincere thanks for their aid and friendship up to the time of his death. Mr. and Mrs. W. J. McRae.

Born August 21, 1891, and died February 4, 1905.

MOLZ, CARALINA - (The Kearny County Advocate, Nov. 30, 1928) Mrs. Caralina Molz, nee Kistner, was born April 12th, 1864*, at Wapenroth, Germany. On the 29th of May 1868, she was married to Christian Molz in Sulzbach, Germany. This union was blessed with ten children. In the year of 1886 the deceased with six of her children

SHOCKEY CEMETERY

followed her husband out of the old country to establish a home in America. Mr. Molz and an older daughter having come here a few months earlier. These people were among the early pioneers of Stanton County. From time to time her children left home to establish their own homes. In the year 1913 on the 23rd of December her husband passed out of this life. Since then she has been staying with her children who cared for her in last and trying years of her life. Three children preceded her in death in the old country and two, a son and a daughter, here in America.

The departed has always been a faithful member of the Lutheran Church, ever ready to hear the preaching of God's word.

Mrs. Molz passed away on the 19th of November 1928, at the age of 87 years, 7 months and 7 days. She leaves to mourn her death three sons, Christian Molz, Adam Molz and Pete Molz; two daughters, Mrs. Minnie Druessel and Mrs. Adela Druessel, 24 grandchildren, 20 great grandchildren; one brother, Mr. Kiistner of Ulysses and a sister who still resides in Germany.

Funeral services were conducted at the Albert Druessel home and at the Shockey School. She was then laid to rest in the Shockey Cemetery. The Lutheran pastor of Deerfield had charge of the services.

"For to me to live in Christ and to die is again." Phil. 21:21.

*(note: this is what the paper has in it but I think the birth date should be April 12, 1841.)

(Pioneer Democrat, May 29, 1886) The family of Christian Molz, consisting of seven children and their mother arrived in Lakin last Monday direct from the German Empire. They left the Rhine, May 5, with their goods marked direct to Lakin, Kansas. Mr. Molz had preceded them in the fall, and has been busy making ready a pleasant home near Shockeyville, where the family has now gone, except one of the boys, Peter, who has secured a situation in the dining room of the Red Front.

MOLZ, CHRISTIAN - (Agnes Molz Letter) Christian Molz, Sr. was born May 20, 1845, near Sulzbach by Rhaunen, Germany and died at his home in the northeast part of Stanton County on Tuesday, December 23, 1913.

He was united in marriage with Carolina Kiistner, May 29, 1868, in his home village of Sulzbach.

He is survived by his sorrowing widow and six children, Mrs. Lena Eichenauer at present in Topeka, Christian Jr. and Peter who live in this

SHOCKEY CEMETERY

county, Adam Molz a resident of Deerfield, Kansas, Mrs. Adela Drussel and Mrs. Minnie Drussel both of Finney County.

Mr. Molz came to Stanton County in February 1886, at which time he filed on a homestead which he proved up and still resided on at the time of his death.

Burial was in the Shockey Cemetery. Then later he and Carolina were moved to the Garden City Cemetery.

MOLZ, ESTHER - Born and died May 10, 1903.

MOLZ, G. - Infant son of Chris Molz, died in 1917.

SHOCKEY CEMETERY

PENNINGTON, INFANT - (Ulysses Plainsman, Feb. 15, 1890) We neglected to mention last week, the mournful visitation at the home of Mr. and Mrs. Charles Pennington. On the 5th inst. death came and took from their home circle their little baby boy. The afflicted parents have the sympathy of the whole community.
(Grant County Register, Ulysses, Grant County, Kansas, Feb. 8, 1890) The infant son of Mr. and Mrs. Charles Pennington died in Ulysses on Wednesday. The remains were placed in the Ulysses Cemetery.

PIERSE, JAMES H. - Born 1829, died 1893, age 65 yr.

PIONEER BABY -

POPE, ARMINA VAUGHN - (The Lakin Independent, Nov. 30, 1923) Mrs. A. Pope died at the home of her daughter, Mrs. Thos. Tuggle, in Scott City, on Friday morning, November 23rd, 1923, after a lingering illness. Mrs. Pope was eighty-six years of age and had been making her home with her daughter, having been a resident of Grant and Kearny Counties for many years. The remains were brought to Deerfield and funeral services conducted at the home of Mr. and Mrs. Karl Corbett at eight o'clock Sunday morning, Rev. R. L. Wells being in charge of the service, after which the body was taken to its final resting place in Shockey Cemetery. Two sons, J. N. Pope, of Hewins, Kansas, and W. E. Pope, of Eldorado and the daughter, Mrs. Thos. Tuggle, were the only immediate member of her family who were there for the funeral.
(Kearny County Advocate, Mar. 7, 1924) Armina Vaughan was born November 2nd, 1840, in Estel County, Kentucky, and died November 23rd, 1923, at the home of her daughter, Mrs. T. B. Tuggle in Scott City.
She was united in marriage to Fielding H. Pope, March 20th, 1865. To this union ten children were born, five dying in early childhood. Four sons, and one daughter grew to womanhood, being; J. M., John H., F. E., and W. E. and Mrs. T. B. Tuggle.
Mrs. Pope joined the Christian Church at the early age of fifteen years. In later years she joined the Church of Christ, which she attended so long as she was able. In the early days in Grant County, she used to take her family and drive in a wagon six or eight miles to Sunday School, picking up folks along the way until she had a wagon full by the time she reached Sunday School.
The family located in Grant County, Kansas, in 1885, locating on a

SHOCKEY CEMETERY

homestead. Mr. Pope was in poor health resulting from his three years serving in the 8th Kentucky Infantry, he being among the first volunteers. During his service he was captured and confined in Libby Prison, which with other hardships of the war, broke his health. Shortly after coming to Kansas, he died. At the time of his death there was no cemetery, and he was buried in the yard on his homestead. About a year later, when the old soldiers of that county wished to hold Decoration Day services, his remains were removed to the newly established Shockey Cemetery, he being the first to be buried in it. And to this hallowed spot we took mother fore her final resting place by the side of father.

After proving up the homestead, mother took the family to Chautauua County, Kansas, where for many years she lived with a son until she became unable to care for herself, after which she made her home with her daughter. Since coming to Scott City she was confined to her bed except when moved in a wheel chair.

She was patient and uncomplaining, looking forward to the inevitable with Christian fortitude. The best of medical skill and tender loving care was always given her. She suffered no pain, but gradually grew weaker until she quietly passed to the great beyond in restful sleep.

Her last days were made cheerful by the daily visits of the many friends who came to minister and comfort. The Church of Christ ladies came out and held prayer and read Scripture, and Brother Mell, Christian minister, visited with her in her last hour.

One son, W. E. Pope, of Eldcado came before she died but the other boys visited her frequently during the summer, one of them being with her on the summer preceding. Many beautiful floral offerings were sent, among them being on from the Missouri Pacific clerks at Eldcado, where one son is agent for that company. The Junior class of Scott High School, American Legion Auxiliary, W.C.T.U., Church of Christ, Baptist Sunday School of this city and the ladies Sunday School class at Deerfield, all sent beautiful flowers.

Funeral services were held at the Scott City Church of Christ, and the remains then taken to Grant County to the home of a granddaughter, Mrs. Carl Corbett, where former neighbors and friends gathered to pay their last respects to one they had known and loved.

We wish to thank all for their kind acts, floral offerings and sympathy, rendered and given during her sickness and following. Contributed

POPE, FIELDING H. - (Shockeyville Eagle, Shockeyville, Grant Co.,

SHOCKEY CEMETERY

Kansas, June 16, 1887) Died at his home near Shockeyville, Kansas, June 12, 1887, Fielding H. Pope, aged 49 years.

Deceased had been an invalid for many years, by reason of diseases caused by his three years service in the volunteer army, from which he suffered constantly. He removed to this locality about a year and a half ago, with his family and has always held the esteem of those who knew him as a kindly neighbor and an upright citizen. He was a member of Mountain Lodge, No. 187, A.F.& A.M., of Kentucky, also of the G.A.R. He had long been a member of the M.E. Church, and died with a lively faith, and hope of a glorious resurrection. Funeral services were conducted by Rev. D. Holmes, and attended by a large number of sympathizing friends. The Grant Army Post of this place also assisted in paying the last sad rites to their deceased comrade. A wife and five children are left to mourn the loss of husband and father.

He was born in 1838.

PRYOR, DR. GEO. O. - (Shockeyville Eagle, August 10, 1886) Dr. Pryor died suddenly last Sunday morning at his place 10 miles south of Shockeyville. His death resulted from prostration caused by a painful rupture.

(The Surprise Post, Surprise, Hamilton County, Ks., Aug. 12, 1886) We regret very much to chronicle the death of Mr. Geo. O. Prior. His last illness was very short. He will be missed very much by his many friends and neighbors, as he was always ready and willing to aid and oblige them. He leaves one sister and two daughters to mourn his loss, who have the sympathy of the entire community in their sad bereavement.

Died, at his residence at Cognac, Hamilton County, Kansas, on Sunday, August 8th, Geo. O. Prior, aged 41 years.

Mr. Prior was born in Muskingon County, Ohio, February 16, 1845. He came to Kansas about 7 years ago, and settled in Wabaunsee County, where he lived until he came to Hamilton County, about one year ago. Since he located at Cognac, he has worked unceasingly for his community. By his efforts he has secured a post office at Cognac, and was appointed postmaster. He leaves one sister and two little orphan girls aged 6 and 12 years to mourn his loss. He will be greatly missed by the entire community.

SHOCKEY CEMETERY

RANDEL, THEODORE - (Funeral Records) Child of E. A. Randel died in July 1931. Buried at Shockey.
(7/23/31) Death took the babe of Mr. and Mrs. E. H. Randel, last Sunday before the little one saw light of day, leaving bereaved parents with their dreams of a happy, loving child shattered. The little one was laid to rest Sunday afternoon in Shockey Cemetery, Rev. Roxie T. Powell, in charge of the services.

REYNOLDS, BENJAMIN F. - (Grant County Republican, July 15, 1905) George Reynolds' baby is quite sick. Uncle Isaac was in Ulysses, Friday morning, to phone for Dr. Johnston.
Head stone reads aged 9 months, 17 days.

REYNOLDS, NELLIE - (The Lakin Investigator, August 14, 1908) The little two year old daughter of Mr. and Mrs. George Reynolds died Friday afternoon from a snake bite. The family had been visiting relatives in Kingman County, returning Wednesday. Mrs. Reynolds was cleaning the house and the two children were playing in the yard. They were attracted by the strange actions of the chickens that had found a large snake. The baby was bitten just above the ankle. Everything was done to keep the poison from spreading, but is was useless. The baby died in a few hours.
Head stone reads aged 3 years, 26 days.

RIDER, ADA - (The Ulysses News, July 5, 1956) A pioneer Grant County woman who had lived in the county for sixty-nine years died at Ulysses on Saturday, June 30.
She was Mrs. Ada Rider, known to many friends as Grandma Rider. Mrs. Rider was 85.
After her marriage to George R. Rider in 1887 she came to Grant County and had lived here continuously since that time. As a girl she had come to Kansas with her parents in 1881.
Her husband, who preceded her in death in March 1952, was one of the first settlers of Grant County. He had come to this county in 1883. Mr. and Mrs. Rider were residents of the early day town of Shockey in the Bear Creek vicinity of northwest Grant
Mrs. Rider was one of the very few early day homemakers remaining in this county. Many settlers came to this region in the years of 1885-87 and the children of those families are now the only ones left who

SHOCKEY CEMETERY

remember the pioneer settlement.

Funeral services for Mrs. Rider were held in the Church of Christ at 10:00 a.m., Monday, July 2, and were conducted by Mrs. Gordon Maylor.

Music was by Mrs. Glenn Tuttle, Mrs. Merle Mawhirter, Glenn Tuttle and Leo Anderson, who sang, "I Can Hear My Saviour Calling", "Rock of Ages", and "Does Jesus Care".

Pallbearers were George Rexroat, Ramon Rexroat, Merl Rider, Alan Anderson, Phil Shorter and Walter Waechter.

Interment was at the Shockey Cemetery. The Phillips Mortuary was in charge.

Mrs. Rider is survived by two sons, C. D. Rider and Ralph Rider, both of Ulysses; and four daughters, Mrs. Ruby Mosher of Cortez, Colorado, Mrs. Charles R. Andes of Curreyville, Missouri, and Mrs. Everett Rexroat and Thelma Frazee of Ulysses.

Headstone reads born June 1, 1871.

RIDER, AMY - (Grant County Republican, Nov. 27, 1930) The many friends of Mrs. Amy Rider were greatly surprised to learn of her death which occurred Saturday, November 22, 1930, at eight p.m.

Mrs. Rider has been quite ill during the past year. She has been making her home with her two sons, Frank and Claude, during this time and has had the very best of care that could be given.

Miss Amy Davis was born July 31, 1859, in Whiteside County, Illinois. She came with her parents, Mr. and Mrs. Lee Davis, a sister and two brothers in Barber County, Kansas, where they operated a hotel. It was here that she secured her education in a common pioneer school. She assisted her parents and many friends to fight off the many plains Indians who were still dangerous and full of enmity toward the whites.

The first day of January 1867, she was married to Frank G. Rider who was a resident of Chase County, Kansas. In 1882 Mr. and Mrs. Rider, with their four children, came into this country from Barber County, bringing with them 500 head of cattle and 100 head of horses. A dugout was constructed for the protection of the family and for many years this place was a well known "cow camp" to all who had any experience on the frontier.

In later years the Riders with their children moved to a frame house where until the last few years they lived.

Mr. and Mrs. Frank G. Rider lived in New Ulysses and were well

SHOCKEY CEMETERY

known. Mr. Rider died January 20, 1925, and Mrs. Rider remained in Ulysses until her illness when she went to make her home with her two sons.

Mr. and Mrs. Rider were the parents of eleven children, six of which has preceded them in death. The remaining five are Frank W. Rider, Claude C. Rider, Mrs. Goldie Reynolds, Mrs. Dearie Cowden and Mrs. Pearl Anderson.

Mrs. Riders first and last thought were for the welfare of others. She was a most kind and patient mother and friend to all. She will be greatly missed by all who knew her.

Just before she passed away she told her children that she was ready to go home to her Father whenever he called for her.

Funeral services were held at the home Sunday afternoon at 3 o'clock and she was laid to rest beside her loved one in the Shockey Cemetery. Rev. Roxie Powell was in charge of the services.

RIDER, BABY - (Grant County Republican, Sat., May 28, 1921) Shockey Items. We are sorry to report that the baby born to Mr. and Mrs. Frank Rider, Jr. was born dead on Monday, May 19, of this week and was buried in the Shockey Cemetery.

RIDER, CANARY - 1 yr., 6 mo. Daughter of Frank and Amy Rider. Headstone in memory only.

RIDER, CARRIE - 8 mo. Daughter of Frank and Amy Rider. Headstone in memory only.

RIDER, CLAUD - 1 yr., 6 mo. Son of Frank and Amy Rider. Headstone in memory only.

RIDER, COLUMBUS D. - (Garden City Telegram, June 3, 1983) Columbus Dewight Rider, 89, died Wednesday, June 1, 1983, at Bob Wilson Memorial Hospital at Ulysses after a long illness. Born June 1, 1894, in Grant County, he was a retired farmer and rancher and had lived in Ulysses all his life.

Survivors are a brother, Ralph, Ulysses; and two sisters, Dove Rexroat and Thelma Frazee, both of Ulysses.

Funeral was held at Phillips Mortuary Chapel, Ulysses, the Rev. Leon Brodrick officiating. Burial at Shockey Cemetery.

SHOCKEY CEMETERY

RIDER, FRANK G. - ((The Kearny County Advocate, January 23, 1925) Frank Rider, a prominent Grant County farmer and stockman, was taken suddenly ill Tuesday morning, just after partaking of breakfast, and passed away in a very short time. His many friends here will learn with deep sorrow of his demise.
Born February 12, 1885, and died January 21, 1925.

RIDER, GEORGE - (The Lakin Independent, March 21, 1952, Southwest Kearny News) A number of people of this community attended the funeral Saturday afternoon of Geo. Rider, a pioneer, who passed away at his farm home in northwest Grant County, Thursday night, March 13, 1952. The funeral was held in the Methodist Church at Ulysses. He was born May 17, 1857.

RIDER, GEORGE 'RALPH' - (Garden City Telegram, November 27, 2000) Vigil service and Funeral Mass for George 'Ralph' Rider, 84, was held at Mary Queen of Peace Catholic Church, Ulysses, with the Rev. Louis Hoang officiating. Burial in Shockey Cemetery, Ulysses.
Mr. Rider died Saturday, November 25, 2000, at Western Prairie Care Home in Ulysses.
He was born February 18, 1916, in Grant County, the son of George R. and Ada (Smethers) Rider.
A lifetime resident of Ulysses, he was a farmer and rancher. He belonged to Mary Queen of Peace Catholic Church and served in the 83rd Infantry Division of the U.S. Army during World War II.
On April 3, 1948, he married Alice Marie Doerr at Evansville, Indiana. She survives. He is also survived by a son, David Rider, Ulysses; three daughters, Kathy Goff, Janet Curl and Mari Honstead, all of Ulysses; 11 grandchildren; seven great grandchildren; and two sisters, Dove Rexroat, Lakin, and Thelma Frazee, Ulysses. He was preceded in death by two brothers; an infant brother, C. D. Rider; and two sisters, Flossie Andes and Ruby Mosher.
Memorials to Western Prairie Care Home in care of Garnand Funeral Home, Ulysses.

RIDER, GRACE - (The Lakin Investigator, March 27, 1908) Grace Ryder, aged thirteen, youngest daughter of Mr. and Mrs. Frank Ryder, of Grant County, died last week, and the funeral was held at Shockeyville, Friday.

SHOCKEY CEMETERY

(Grant County Republican, March 28, 1908) Miss Grace Rider, the daughter of Mr. and Mrs. F. G. Rider who are among the first settlers of this county, was born in Grant County, Kansas, on February 20, 1895, and died March 18, 1908, at the age of 13, of appendicitis after an illness of about three weeks. The funeral service was conducted by Elder Freed at Shockey and was attended by a large number of sorrowing neighbors and friends after which interment was made in Shockey Cemetery. The deceased had scores of friends who mourn that she was cut down in the dawn of her life, as an opening flower which falls as soon as its beauty is revealed.

RIDER, INFANT SON - Died in 1905, son of Mr. and Mrs. G. R. Rider, aged 4 mo.

RIDER, OLA - 2 yr. Daughter of Frank and Amy Rider.
Headstone in memory only.

RIDER, PRESTON - 2 yr., 6 mo. Son of Frank and Amy Rider.
Headstone in memory only.

SHOCKEY CEMETERY

SALSER, ELZINA - Died May 30, 1896. (Shockeyville Ind., Jan. 4, 1888) Married at the residence of the bride's parents, seven miles southwest of Shockeyville, on Saturday evening, December 31, 1887, Mr. Elias Salser to Miss Mattie Bloom, Rev. S. H. Dunkleberger officiating. We wish the young couple a long life of happiness and prosperity.

SCHAFFER, GEORGE B. T. - (The Grant County Republican, June 6, 1896) A child of Mr. Schaffer of Shockey died of scarlet fever last Saturday.
Born October 11, 1894 and died May 30, 1896. Son of J. P. and M. E. Schaffer.

SHOCKEY, EFFIE B. - (Ulysses Tribune, Oct. 15, 1892) Miss Effie Shockey, daughter of Mid Shockey, died Friday morning, October 14, at the home of her parents at Shockeyville after an illness of ten days. Miss Effie had a large acquaintance for one so young, and was a great favorite with all. Her sudden taking off was quite a shock to the community and the occasion of much sincere regret. To her parents however, whose idol she was, comes the severest blow, and the sympathy of all our people goes out to them in their great affliction
She was born February 22, 1877.

SMITH, CECIL - (Grant County Republican, March 13, 1909) A young son of Mr. and Mrs. Rolla Smith died very suddenly last week of grip or pneumonia and was buried at Shockey on Sunday. The parents have the sympathy of many friends in their dark hour.

SMITH, ORAH MAY - (Funeral Record) Mrs. Rolla B. Smith died at Ulysses and was buried at Shockey Cemetery, April 24, 1925. Died of Influenza and pneumonia. Born January 23, 1882, and died April 20, 1925.

STAPLES, FLORA BELLE - (Grant County Republican, April 7, 1923) Flora Belle Staples was born to George and Allie Staples, April 10, 1867, in Brown County, Indiana, died March 29, 1923, age 55 years, 11 months, 19 days. She leaves to mourn her loss, one sister, one brother, three half sisters, and one half brother and a host of relatives and friends. She was preceded to rest by her father and mother.

SHOCKEY CEMETERY

She united with the Seventh Day Adventist Church in 1893 and lived faithful to her pledges to that faith. She was of a very sunny disposition despite her afflictions. After the death of her mother she came to live with her sister. Her life was given almost entirely to the work of the Master, and she was never happier than when she was reading from the precious word of God.

Her funeral text was Revelations 14:13. Seventh Day Adventist preacher came from Topeka and preached her funeral.

Card of Thanks: We wish to thank the friends and neighbors for their kindness in assisting us during the sickness and death of our afflicted sister and aunt. Mrs. A. W. Anderson and family.

STRUTHERS, VETTA - (Hartland Herald, Dec. 17, 1887) The daughter of Mr. and Mrs. W. P. Struthers of Shockeyville, died suddenly of diphtheria early last Tuesday morning.

(Shockeyville Independent, Shockey, Grant County, Kans., Wed. Dec. 14, 1887) A mournful visitation came upon our fellow townsman, W. P. Struthers and his wife, yesterday morning. Yetta, their little eight year old daughter and only child, had been ill for over a week with diphtheria, and was considered out of danger when she suddenly took worse, and after intense suffering of several hours duration, death came to her relief. To the bereaved parents and friends of little Yetta, we tender the heartfelt sympathy of this whole community. No words of ours however, can be a balm for the heart broken parents. Let them reflect that "little children" are guileless, and that "of such is the kingdom of heaven." We commend the agonizing parents to Him who is the support of the bereaved and desolate.

Yetta, aged 8 years and 6 months, only child of W. P. and E. M. Struthers, departed this life at 4 o'clock a.m. December 13, 1887. Her fatal disease was diphtheria. All that medical skill, loving hearts and tender hands could do, was done for her; but Alas! Death had chosen her as a victim. Oh! How fresh in our memory is the remembrance of the innocence and purity of the lovely departed! All that was mortal of little Yetta is changed now, and forever clouded; but death cannot enter that bright and immortal sphere where she has gone. How sad indeed, is this dispensation of heavenly Father's chastening hand; yet, we can see many merciful preparations for it, the chief one being, the dear child's inner life. Our hope and prayer is, that, although no longer with us, she may be a ministering angel in our desolate home; and that her desire to bless us

SHOCKEY CEMETERY

and make us happy, may receive a deeper and more inward power.

> She is gone! our darling Yetta,
> To that land so bright and fair;
> To the arms of her Redeemer,
> She will ever wait us there. W.P.S

(Shockeyville Independent, Dec. 21, 1887) The funeral service of little Yetta Struthers was held last Friday, conducted by Rev. Dunkelberger, and the remains interred in the Maple Grove Cemetery, east of town.

SWINNEY, HANNAH J. - (Grant County Republican, July 7, 1900) Died at her home in Sherman Township, Mrs. T. W. Swinney on Tuesday, July 3rd at 11 o'clock a.m. Mrs. Swinney was sick but a few days, and had the best of care and nursing, but of no avail. She leaves a husband, son and two daughters to mourn her loss.

She was born October 23, 1844.

SHOCKEY CEMETERY

TUTTLE, BABY - (Has a small marker. No information available.)

SHOCKEY CEMETERY

WHITE, EDNA FAY - (Shockeyville Ind., Jan. 4, 1888) Died, Edna Fay, infant daughter of Mr. and Mrs. Augustus White, December 30, 1887, aged 5 months and 10 days. The funeral services were conducted at Prairie Star, Sunday, January 1, 1888, by Rev. C. E. Swinney.

WHITE, HARRY - (The Kendall Boomer, Nov. 17, 1888) Died on Thursday, November 9th, at 11 o'clock a.m., Harry, son of Mr. and Mrs. L. R. White of Shockeyville, of diphtheria, aged 3 years, 11 months, 9 days, was buried in the Maple Grove Cemetery at Shockeyville, November 11, at 2 p.m.

Little Harry was beloved by all who knew him and for his mild and gentle way. His death was a great shock to the bereaved parents who have the sympathy of the community in which they live as well as of friends abroad.

> "Jesus has called our darling,
> Away from this world of care
> In that bright land above us
> Dear Harry awaits us there" W.P.S.

WRIGHT, INFANT SON - (Shockeyville Plainsman, Shockey, Grant Co., Kans., Sat., Feb. 9, 1889) Died February 5, of whooping cough, the infant son of Mr. and Mrs. John B. Wright. The whole community join in sympathizing with them in their bereavement.

DIGGIN' UP BONES BOOK IV

BIBLIOGRAPHY

Birth And Death Records. East Hibbard Township, Kearny County Ks.: March 1, 1908 & March 1, 1909.

Cemetery Records. Kendall Cemetery, Kendall, Ks.: 2000.

Funeral Records. J. J. Nash. Lakin, Ks. 1916.

Grant County New Era. Ulysses, Ks.: 1930-1933.

Grant County Register. Ulysses, Ks.: 1885-1890.

Grant County Republican. Ulysses, Ks.: 1892-1937.

Hamilton County Census. Syracuse, Ks.: 1910.

Hamilton County Bulletin. Syracuse, Ks.: Feb. 1892.

Hamilton County Cemetery Records. Syracuse, Ks.: 2000.

Hartland Herald, Hartland, Ks.: 1886-1891.

Hartland Standard, Hartland, Ks.: 1886-1889.

Hartland Times. Hartland, Ks.: 1886-1887.

Kearney County Advocate or The Advocate. Lakin, Ks.: 1885-1937.

Kearney County Coyote. Chantilly & Omaha, Ks.: 1887-1890.

Kearney Koyote. Kearney, Ks.: Jan.-May 1887.

Kearny County Historical Society. The Kearny County History Book, Vol. I. Dodge City, Ks.: Rollie Jack, Inc., 1964.

Kearny County Historical Society. The Kearny County History Book, Vol. II. North Newton, Ks.: Mennonite Press Inc., 1973.

DIGGIN' UP BONES BOOK IV

Kendall Free Press. Kendall, Ks.: April 1890.

Kendall Gazette. Kendall, Ks.: May-June 1887.

Kendall Weekly Signal. Kendall, Ks.: April-Sept. 1886.

Lakin Eagle. Lakin, Ks.: 1878-1879.

Lakin Pioneer Democrat. Lakin, Ks.: 1885-1890.

Lakin Union. Lakin, Ks.: 1895.

Syracuse Journal. Syracuse, Ks.: 1930-Date.

The Garden City Telegram. Garden City, Ks.: 1912-Date.

The Kendall Boomer. Kendall, Ks.: 1886-1887.

The Lakin Herald. Lakin, Ks.: 1881-1884.

The Lakin Independent. Lakin, Ks.: 1915-Date.

The Lakin Index. Lakin, Ks.: 1890-1898.

The Lakin Investigator. Lakin, Ks.: 1898-1911.

The Leoti Standard. Leoti, Ks.: 1890-Date

The Syracuse Journal. Syracuse, Ks.: 1885-1929.

The Ulysses News. Ulysses, Ks.: 1937-Date.

The Wichita Standard. Leoti, Ks.: 1886-1887.

Ulysses Tribune. Ulysses, Ks.: 1891-1893.

Wichita County History Association. History of Wichita County Kansas, Vol. I. North Newton, Ks.: Mennonite Press Inc., 1980.

www.ingramcontent.com/pod-product-compliance
Lightning Source LLC
Chambersburg PA
CBHW071422160426
43195CB00013B/1771